THE POLITICS OF EUROPEAN
DEFENSE COOPERATION

THE POLITICS OF EUROPEAN DEFENSE COOPERATION
Germany, France, Britain, and America

David Garnham

BALLINGER PUBLISHING COMPANY
Cambridge, Massachusetts
A Subsidiary of Harper & Row, Publishers, Inc.

International Standard Book Number: 0–88730–302–1

Library of Congress Catalog Card Number: 88–19314

Printed in the United States of America

Library of Congress Cataloging-in-Publication Data

Garnham, David, 1942–
    The Politics of European defense cooperation.

    Includes bibliographies and index.
    1. Europe—Defenses. 2. European cooperation.
3. North Atlantic Treaty Organization. I. Title.
UA646.G39   1988   355'.03304   88–19314
ISBN 0–88730–302–1

For my parents with love and gratitude

CONTENTS

LIST OF TABLES

LIST OF ABBREVIATIONS

ACE	avion de combat européen
ALCM	air-launched cruise missile
ASMP	air-sol à moyenne portée (French ALCM)
BAOR	British Army of the Rhine
Benelux	Belgium, the Netherlands, and Luxembourg
CCFR	Chicago Council on Foreign Relations
CDU	Christian Democratic Union (FRG)
CNAD	Conference of National Armaments Directors
CSCE	Conference on Security and Cooperation in Europe
CSI	Cours supérieur interarmées
CSU	Christian Social Union (FRG)
DGA	Délégation générale pour l'armament
DoD	Department of Defense (United States)
EC	European Community
EDC	European Defense Community
EEC	European Economic Community (Common Market)
EFA	European Fighter Aircraft
EPC	European Political Cooperation
ESA	European Space Agency
FAR	Force d'action rapide
FDP	Free Democratic Party (FRG)
FRG	Federal Republic of Germany
FY	Fiscal Year
GDP	Gross Domestic Product (GNP minus net income from abroad)

GDR   German Democratic Republic
GLCM   ground-launched cruise missile
GNP   Gross National Product
IEPG   Independent European Programme Group
IHEDN   Institut des hautes études de défense nationale
IISS   International Institute for Strategic Studies (London)
I NF   intermediate nuclear forces
IRBM   intermediate range ballistic missile
MBFR   Mutual and Balanced Force Reduction Talks
MoD   Ministry of Defence (United Kingdom)
NASA   National Aeronautics and Space Administration
NPT   Non-Proliferation Treaty
PS   Parti Socialiste (France)
RAF   Royal Air Force (United Kingdom)
RPR   Rassemblement pour la République (France)
RUSI   Journal of the Royal United Services Institute for Defence Studies
SACEUR   Supreme Allied Commander Europe
SDI   Strategic Defense Initiative
SDP   Social Democratic Party (United Kingdom)
SLBM   submarine-launched ballistic missile
SPD   Social Democratic Party (FRG)
UDF   Union pour la Démocratie Française (France)
UK   United Kingdom
WEU   Western European Union
WTO   Warsaw Treaty Organization

ACKNOWLEDGMENTS

I began this book during a sabbatical leave provided by the University of Wisconsin-Milwaukee. Many people assisted its completion. Anne Flohr helped greatly to locate and translate German language literature and to organize my interview schedule in the Federal Republic. Hans-Adolf Jacobsen was also extremely helpful in arranging interviews in Bonn. Parts of the manuscript profited from comments by Arthur Cyr, Karen Greenstreet, Joseph Lepgold, Reinhardt Rummel, Peter Schmidt, Stanley Sloan, and Steve Smith. Meredith Watts generously shared his knowledge of German politics. My major debt is to Carla Garnham who read the entire manuscript with her usual skepticism and provided writing time by excusing me from dishwashing for many months.

My thanks to the staff of the University of Wisconsin-Milwaukee Library and the staffs of the following libraries in the United States and Europe: the British Library, Fondation Nationale des Sciences Politiques, Les Instituts Français (Bonn and London), International Institute for Strategic Studies, Library of Congress, Marquette University, Milwaukee Public Library, Royal United Services Institute, University of California-Berkeley, University of California-Santa Barbara, University of Reading, and the University of Wisconsin-Madison.

Earlier versions of portions of this book appeared in *International Security*; C.E. Baumann, ed., *Europe in NATO: Deterrence, Defense, and Arms Control*; and R. Rummel, ed., *West European Self-Assertiveness: Fact or Fiction.*

1 INTRODUCTION

Since 1945, Europe has experienced one of the longest periods of peace in modern history. After two devastating twentieth century wars, Europeans are determined to preserve this peace, which most attribute to nuclear deterrence and America's commitment to European defense. Until recently, most Europeans looked primarily to the Atlantic Alliance to preserve peace, rather than to national or regional defense arrangements. Only the French, who emphasized their national deterrent force, chose a different option.

Now Europeans are beginning to question the American defense commitment, and this concern fuels renewed interest in European defense cooperation, a concept which became moribund when France's National Assembly defeated the European Defense Community (EDC) proposal in August 1954. This book will examine the politics of military cooperation among the NATO (North Atlantic Treaty Organization)–European states and especially the likelihood that a viable "European pillar" could evolve to reduce or replace America's postwar role as the ultimate guarantor of Western European security.

This study emphasizes relations among the three most powerful Western European states (the Federal Republic of Germany or West Germany, France, and Great Britain) which in 1985 accounted for over 60 percent of the total Gross Domestic Product (GDP) of non-North American NATO members.[1] Compared to these three, the remaining European countries are substantially less influential: none possesses nuclear

Table 1–1.   Capabilities of Selected NATO–European Countries.

	Nuclear Weapons	Number of Males 18–30 years (millions)	GDP 1985 (in billions)	1986 Defense Budget (in billions)	Military Personnel
Belgium		1.0	$80	$2.4	91,428
Denmark		0.5	$57	$1.5	29,525
France	x	5.6	$511	$22.3	463,320*
Italy		5.7	$361	$14.1	387,800
Netherlands		1.6	$124	$5.5	105,134
Norway		0.4	$58	$2.1	37,300
Spain		4.1	$169	$5.6	320,000
United Kingdom	x	5.7	$481	$24.9	323,800
West Germany		6.5	$622	$22.5	485,800

Source: *The Military Balance 1986–1987* (London: International Institute for Strategic Studies, 1986), pp. 56–76.

*Not including Gendarmerie (constabulary) (85,708) and Service de Santé (health service) (8,465).

weapons, and the largest (Italy and Spain) are isolated geographically. Furthermore, Spain is outside both the Western European Union (WEU) and NATO's integrated military structure. The Benelux (Belgium, the Netherlands, and Luxembourg) countries are geographically central and active members of the WEU and NATO, but their size precludes a substantial impact on European defense.

WEST GERMANY

Geography makes West Germany the keystone of Western European defense and the most vulnerable member of NATO. Among the NATO countries that border the Eastern bloc (Norway, Greece, and Turkey), only the FRG has 30 percent of its population and 25 percent of its industrial capacity located within sixty miles of the East-West frontier. This proximity, and the absence of a national nuclear deterrent capability, makes the Federal Republic the most exposed member of the Atlantic Alliance.

The Federal Republic is also the most populous Western European country (57 million inhabitants in an area the size of Oregon), the largest Western European economy (see Table 1–1), and the fourth largest global economy. In 1986, the FRG overtook the United States to become the world's principal exporting country.[2]

The world wars were disastrous and left Germany defeated and divided. This experience, combined with feelings of guilt for Nazi atrocities, convinced many Germans that warfare was immoral, ineffective, and dangerous.[3] Article 26 of Bonn's constitution prohibits "Activities tending and undertaken with the intent to disturb peaceful relations between nations, especially to prepare for aggressive war. . . ." This dovish inclination is reinforced by Germany's precarious position as the likely battleground for any European war. By comparison, France, and especially Britain and the United States, enjoy more favorable geopolitical positions. Moreover, only diplomacy—not force of arms—can advance the goals of *Deutschlandpolitik*, because the Soviet Union can effectively block improved inter-German relations as General Secretary Chernenko demonstrated by preventing East German leader Erich Honecker's proposed visit to the Federal Republic in 1984.[4]

Following World War II, West Germans renounced aspirations to great power status and rejected strategic concepts based on *Realpolitik* and Vegetius' maxim "Let him who desires peace, prepare for war."[5] Contemporary German thinking is influenced more by notions of "common security," which Egon Bahr, a leading member of the Social Democratic Party (SPD), defined as an awareness that "the security of the potential enemy is my own, and vice versa. Both sides will survive together, or be destroyed together."[6] Or, as one Bonn foreign policy specialist expressed it, "We cannot sleep very well if our Eastern neighbor is afraid of us."

The philosophy of common security dominates the Left, but its influence extends across the political spectrum. There is a broad consensus among German elites that ultimate security cannot come from military preparedness; it must be based on arms control and other diplomatic approaches which recognize the East's legitimate security concerns. This prompted an American diplomat to remark that "these people have simply had power politics bred out of them,"[7] and a recently retired Bundeswehr (German-armed forces) officer exaggerated only slightly in stating, "I do not think there are any hawks in this country."

FRANCE

Compared to the Federal Republic, France enjoys a preferable security situation in two major respects: the West German buffer shields French territory from direct exposure to Warsaw Pact aggression, and France possesses its own nuclear deterrent force. France's policy of "deterrence by the weak of the strong" (*la dissuasion du faible au fort*) presumes that the Soviets will be deterred if the damage that France can credibly threaten to inflict on Soviet territory exceeds Soviet benefits from defeating France.[8] French military forces consist of strategic nuclear forces, tactical nuclear weapons, conventional forces, and the more recently created Force d'action rapide (FAR), which is a highly mobile intervention force of 47,000 soldiers intended for use in Europe or the Third World. Except for the FAR, all of these forces have deterrence rather than fighting a war as their principal or sole mission.

French military thought differentiates three strategic circles: the first circle (French national territory, often called the Hexagon), the second circle (Europe), and the third circle (the rest of the world).[9] Strategic nuclear policy pertains to the first circle, but since the mid-1970s when French President Giscard d'Estaing and General Méry introduced the concept of "enlarged sanctuary," the consensus has progressively embraced a more expansive definition of French interests to include some portion of the second circle.[10] At least rhetorically, the enlarged sanctuary is now endorsed by the three principal political groupings: Parti Socialiste (PS), or the Socialist Party; Rassemblement pour la République (RPR), or Rally for the Republic; and Union pour la Démocratie Française (UDF), or Union for French Democracy.[11] However, specifications of French vital interests remain enigmatic and are left ultimately for the president to interpret in extremis. According to French specialists, nuclear weapons "would be employed for the defense of the 'vital interests' of the country and . . . it is for the president of the republic to define them when the moment comes."[12]

In addition, although West Germany's defense consensus unraveled in recent years, the Gaullist doctrine for autonomous defense of French territory with nuclear weapons is embraced with various nuances by all major French political parties.[13] The consensus runs so deeply that French defense policy is insulated from electoral shifts such as those from Giscard to Mitterrand in 1981 and to *cohabitation* (with the right controlling the parliament and the Socialists the presidency) between March 1986 and June 1988. It is notable that the Socialists abstained (rather than oppose) when the 1987 and 1988 defense budgets passed the National Assembly, and they supported the new five-year military plan (*loi de programme militaire* 1987–91) drafted by the Chirac government (albeit with a substantial input from President Mitterrand) when it passed in April 1987.[14]

UNITED KINGDOM

Britain's military has four principal missions: the independent nuclear deterrent; conventional defense of the United Kingdom; a continental commitment focused on the British Army of the Rhine (BAOR) and the Royal Air Force (RAF) in Germany; and a naval role which emphasizes the Eastern Atlantic and Channel areas. For more than thirty years following World War II, a broad political consensus sustained these missions. They were considered essential to maintain Britain in its rightful position as the first power of the second tier, immediately below the superpowers.

Now, this unity has disintegrated. The nuclear consensus was always fragile, and it crumbled when Labour's left wing captured control of the party in the late 1970s and adopted a policy of unilateral nuclear disarmament for Britain and a non-nuclear defense strategy for NATO.[15] Since 1983, polls have routinely indicated that the public preferred the Conservative Party's defense policy by a margin varying between two-to-one and three-to-one, and this policy may have cost Labour 5 percent of the vote and several dozen seats in the 1987 general election.[16] An October 1987 poll found that overall Labour support had dwindled to only 34 percent of the electorate. Although this indicated that only hard-core Labour partisans remained, 40 percent of self-identified Labour sympathizers still broke with Labour on the defense issue and favored a British nuclear deterrent. Among the total electorate, 65 percent favored either a national nuclear deterrent within NATO (39 percent) or a European nuclear deterrent within NATO (26 percent).[17]

Consequently, Labour reconsidered its defense policy. A policy review group was formed which will report to the 1989 party conference, and there is an apparent retreat from unilateral nuclear disarmament while remaining committed to the eventual goal of non-nuclear defense. In 1987, Labour leader Neil Kinnock outlined a policy of trading Trident for Soviet nuclear reductions. He told the BBC:

> I have made it clear many times that the Soviet Union was willing to dismantle a precisely similar weapon system to that of Polaris as a consequence of our doing so. It is conceivable that the same kind of arrangement could be undertaken against the background of strategic arms reductions in the case of Trident.[18]

And Kinnock was more specific in June 1988; he said, "We want to get rid of Trident. But the fact is that it does not have to be something for nothing. The fact is now it can be something for something."[18]

Despite this shift, Kinnock's position remains very ambiguous, and there is considerable residual support for unilateralism among Labour party activists. There is also substantial support for non-nuclear policies among members of the former Liberal party (now part of the Social and Liberal Democratic Party).

Britain allocates 4.9 percent of its Gross Domestic Product (GDP) to defense spending, a level substantially greater than that of France (4.0 percent) or the Federal Republic (3.0 percent).[19] After adjusting for inflation, British defense expenditures rose 20 percent between 1978–79 and 1985–86, but now the tide has turned, and real defense spending will *decrease* by 2.5 percent in real terms between 1986–87 and 1988–89.[20] Some observers predict a shortfall of 20 percent (£5 billion) in the defense budget,[21] and many now argue that Britain's economy can no longer sustain all four missions. In particular, these budgetary pressures intensified clashes between advocates of Britain's postwar "continental" strategy, which emphasizes forward defense of the Central Front in Germany, and Britain's more traditional "maritime" orientation.

THE TASK OF EUROPEAN DEFENSE

If deterrence failed, a Warsaw Pact attack on Europe would probably be limited to use of conventional arms. The Soviets would hope to prevail in a blitzkrieg war and to avoid nuclear escalation. Nonetheless, NATO must prepare for possible use of battlefield or longer range nuclear weapons, and Europe requires *both* conventional and nuclear forces to deter the spectrum of possible attacks. Although there is strong minority support for non-nuclear deterrence in both the Federal Republic and Britain (unlike France), a purely conventional deterrent is insufficient. Only the threat of nuclear reprisals can deter nuclear aggression. Furthermore, NATO countries remain unwilling, as in the past, to fund conventional forces sufficient to match those of the Warsaw Treaty Organization (WTO). Especially in the face of conventional inferiority, European deterrence is strengthened if the Soviets must fear European first use of nuclear weapons if its conventional defense is failing. Many observers also argue that European deterrence requires a threat that Soviet aggression will jeopardize major Soviet assets. If the Soviets were confident that no

NATO country would initiate the use of nuclear weapons against them, they could attack Western Europe confident that unsuccessful aggression would be their maximum loss. Deterrence is reinforced if nuclear retaliation against Soviet territory is possible.[22] Because any European war would be disastrous, and could escalate to general nuclear war, deterrence must be as dependable as possible.

Conversely, nuclear weapons are not sufficient. Even the most limited use of nuclear weapons would be so damaging that Europe's defense could not credibly threaten nuclear retaliation in response to all provocations.[23] Even without accepting the contention of Robert McNamara and General Etienne Copel that nuclear weapons can *only* deter nuclear aggression,[24] it is clearly not credible to threaten nuclear responses to minor attacks. Even French strategy, which is based on a rather pure form of "deterrence by punishment" through threatened countercity reprisals, recognizes the need to probe the adversary's intentions with conventional forces to assess whether the aggression imperils vital interests and thus justifies the use of nuclear weapons.[25] Deterrence is strongest when a robust conventional capability is married to a potential for nuclear escalation.

For more than a generation, the United States has served as the ultimate guarantor of both conventional and nuclear deterrence in Europe. This book examines the factors which are eroding this security structure and prodding Europeans, however reluctantly, to assume greater responsibility for their continent's defense.

NOTES

1. Computed from data in Caspar W. Weinberger, Secretary of Defense, *Report on Allied Contributions to the Common Defense: A Report to the United States Congress* (Washington: U.S. Department of Defense, April 1987), p. 87.
2. See "West Germany Top Exporter," *The New York Times*, 6 August 1987.
3. This contrasts with the American lesson that it is dangerous to "appease" aggressors. As Gerhard Wettig wrote:

   There is an elementary mood of 'Never again!' Never again should the German people and the territory of Germany originate a threat to peace. Never again should militaristic attitudes and armament activities be prevalent in Germany. Never again should feelings of enmity be allowed to spoil German minds and hearts. The idea, therefore, that there is a potential adversary who poses a challenge may not be admitted. Instead one has to be unconditionally friendly toward anyone who is supposedly antagonistic.

Gerhard Wettig, "Europe and the Idea of Common Security," *The Washington Quarterly* 8 (Spring 1985): 94.

4. Honecker said in a *Die Zeit* interview that he lacked "unlimited scope" for normalizing inter-German relations. Quoted by Hermann Dexheimer, "Tragic reality of the two German states," *The German Tribune*, 2 March 1986 (translated from *Allgemeine Zeitung*, Mainz, 15 February 1986).

5. See Hans-Peter Schwarz, *Die gezähmten Deutschen: Von der Machtbesessenheit zur Machtvergessenheit* (Stuttgart: Deutsche Verlags-Anstalt, 1985), pp. 107–51 and Simon Bulmer and William Patterson, *The Federal Republic of Germany and the European Community* (London: Allen & Unwin, 1987), pp. 9–10.

6. Egon Bahr, "Observations on the principle of common security," in R. Väyrynen, et al., *Policies for Common Security* (London and Philadelphia: Taylor & Francis, 1985), p. 34. This volume also contains an article by the late Alois Mertes, a foreign ministry official in the Kohl government, "Common security and defensive security," pp. 187–91.

7. Quoted in James M. Markham, "The Uneasy West Germans: Yearnings Despite Prosperity," *The New York Times*, 2 August 1987.

8. See David S. Yost, *France's Deterrent Posture and Security in Europe: Part I: Capabilities and Doctrine*, Adelphi Paper Number 194 (London: International Institute for Strategic Studies, Winter 1984/5), pp. 14–15.

9. See Charles Hernu, *Défendre la paix* (Paris: Editions J.-C. Lattès, 1985), pp. 26–27 and Lucien Poirier, "Le deuxième cercle: La défense égoïste de la citadelle et la grande aventure au-delà de la contrescarpe," in Lucien Poirier, *Essais de stratégie théorique* (Paris: Fondation pour les études de Défense Nationale, *Collection les sept épées*, No. 22, premier trimestre 1982), p. 293.

10. See General Guy Méry, "French Defense Policy," *Survival* 18 (September–October 1976): 226–28 and Charles Hargrove, "Valéry Giscard d'Estaing," *Politique étrangère* 51 (Spring 1986): 121. However, General Lucien Poirier is correct that it is actually "enlarged deterrence" rather than an "enlarged sanctuary," as there is no intention to use strategic nuclear weapons to defend interests in the second circle. See Lucien Poirier, "La Greffe," *Défense nationale* 39 (April 1983): 21.

11. See Paul-Marie de La Gorce, "Dissuasion française et défense européenne," *Le Monde diplomatique* (September 1985): 1, 22–23; Le Parti Socialiste, *La Sécurité de l'Europe* (Paris, 1985); Rassemblement pour la République, *La défense de la France: 4 ans de gestion socialiste, Propositions pour le renouveau* (Paris: June 1985), pp. 89–91; Union pour la Démocratie Française, *Redresser la défense de la France* (Paris: November 1985), pp. 159–73.

12.   Paul-Marie de La Gorce, "Dissuasion française et défense européenne," p.23. Also see writings by two former Socialist defense ministers—Paul Quilès wrote that "the implication of French vital interests cannot be defined a priori: the assessment of that comes back, on a case-by-case basis, to the chief of state, the only one empowered to trigger the nuclear fire." In "Au-delà des fausses querelles," *Le Monde*, 7 March 1986; and Charles Hernu wrote that, "The president of the republic, and he alone, is charged to appreciate if these interests are threatened and to take the measures demanded by the circumstances." *Défendre la paix* (Paris: Editions J.-C. Lattès, 1985), pp. 28–29.

13.   The Communists accepted nuclear deterrence in 1977 and the Socialists followed in 1978; see Michel Dobry, "Le jeu du consensus," *Pouvoirs* (September 1986): 48. A softening of Communist support for the nuclear deterrent is described in Olivier Biffaud, "Le PCF rompt le consensus nucléaire," *Le Monde*, 10 April 1987.

14.   See Paul Lewis, "France Approves Arms Plan Linked to European Allies," *The New York Times*, 11 April 1987, and "Défense: les agacements de M. Giraud," *Le Monde*, 12 November 1987.

15.   See, for example, the Labour Party's defense brochure prepared for the 1987 general election, *The Power to Defend Our Country* (London: Labour Party, n.d.); Dennis Healey, "A Labour Britain, NATO and the Bomb," *Foreign Affairs* 65 (Spring 1987): 716–29; and Neil Kinnock, "How Labor Would Defend Britain," *The New York Times*, 27 March 1987.

16.   The MORI (Market and Opinion Research International) poll found the following opinion on the question "Which party has the best defence policy?"

	Conservative (%)	Labour (%)	Liberal/SDP (%)	Don't Know (%)
June 1983	53	19	14	14
June 1987	50	24	16	9
September 1987	53	17	7	22

Source: Robin Oakley, "Battle for Alliance deserters," *The Times* (London), 5 October 1987.

R.W. Johnson, "Now for a real alliance," *The Times* (London), 7 July 1987 calculates the 1987 electoral effect as 3 percent, but Andrew Gamble, in "Cutting defence down to size," *The Times* (London), 23 June 1987 cites a private Labour poll indicating 5 percent. Apparently, the MORI polling organization informed Labour ten days prior to the June 1987 general election that the defense policy was "the greatest liability of all." Robin Oakley, "Labour relents over defence," *The Times* (London), 28 September 1987. Also see Tom Lister and Bruce George, "Defence: The 1987 General Election and Beyond," *RUSI: Journal of the Royal United Services Institute for Defence Studies* 132 (September 1987): 69–71.

17. "Most Labour voters 'favour nuclear deterrent'," *The Times* (London), 26 October 1987. The survey was conducted by MORI on October 19, 1987; the sample equaled 1,109 adults aged eighteen or more.

18. Quotations from Robin Oakley, "Kinnock's credibility on trial," *The Times* (London), 15 June 1988.

19. See *Financial and Economic Data Relating to NATO Defence*, M-DPC-2(87)48 (Brussels: NATO Press Service, December 1, 1987), p. 4.

20. See Nicholas Wood, "Defence spending rise eases cash pressure on equipment," *The Times* (London), 4 November 1987. Previously, the British government had estimated a 5 percent real reduction during this period; see *Survey of Current Affairs* 17 (June 1987): 198.

21. See Peter Hennessy, "Waiting for Defence Review No. 8," *New Statesman*, 17 July 1987 and "The best form of defence..." *The Independent*, 8 October 1986 (editorial).

22. See François de Rose, *European Security and France* (Urbana: University of Illinois Press, 1984), pp. 57–79; Samuel P. Huntington, "Conventional Deterrence and Conventional Retaliation in Europe," *International Security* 8 (Winter 1983–84): 32–56; John J. Mearsheimer, "Nuclear Weapons and Deterrence in Europe," *International Security* 9 (Winter 1984–85): 19–46, and Major Bruce K. Scott, "A NATO Nonnuclear Deterrence: Is It Affordable?" *Military Review* 64 (September 1984): 57–69. As Stanley Hoffmann has written, President Mitterrand opposes "relying purely on conventional weapons to defend Europe, which the French believe might make war more likely." Stanley Hoffmann, "Gaullism By Any Other Name," *Foreign Policy* (Winter 1984–85): 48.

23. This was a principal criticism of America's strategy of massive retaliation during the 1950s. See Michael Mandelbaum, *The Nuclear Question: The United States and Nuclear Weapons, 1946–1976* (New York: Cambridge University Press, 1979), pp. 59–60.

24. See, for example, Robert S. McNamara, "The Military Role of Nuclear Weapons," *Foreign Affairs* 62 (Fall 1983): 73 and General Etienne Copel, *La puissance de la liberté: Les chances d'une défense de l'Europe* (Paris: Lieu Commun, 1985), pp. 85–86 and p. 99.

25. See Etat-Major des Armées, "Le Concept de défense français," *Armées d'aujourd'hui* (January/February 1985): 7; "Les missions des forces classiques," *Armées d'aujourd'hui* (January/February 1985): 20; and Général C. Dellamby, "L'Engagement des forces terrestres en centre Europe," *Armées d'aujourd'hui* (April 1985): 30–31.

2 EUROPE AND AMERICA

America's current commitments to Western European defense date from the Truman administration. The outbreak of the Korean War (1950) convinced the signatories of the North Atlantic Treaty (1949) that an integrated military organization, rather than a mere American guarantee, was required to safeguard European security. The Truman administration also extended the nuclear guarantee, although tactical nuclear weapons were not introduced until the Eisenhower administration. Prior to the deployments of national nuclear deterrents by Britain (1956) and France (1963),[1] NATO's nuclear deterrent was entirely American. Even today, the British and French forces are relatively small, and former U.S. Defense Secretary James Schlesinger estimates that the United States still "bears the cost of 97 percent of the total nuclear capabilities of the alliance . . . ."[2]

NATO's conventional burden is more evenly divided between the United States and Europe. As European leaders frequently proclaim, Europe provides 90 percent of the ground forces, 80 percent of the combat aircraft, 80 percent of the tanks, and 90 percent of the armored divisions stationed in Europe during peacetime.[3] Nonetheless, the role of America's 330,000 troops is not merely to serve as symbolic hostages intended to activate the nuclear guarantee. In fact, these troops are integral to Europe's conventional defense.[4] U.S. troops constitute approximately one-quarter of NATO forces on the Central Front, and America's percentage contribution would increase with full mobilization.[5] Only West Germany exceeds the U.S. contribution to the forward defense of Western Europe.

In 1985, aggregate defense spending by NATO countries equaled approximately $355 billion; the U.S. paid 73 percent[6] of this although America's GDP equaled only 57 percent of the Alliance total.[7] Similarly, in 1985 when NATO-European countries averaged 3.8 percent of Gross Domestic Product (GDP) for military expenditures, the U.S. rate was 6.7 percent, which was nearly twice as high.[8] Europeans are quick to identify the limitations of this comparison. Every NATO-European country except the United Kingdom, Luxembourg, and Iceland has conscription. It is estimated that volunteer armies increase defense budgets by approximately 25 percent.[9] The British example is illustrative. Among NATO-European countries, only Greece spends a higher percentage of GDP for defense than Britain does, but only Luxembourg and Denmark have a lower proportion of their populations under arms. The Germans rightly point to the invisible costs of supporting a density of military personnel twenty–six times greater than that in the United States. These costs include more than 40,000 military installations valued at $18 billion, 5,000 military exercises annually (which caused damage of $40 million in 1984), and 580,000 military flights annually (approximately 20 percent of the flights at low altitude).[10] At the beginning of 1988, ten American, British, and French military aircraft crashed in the Federal Republic during a three month period.

Nonetheless, Europe does not cover most of the costs of European defense. Recent studies by the U.S. Department of Defense and the General Accounting Office estimate that more than 55 percent of the U.S. defense budget goes to defend Western Europe.[11] This means that American per capita expenditures for Western European defense exceed those of most European nations. In 1986, total U.S. defense expenditures equaled $830 per capita and approximately $457 per capita[12] (55 percent of $830) *for Western European defense*; Britain ($513), France ($518), and Norway ($480) were the only European countries that exceeded America's per capita level of expenditure for European defense, and most NATO members were substantially lower.[13]

To summarize, America bears more than one-half the cost of Europe's conventional defense while also supplying the overwhelming portion of the nuclear deterrent and assuming principal responsibility for global security including Northeast Asia, the Persian Gulf, and other regions. American foreign policymakers accepted this skewed division of labor for two reasons: they believed, as Defense Secretary Weinberger wrote, that "the security of America and Europe is indivisible . . ."[14] and because America occupied a hegemonic position in the early postwar years.

Following World War II, much of Western Europe remained enfeebled by war damage, and West Germany was occupied until May 1955. By comparison, the United States ended the war with a robust economy and a nuclear monopoly. In 1950, the United States produced 40 percent of the world's gross national product (GNP) compared to only 21 percent for Europe.[15] Given the disparity of material and military capabilities, it was natural for the United States to become the ultimate guarantor of Western European security. What is surprising is that the United States has filled this role for more than forty years. General Eisenhower was the first Supreme Allied Commander Europe (SACEUR), and he notified the Senate Foreign Relations and Armed Services Committees in 1951 that U.S. troop commitments would provide "the needed active strength *pending the time* that the European nations can build up their own defense forces."[16] As long ago as 1963, after leaving the presidency, Eisenhower argued that U.S. troop deployments could be cut. He believed that Europe had substantially recovered from World War II and that the continuing need for a symbolic U.S. presence could be fulfilled more cheaply. In Eisenhower's words, "One American division in Europe can show the flag as definitely as can several."[17] But although the international system changed, the U.S. commitment remained.

By the 1980s, the Soviets had achieved nuclear parity while retaining superior ground combat forces, and in 1986 the combined gross national products of the European community member states ($3.9 trillion) equaled that of the United States ($4.2 trillion).[18] Nonetheless, the United States continued to maintain 330,000 troops and (even after the reductions agreed to at NATO's Montebello meeting in 1983) 4,600 nuclear weapons in Western Europe.[19]

Disagreements regarding the current balance of conventional arms between NATO and the Warsaw Pact complicate efforts to realign the defense burden. Many American and European observers, including *a fortiori* the Reagan administration, argued that the Warsaw Pact enjoyed a decisive edge. For example, Defense Secretary Caspar Weinberger's 1987 annual report asserted that the WTO's (Warsaw Treaty Organization) advantage "in terms of forces within the NATO guidelines area" was two-to-one in main battle tanks, combat aircraft, surface-to-air missiles, and combat helicopters and greater than three-to-one in artillery.[20] Overall, Secretary Weinberger concluded that "By one measure, which accounts for both quantity and quality of forces, the Pact's advantage in in-place ground force combat power has increased from around 1.5-to-1 in 1965 to more than 2.2-to-1 today."[21]

Nonetheless, many other observers asserted that NATO did possess a credible conventional deterrent. Horst Ehmke (deputy SPD Bundestag chairperson) went further than most in asserting that "Soviet advantages are greatly exaggerated, if they exist at all."[22] However, many concur with former Ambassador Jonathan Dean that "NATO forces would be considerably more evenly matched with Soviet forces than most analyses allow for. . . . "[23] And reportedly, a classified Joint Chiefs of Staff "net assessment" completed in 1987 concluded that NATO possessed, and would continue to possess through 1994, a strong capacity for conventional deterrence in Europe. This analysis examined both quantitative and qualitative factors such as morale, leadership, and training.[24]

Although the status of the East-West balance is disputed, two things are clear: America's conventional contribution is vital, and notwithstanding ritualized assurances at NATO meetings,[25] European states obdurately refuse to increase their conventional expenditures.[26] Europeans resist for three reasons. First, they fear that stronger conventional forces would weaken overall deterrence by diminishing the threat of rapid nuclear escalation if deterrence failed. In Europe, even a conventional war would be catastrophic, so the only politically acceptable alternative is a "non-war" deterrent policy.[27] Second, they fear that more powerful conventional forces could "decouple" America from European security. If Europe appeared capable of self-defense, the United States could safely downgrade its commitment to Europe. Finally, Europeans shirk the cost of self-defense, and economic troubles during the 1980s intensified this deep-seated aversion to increased defense burdens.

These factors explain why average inflation-adjusted military expenditures by European NATO states have not achieved the 3 percent level agreed to in 1977.[28] For example, between 1981 and 1985 France averaged a *real* annual growth rate of 1.4 percent.[29] This increased somewhat under *cohabitation*. Jacques Chirac's government approved a nominal 4.5 percent increase from 1987 to 1988, for a real increase of approximately 2 percent; the entire gain came in the equipment portion of the budget, which rose 6 percent and constituted more than one-half the defense budget for the first time, while the operations budget declined in real terms.[30]

Measured in current dollars, the Federal Republic's defense budget will increase approximately 5 percent between 1987 and 1989.[31] Even considering Germany's extremely low inflation rate, the level of real growth is not large. Defense spending was a principal priority of the Thatcher government, and British defense expenditures rose dramatically between 1979 and 1986. Now that the tide has turned, the question is how much British defense spending will decline.

Actually, NATO's central problem is not inadequate spending; aggregate NATO spending approximates the Warsaw Pact's, and by some calculations exceeds it.[32] The problem is inefficient spending because of competitive military organizations and arms industries, small production runs, incompatible objectives, and lack of standardization or even interoperability. As Robin Beard has written:

> ... we have four Main Battle Tanks in Europe, developed at great cost to the taxpayer, that cannot fire the same ammunition. ... money and energy are having to be spent designing gateways to ensure that seven otherwise non-interoperable national developments of tactical communications battlefield systems are rendered interoperable between themselves, and with NATO's own communications system. ... eleven different firms in seven countries are working on anti-tank weapons, eighteen firms in seven countries are making ground-to-air weapons; eight firms in six nations are making air-to-air weapons; sixteen firms in seven nations are working on air-to-ground weapons, and ten firms in seven countries are working on ship-to-ship weapons.[33]

This situation prompted former NATO Secretary General Lord Carrington to comment that "the allies have only one thing in common, the air that inflates the tires of their vehicles."[34] It also recalls Marshall Foch's pungent observation after serving as commander in chief of allied armies in France during World War I: "Since I know what a coalition army is, I have much less admiration for Napoleon." More spending may be desirable, but improved coordination is imperative.

Prospects for European defense cooperation are affected by domestic politics within Germany, France, and Britain as well as external factors including American policies, East-West relations, and bilateral and multilateral Western European relations. American behavior is especially important. Without America's commitment to Europe's security, European governments would be compelled to accommodate the Soviet Union or to devise a national or European solution to their security problem. Ambassador Richard Burt and others have argued that "American withdrawal would strengthen those in Europe—such as the Greens in Germany or the

Labour Party in Britain—who favor a unilateral disarmament as a way of seeking an accommodation with the Soviet Union."[35] The author believes this supposition is mistaken, and the concluding chapter will discuss the historical and contemporary evidence showing that Western European governments are actually more likely to coalesce to offset Soviet power. This chapter discusses the evolution of American policy toward the Atlantic Alliance.

THE CONVENTIONAL COMMITMENT

Many Europeans see worrisome trends which undermine American support for European security. These trends include: nuclear isolationism (as reflected by the Strategic Defense Iniatiative, or SDI, and the Reykjavik summit), record U.S. budget deficits, shifting American attention from the Atlantic toward Latin America and the Pacific Basin,[36] and American resentment at Europe's failure to assume its fair share of the alliance burden and to support America's out-of-area initiatives.

Within the United States, the conventional troop deployments have received more political attention than the nuclear guarantee. This is somewhat baffling, for it is the nuclear commitment that entails existential threats to American survival. As Klaus Knorr has written, "The most consequential burden . . . is the commitment to initiate intercontinental nuclear war with the USSR in the event a Soviet attack in Europe overcame NATO defenses. . . . Beside such a risk, budgetary considerations simply pale into insignificance."[37] But most Americans avoid thinking about the unthinkable and the troop commitment involves the more costly and more tangible burden.

Former Senate majority leader Mike Mansfield's (D-Montana) long crusade to withdraw American troops from Europe gave substantial attention to the conventional commitment. In 1966, Mansfield began by introducing nonbinding "sense of the Senate" resolutions which attracted numerous cosponsors but never reached the Senate floor. His tactics altered in 1971 when he attached an amendment to the selective service bill which called for a 50 percent troop reduction. This amendment was defeated, 61 to 36, but only after substantial debate and several prior votes on weaker substitutes.[38] Mansfield's efforts continued, and by 1973 even strong NATO supporters such as Senators Henry Jackson and Sam Nunn were willing to sponsor a successful motion (passed 84 to 5 in September 1973) stipulating that U.S. troop reductions should take place to the degree that America's allies failed to offset the negative balance of payments effects from European troop costs.[39] The Senate also passed (48 to 36) an amendment sponsored by Democrats Hubert Humphrey and Alan Cranston which called for withdrawing 95,000 troops from abroad by the end of 1975. The measure died in a conference committee.

After 1973, several factors diminished the effectiveness of Mansfield's efforts: superpower detente deteriorated following the 1973 October war; the balance of payments issue was erased by floating exchange rates and investments of surplus oil revenues in the United States; and support for unilateral troop withdrawals was undercut by the fall of South Vietnam and the ongoing Mutual and Balanced Force Reduction (MBFR) talks in Vienna. As superpower relations continued to deteriorate after 1975, the issue of American troop withdrawals remained quiescent until the early 1980s. Then, Senator Carl Levin (D-Michigan) successfully amended the fiscal year (FY) 1981 Defense Authorization Act to require a report by the secretary of defense on contributions to the common defense by NATO allies and Japan, and in 1982 Senator Ted Stevens (R-Alaska) proposed that European troop deployments be reduced by 19,000.

The major recent initiative was introduced by Senator Sam Nunn (now Senate Armed Services Committee chairman) in June 1984. Nunn's action was especially significant because he possessed solid credentials as a stalwart NATO supporter and because his intent was not U.S. disengagement but to stimulate more military effort from NATO-Europe. Nunn's proposal called for annual U.S. troop reductions as large as 30,000 during each of three consecutive years unless America's allies met either of two goals: 3 percent increases in inflation-adjusted defense spending; or implementation of a concrete program to build stocks of conventional munitions sufficient to fight for thirty days, construction of bombproof shelters and other facilities to receive American aircraft scheduled for European deployment in case of war, and enhanced conventional capabilities that raised the nuclear threshold. Senator Nunn argued that the proposed troop reductions were not intended to "blackmail" the Europeans. In his words:

... the simple reality is, if we do not have allies that are going to do their part, there is no need for the American taxpayer to continue to spend billions and billions and billions of dollars on troops, on ammunition, on airlift, on all types of equipment for modernization. We can have a tripwire—that is, having our forces basically link the American nuclear deterrent to the defense of Europe—for a lot less money.[40]

The Nunn Amendment was defeated (by tabling) 55 to 41, but the Senate overwhelmingly passed (94 to 3) the same basic measure with the penalties removed.

After 1984, Senator Nunn became more satisfied with Europe's conventional efforts in such areas as ammunition supplies and sheltered aircraft hangars. Meanwhile, others in Congress took up this cause. Indeed, Stanley Sloan of the Congressional Research Service said in 1987 that there was more congressional interest in burden sharing and troops abroad than at any time during the preceding decade.[41]

Particularly among House of Representatives members, there was a tendency to link troop deployments to America's massive trade deficit, which grew from $38 billion in 1982 to $156 billion in 1986 and $171 billion in 1987.[42] Representative Patricia Schroeder (D-Colorado) said she had, "tried the troop reduction approach, and everybody goes cuckoo. We've been Uncle Sucker for so long, [but] the trade and budget deficits will drive us to have to do something about it."[43] Schroeder proposed a Defense Protection Act to link U.S. tariffs to a foreign country's level of defense spending. If enacted, this legislation would raise tariffs on Japanese imports by 5.3 percent, Canadian by 4 percent, and West German by 3 percent.

Even more than protectionist sentiments, the gargantuan federal budget deficits are likely to increase pressure toward disengagement. Budget deficits soared during the Reagan administration, from 2.6 percent of GNP in 1981 to 6.3 percent in 1983.[44] The cumulative federal debt more than doubled from $1 trillion to more than $2.5 trillion in seven years,[45] rising from 27 percent of annual GNP to 43 percent.[46] Toward the end of Reagan's second term there was some success in reducing the size of the annual deficit, to $148 billion in FY 1987 down from a record $221 billion in the previous year. But 1986 tax receipts were artificially inflated because many investors took capital gains during 1986 to avoid higher 1987 tax rates. With nonrecurrent factors excluded, most economists calculated the underlying FY 1987 deficit at approximately $180 billion, and in August 1988 the Treasury Department predicted that the FY 1988 deficit would exceed $152 billion, $8 billion above the deficit limit of $144 billion mandated by the 1987 budget-balancing law.[47] Even prior to the stock market crash of October 19, 1987, former Commerce Secretary Peter Peterson of the Nixon administration had written that "it is totally incredible that we could fund both our domestic obligations and our current global military obligations."[48]

After growing more than 50 percent in real terms between FY 1980 and FY 1985,[49] the defense budget failed to match inflation during three successive fiscal years, 1985–88. Public opinion reinforced this decline. For example, in a November 1987 *Newsweek* poll, 43 percent of those surveyed thought "major cuts in defense spending" should be "the main approach used to reduce the federal budget deficit." This compared to 23 percent of persons who favored "major cuts in nondefense domestic spending," 9 percent who supported higher taxes, and 8 percent who advocated limits on cost-of-living increases of entitlement programs.[50]

The budgetary squeeze was intensified by the fact that President Reagan's defense buildup emphasized force modernization more than readiness and sustainability. Therefore, costs put into weapons development will be lost unless the Pentagon continues to acquire new hardware as it emerges from the procurement pipeline. Moreover, all the new ships, planes, and other equipment will inflate operating costs for U.S. armed services. As a result, François Heisbourg envisioned U.S. Army units in Europe as the more tempting targets for Pentagon or Congressional cost cutters, because Air Force and Navy units were the focus of modernization programs, and these units are essential to the unilateral force projections that Europeans believe Washington now prefers.[51]

Heisbourg's prediction may prove prescient. Although Secretary Weinberger reduced readiness and procurement to protect personnel under the FY 1988 budget, his successor, Secretary Frank Carlucci, made it clear from the outset that he (Carlucci) "would rather have a smaller force that is effective, and that has the necessary ammunition, the necessary personnel, than to have a larger force that is not effective."[52] Soon after Carlucci assumed office, the Pentagon announced that military personnel would decline by 100,000 over a five-year period.[53] While the administration remains committed to current European troop deployments, and Army cuts are expected to be smaller than those of the other services, it will become increasingly difficult to justify large permanent European conventional commitments as military personnel is cut. This difficulty is reinforced when the U.S. dollar weakens against European currencies— especially the German mark. As the dollar slides, expenses for overseas housing allowances and foreign cost-of-living adjustments rise. Only two months into FY 1988, the Department of Defense (DoD) already foresaw a 40 percent shortfall in that category of the defense budget.[54]

In recent years, European anxieties were fed by a spate of recommendations to pare America's European commitment. In addition to Senator Nunn, prestigious advocates of reductions included former Secretary of State Henry Kissinger and President Carter's national security adviser,

Zbigniew Brzezinski. In a widely quoted *Time* article, Kissinger argued that Europe "should assume the major responsibility for conventional ground defense,"[55] that a European (not an American) should serve as Supreme Allied Commander Europe (SACEUR), and advocated gradually withdrawing as many as 50 percent of U.S. ground forces. Brzezinski argued that the United States should reallocate resources from Europe, where the allies are most capable of filling the gap, to counter Third World contingencies where threats are greater and capabilities are more limited. He argued that "A gradual reduction of approximately 100,000 troops would also free U.S. budgetary and manpower resources for the flexibility needed to respond to other geostrategic threats."[56]

Conservative support for European troop withdrawals typically comes from "libertarians" (who are most interested in reducing federal expenditures) and "neoconservatives," who believe that the United States requires a capacity for unilateral intervention. The neoconservatives dismiss the libertarians as right-wing isolationists and echo Brzezinski's argument that resources should be redeployed from Europe to strengthen American capabilities elsewhere. Irving Kristol and Melvyn Krauss are among the more prominent and persistent advocates of this position,[57] but it is also articulated by the conservative *New York Times* columnist William Safire and by Mortimer Zuckerman, chairman and editor-in-chief of *U.S. News and World Report.*[58]

According to Krauss' "supply side" analysis, "When the United States gave Europe a defense guarantee, it also gave the Europeans an incentive to minimize their own defense efforts."[59] Even worse, the American commitment has actually impaired U.S.-European solidarity:

> U.S. troops have been in Europe for the past forty years and, during the last twenty at least, Western Europe has become increasingly contentious with the United States at the same time that it has become increasingly accommodating to the Soviet Union. This is evidence that the U.S. troops in Europe have hurt, not helped, containment.[60]

There are also liberal advocates of withdrawal including James Chace, David P. Calleo, Gar Alperovitz, and *The New Republic*.[61]

Although the European commitment is attacked from all points of the political compass, it remains a first principle of postwar U.S. foreign policy with equally wide support.[62] There is deep bipartisan agreement with Caspar Weinberger's argument that "A world in which Western Europe fell under the yoke of Soviet domination would be an intolerable world for the United States . . . . [Therefore] American and European

Table 2–1.   Attitudes Toward NATO (percent).

Question: Some people feel that NATO, the military organization of Western Europe and the United States, has outlived its usefulness, and that the United States should withdraw militarily from NATO. Others say that NATO has discouraged the Russians from trying a military takeover in Western Europe. Do you feel we should increase our commitment to NATO, keep our commitment what it is now, decrease our commitment but remain in NATO, or withdraw from NATO entirely?

| | 1986 | | 1982 | | 1978 | |
	Public	Leaders	Public	Leaders	Public	Leaders
Increase commitment	8	8	9	7	9	21
Keep commitment						
what it is	62	77	58	79	58	65
Decrease commitment	11	13	11	12	9	12
Withdraw entirely	5	1	4	1	4	1
Not sure	14	1	18	1	20	1

Source: John E. Rielly, ed., *American Public Opinion and U.S. Foreign Policy 1987* (Chicago: Chicago Council on Foreign Relations, 1987), p. 21. Survey by Gallup, October 30 to November 12, 1986; N = 1,585; the leadership survey was conducted between mid-September and mid-November 1986; N = 343.

security is indivisible. . . . "[63] In fact, American leadership support for the NATO commitment is overwhelming, and there is also extremely high support among the mass public. Studies by the Chicago Council on Foreign Relations (CCFR) confirm this for the period 1978 through 1986 as Table 2–1 illustrates. There is also very high support (93 percent of leaders and 68 percent of the public) for using U.S. troops if the "Soviets invade Western Europe."[64]

A similar survey was conducted in October 1987 for the World Policy Institute. It found that although 86 percent of the respondents favored "requiring the Japanese, Koreans, and Europeans to pay for their own defense" (8 percent opposed),[65] only 33 percent favored withdrawing U.S. troops while 46 percent opposed withdrawal.[66]

The 1986 CCFR study also examined the relative priority of Europe and Asia to global U.S. security interests. One question stated, "Some Europeans are worried that both American popular attention and leadership attention are shifting away from Europe to Asia. Which area do you think is more important to the United States, Europe or Asia?" Forty-six percent of the leadership sample replied that Europe was more important, 18 percent said Asia was more important, and 34 percent said they were equally important.[67] Even if this reflects a diminution of relative interest in Europe compared to the past, Europe retains a considerable advantage. Moreover, Europe's edge was higher in the Congressional sample (which is representative of the whole nation) than among administration officials (where Westerners were more prevalent).[68] Considering that it is the U.S. Congress, rather than the executive branch, which has traditionally questioned the European commitments, and the likelihood that the influence of Westerners will decline in the next presidential administration, this should reassure Europeans.

These public opinion data suggest that Europeans may exaggerate the probability of early troop withdrawals. But even twenty years ago, Senator Mansfield marshalled considerable support for his proposals, and today many more highly respected politicians and policy analysts advocate troop cutbacks.

The trade and budget deficits, accentuated by the October 1987 financial crash, highlight significant problems which American policymakers must address. It is true that redeploying troops, as the neoconservatives advocate, generates no savings.[69] But even granting that demobilization is the *sine qua non* for deficit reduction, *The Economist*'s conclusion is irrefutable: "sooner or later, America will do less to defend Western Europe."[70] *The Times* drew this conclusion from President Reagan's October 1987 speech at West Point in which he said that "the alliance should become more and more among equals, indeed an alliance between continents."[71] Evidence is also accumulating that top West German elected officials now anticipate U.S. troop withdrawals in the near future and are even resigned to them so long as significant U.S. forces remain.[72]

THE NUCLEAR COMMITMENT

Burden sharing receives more domestic political attention in the United States, but through the years nuclear policy has largely defined the Euro-American security debate. When the United States possessed a nuclear monopoly (1945-9), or even nuclear superiority (from 1949 through approximately 1968),[73] it could credibly deter Soviet attacks upon Western Europe by threatening nuclear responses. This was true under the Eisenhower administration's policy of massive retaliation and, initially, under flexible response. Since the Kennedy administration (but officially only since 1967, when MC-14/3 was approved as NATO doctrine) flexible response has threatened that NATO might initiate the use of tactical nuclear weapons if the Warsaw Pact nations attacked and NATO's conventional defense was failing. As a final stage, flexible response threatens direct American nuclear attacks against the Soviet Union if NATO is losing a limited nuclear war.

As the Soviets' capacity to annihilate the United States with nuclear weapons grew, self-deterrence undermined the credibility of this threat, and it became increasingly dubious that the United States would honor its commitment. As early as 1959, when massive retaliation remained America's declaratory policy for extended deterrence, Secretary of State Christian Herter told the Senate Foreign Relations Committee, "I cannot conceive of any President engaging in all-out nuclear war unless we are in danger of all-out devastation ourselves."[74] And despite the declared policy of flexible response, former Secretary of Defense Robert McNamara wrote that "in long private conversations with successive Presidents—Kennedy and Johnson—I recommended, without qualification, that they never initiate, under any circumstances, the use of nuclear weapons."[75]

The most publicized example of such reservations by a senior American national security official is former Secretary of State Henry Kissinger's speech in 1979, which stated:

> it is absurd to base the strategy of the West on the credibility of the threat of mutual suicide. . . . European allies should not keep asking us to multiply strategic assurances that we cannot possibly mean, or if we do mean, we should not want to execute because if we execute, we risk the destruction of civilization.[76]

Senator Sam Nunn asserted that, "Under conditions of strategic parity and theater nuclear inferiority, a NATO nuclear response to non-nuclear Soviet aggression in Europe would be a questionable strategy at best, a self-defeating one at worst."[77] And Admiral Stansfield Turner, director of Central Intelligence during the Carter administration, wrote that

> a nuclear attack against Western Europe would provoke a response only against Eastern Europe. All reprisals must be symmetrical. . . . You Europeans must understand well the following: the Soviets have considerably augmented their nuclear power. Today, they have become dangerous. If we attack Moscow to defend one of your European cities, we would risk receiving a bomb on New York; therefore, we will not do it. Stop believing that the United States protects you. . . .[78]

These avowals by national security officials from five successive administrations (Eisenhower, Kennedy, Johnson, Nixon, Ford and Carter), as well as Senator Nunn, proclaim the improbability that the United States would initiate the use of nuclear weapons—or perhaps even retaliate against Soviet territory—to deter or defend Western Europe, as NATO doctrine stipulates.[79]

European confidence in the American nuclear umbrella eroded as the United States became increasingly vulnerable to Soviet attack. The Reagan administration introduced new shocks when the Strategic Defense Initiative (SDI), the 1986 Reykjavik summit, and the "double zero" arms control treaty for the removal of intermediate nuclear forces challenged the very legitimacy of nuclear deterrence.

SDI

As outlined by President Reagan's initial speech (March 1983), SDI foresaw a "leakproof" population defense which, in the president's words, would "give us the means of rendering these nuclear weapons impotent and obsolete." Nearly everyone, except the president himself, soon acknowledged the futility of that goal, at least in the foreseeable future. So the Reagan administration retained population defense as the ultimate goal but redefined SDI's short-term objective as "enhancing the basis of deterrence, strengthening stability, and thereby increasing the security of the United States and our allies."[80] Most analysts also accept the view of Reagan administration arms control adviser Paul Nitze that a workable defensive system must be defensible, that is sufficiently invulnerable to preemptive attack, and "cost-effective at the margin. . . . " This means "cheap enough to add additional defense capability so that the other side has no incentive to add additional offensive capability to overcome the defense."[81]

The SDI debate has stressed two issues: the program's technical feasibility and its strategic effects. These concerns are interrelated, but the strategic implications are more salient to the politics of European defense cooperation. Therefore, the author will sidestep the vital issues of technical practicality, survivability, and cost to focus on the probable political effects of SDI—particularly its implications for United States-Western European relations.

Increasingly, the SDI program has stressed defending American military assets—especially land-based ballistic missiles—from Soviet attack. There is nothing revolutionary about that: the United States once maintained a substantial air defense against bomber attacks,[82] and the Nixon administration built a Safeguard anti-ballistic missile (ABM) system at Grand Forks, North Dakota to defend Minuteman missiles.[83] The distinctive element of recent American nuclear policy is President Reagan's vision of a world made safe from nuclear weapons. Heretofore, nuclear weapons were considered so destructive that a leakproof population defense was dismissed as preposterous. Therefore, in its more utopian presidential formulation, SDI was a revolutionary concept with profound implications for all facets of U.S. national security and arms control policy, including extended deterrence.

If the superpowers deployed leakproof population shields which were both survivable and cost effective at the margin,[84] they *might* agree to massive reductions in nuclear arsenals as President Reagan has predicted.[85] However, the superpowers are more likely to pursue ways to foil the other's defenses, even including such unconventional and destabilizing vectors as "suitcase" bombs.

Leakproof defenses could strengthen Western European security by reinforcing the credibility of the American nuclear guarantee. As Bavarian Prime Minister Franz Josef Strauss has argued, "we are very much interested in the Americans achieving invulnerability through such a defense system because, as a result, the credibility of their intercontinental missile deterrent would be even greater and more infallible than it is today."[86] However, Soviet defenses will undermine the nuclear umbrella's deterrent effect. Because defense against short-range and subatmospheric weapon systems is more difficult, Western Europe's defenses are likely to be less effective than those of the superpowers.[87] This could encourage the outbreak of limited nuclear war in Western Europe if leakproof defenses diminished superpowers' fears that a limited war might escalate and engulf their homelands.

Even if the Reagan administration's stated goal were achieved, and Western Europe were also defended,[88] this would still confront NATO-Europe with the Warsaw Pact's conventional threat. Since the alliance's creation, NATO has consistently considered its conventional military forces insufficient for an adequate defense, so the United States has buttressed these capabilities with threats to initiate the use of nuclear weapons if conventional defense fails. The United States first extended this commitment when it enjoyed strategic superiority, but in theory the commitment continues today. Having spent hundreds of billions, and perhaps more than one trillion, dollars on strategic defense, the West would then need to increase spending for expensive conventional forces.

Finally, because the British and French nuclear arsenals are substantially smaller than America's, effective Soviet defenses would have more effect on those countries. Given these probable consequences—greater risks of conventional and/or limited nuclear war and a weakened European deterrent—perfect (or nearly perfect) defenses would erode (rather than enhance) European security.

The development of partial defenses suitable to protect retaliatory weapons is more probable. Unlike perfect defenses, a partial shield would not reverse the effects of mutual superpower vulnerability and reestablish the credibility of America's nuclear guarantee. However, a partial Soviet defense could erode the deterrent effect of the British and French forces and undermine America's retaliatory capability. Under present circumstances, if a Soviet first strike demolished every American land-based intercontinental ballistic missile (ICBM), the United States could still retaliate with 4,500 SLBM (submarine-launched ballistic missile) warheads. If both superpowers deployed defensive shields capable of destroying 4,000 reentry vehicles, 2,240 Minuteman warheads might survive the first strike, so the United States could retaliate with 6,740 warheads (4,500 SLBM warheads plus 2,240 ICBM warheads). But fewer warheads (2,740 warheads rather than 4,500) would reach their targets, for the Soviet shield would destroy the remainder.[89] Thus, the existence of the Soviet defense would actually degrade America's riposte. It would also increase the advantage of striking first if war were perceived to be unavoidable, and diminish incentives to control and limit nuclear warfare, for limited strikes would lighten the defender's task.[90]

Finally, although the Reagan administration argued that strategic defense would encourage deep cuts in the superpowers' nuclear stockpiles, partial shields are more likely to stimulate the arms competition and hobble arms control prospects. Neither superpower is likely to cut its arsenal while its adversary is building defenses. Traditionally, military organizations attempt to defeat defenses through saturation or circumvention.[91] Examples include the development of MIRVed (multiple independently targeted reentry vehicle) ballistic missiles, whose original purpose was to inundate ballistic missile defense systems, and Germany's outflanking of the Maginot Line by striking France through Belgium in 1940. Prior to the November 1985 Geneva summit, even Defense Secretary Caspar Weinberger advanced the argument that defense might stimulate the arms race. He described evidence of Soviet preparations for ballistic missile defense that "could have a profound impact on our strategic deterrent forces," and argued that, "Even a *probable* territorial defense would require us to increase the number of our offensive forces and their ability to penetrate Soviet defenses to assure that our operational plans could be executed."[92]

These undesired effects made Europeans very skeptical of SDI, and the bilateral SDI research agreements negotiated with Britain, West Germany, and Italy did not demonstrate European support for SDI as the Reagan administration had alleged. France was SDI's principal European critic, but the French, as Pierre Lellouche observed, "only said aloud . . . what the other Europeans were thinking without, however, daring to say it so bluntly to the Americans."[93] According to an October 1986 resolution (passed 129 to 126, with 3 abstaining), the European Parliament, "profoundly regrets that America's inflexible attachment to the Strategic Defense Initiative caused the failure of an historic opportunity to substantially reduce the number of strategic missiles and to abolish all intermediate range missiles in Europe. . . . " According to the Parliament, it was "absolutely unacceptable that a program like SDI, which serves exclusively the United States, obstructs steps aimed at disarmament."[94]

Germany's initial reaction to SDI was confused but overwhelmingly negative; there was even criticism from conservatives such as Defense Minister Manfred Wörner. But the typical partisan alignment soon asserted itself.[95] Green Party supporters were most critical; they saw SDI as inherently offensive and intended to reestablish U.S. nuclear superiority. The left wing of the SPD shared this viewpoint; for example, the influential SPD parliamentarian Egon Bahr maintained that "Moscow is offering common security, Washington is still bound to the idea that the United States has to remain a power second to none."[96] More conservative Social Democrats also opposed SDI, but they principally feared that SDI might succeed and decouple the United States from Europe.

Although the Free Democrats belonged to the governing coalition, and their leader Martin Bangemann negotiated the German-American SDI agreement, the Free Democratic Party (FDP) was very skeptical. They worried that even an SDI research program could destabilize the European balance because Moscow considers the program an effort to reestablish American superiority. The FDP also feared that SDI could absorb the funding needed to finance the enhanced conventional forces that strategic defense would necessitate.

The FDP also shared the widespread German condemnation of SDI for creating "different zones of security" within NATO. Obviously, geography and history make differing degrees of vulnerability inevitable, but Bonn seeks to minimize them. Germans realize that American invulnerability would make the nuclear guarantee more credible, but it would reduce the likelihood that a European war would escalate out of control and engulf the Soviet and American homelands. This would lessen Soviet risks and weaken deterrence. SDI's model of deterrence assumes, as Albert Wohlstetter wrote, "that the West can deter Soviet attack most effectively by improving its ability and will to respond in a non-suicidal way if deterrence fails." But in Germany, the prevailing concept of deterrence "rests its hopes for deterring on ensuring that if deterrence fails, any response the West could make to an attack would lead uncontrollably to the apocalypse."[97]

Because "deterrence by punishment" is widely accepted in the Federal Republic, even German conservatives extended only tepid support to SDI. This was especially true within the Christian Democratic Union (CDU), and there was no parallel to the American right's dream of shifting from "assured destruction" to "assured survival." Even SDI proponents such as former Defense Minister Kai-Uwe von Hassel and Professor Werner Kaltefleiter justified strategic defense as a necessary response to Soviet programs rather than a transition to a new strategic era.[98] According to Elizabeth Pond, although Chancellor Helmut Kohl

> has been eager to endorse SDI rhetorically—both to demonstrate solidarity with Reagan and to signal to Moscow that the Alliance cannot be split on the subject—he has consistently specified that what he is endorsing is a research programme only.[99]

Therefore, although the strongest German critics of SDI were outside Bonn's center-right coalition, even the government rejected the Reagan administration's basic premise that strategic defense could (or should) supersede nuclear deterrence.[100] Bonn's concerns were made explicit by the conditions attached to SDI participation:

- European security must not be decoupled from the security of the United States;
- The NATO strategy of Flexible Response must remain valid without any revision as long as no more promising alternative of war prevention has been found;
- Instabilities in a possible transition phase from a strategy based exclusively on deterrence to a new form of strategic stability which would rely more on defensive systems must be avoided; and
- Conventional disparities must be reduced.[101]

The German government did not share the Reagan administration's strategic vision, but signed the SDI agreement to avoid alienating Washington and to capitalize on commercial and technological opportunities. For this reason, it was Economics Minister Martin Bangemann, rather than Defense Minister Manfred Wörner, who negotiated the accord.[102] Bonn rejected Washington's argument that defense would lead to disarmament, but hoped that pressure for deep reductions in strategic nuclear arsenals would compel the superpowers to restrict defensive deployments.

The British reaction was much like the German. Labour, the Liberals, and the Social Democratic Party (SDP) opposed SDI, and the Conservatives extended conditional support. In 1986, the Labour Party and the German Social Democrats signed a joint communiqué pledging, if returned to power, to "end their Governments' support for and participation in the SDI programme."[103] And prior to the 1987 British general election, party leaders David Steel (Liberal) and David Owen (SDP) condemned SDI as "breaching the Anti-Ballistic Missile Treaty . . . destabilizing and likely to lead to nuclear escalation [and] . . . a barrier to a disarmament agreement."[104]

Prime Minister Margaret Thatcher's Conservative government also attached four conditions to the Anglo-American SDI agreement which have been labeled "the holy writ of European conditions for supporting SDI research. . . ."[105] The conditions:

1. The United States and Western aim is not to achieve superiority, but to maintain balance, taking account of Soviet developments;
2. SDI-related development would, in view of treaty obligations, have to be a matter of negotiation;
3. The overall aim is to enhance rather than undercut deterrence; and
4. East-West negotiations should try to achieve security with reduced levels of offensive systems on both sides.[106]

Like Bonn and Paris, London opposed a possible shift to a new deterrent concept. In the words of the late Jonathan Alford, "We don't actually want nuclear weapons to be 'impotent and obsolete;' we really don't like the thought of a world in which nuclear weapons had been disinvented. . . ."[107] Margaret Thatcher said, "I regard dreams of a nuclear-free world as just that—dreams."[108]

The British, like the Germans, were enthralled by SDI's commercial potential. British Defense Secretary Michael Heseltine even sought un-successfully to extract an American guarantee that Britain would receive at least $1.5 billion in SDI research contracts. But Britain's actual bene-fits were disappointing. British firms are expected to receive only $100 million in SDI contracts from 1986 through 1988. By the end of 1987, they had received only $45 million in contracts, just 10 percent of the level anticipated in 1985 when the SDI agreement was negotiated.[109] The commercial debacle deepened British skepticism concerning the program.

Britain and Germany both opposed early SDI deployment, but by 1987 Reagan administration officials were speculating that space-based kinetic defenses could be deployed by the mid-1990s.[110] This prompted British Foreign Secretary Sir Geoffrey Howe, who had earlier cautioned against "a new Maginot Line of the twenty-first century,"[111] to reiterate the strategic and financial arguments against a premature deployment deci-sion.[112] For various reasons, including the realization that no technology was ready for deployment, this possibility faded even before Caspar Weinberger retired as U.S. defense secretary.

FEARS OF DENUCLEARIZATION

The French, and to a lesser extent the British and Germans, were horrified that during the 1986 Reykjavik summit President Reagan and General Secretary Gorbachev agreed to move toward the elimination of interme-diate nuclear forces and endorsed the prospect of eliminating ballistic missiles (some accounts said *all* nuclear weapons) by 1996.[113] After SDI, a strong odor of *déjà vu* surrounded President Reagan's willingness to un-dercut the nuclear deterrent, which most Europeans believed had pre-served the peace since 1945, in the total absence of prior allied consultation. They were not reassured by former Assistant Secretary of Defense Richard Perle's argument that "NATO's deterrent strategy of Flexible Response would also be enhanced by the elimination of ballistic missiles."[114] Of course, the Soviet Union is relatively more dependent upon ballistic missiles (especially ground-based ICBMs), but Europeans understood that countercity threats were insufficient for credible extended deterrence.[115] Reliance upon bombers and cruise missiles might strengthen prospects for American primary deterrence, but it could weaken extended deterrence. This prompted British military historian Sir Michael Howard to describe "the approval at Reykjavik of arms reduc-tions on a scale, and of a kind, which calls the defence of Europe into question."[116] The trauma intensified when the superpowers agreed to eliminate all Soviet and American nuclear missiles in the 500 to 5,500 kilometer range (300 to 3,400 miles).

Gorbachev's acceptance of the global zero option confronted the Bonn coalition with a thorny dilemma. During the heated 1983 domestic debate on Pershing 2 and cruise missile deployments, the German government justified the Pershing 2 and GLCMs (ground-launched cruise missiles) as necessary responses to the Soviet SS-20s. And in 1987, the Reagan administration used this argument to justify the double zero treaty; for example, Richard Perle argued that NATO's INF (intermediate nuclear forces) deployments were "largely conceived to counter the Soviet SS-20s. . . ."[117]

From Europe's perspective, this was not an accurate description of the INF's purpose. The INF deployments were intended to reinforce deterrence by increasing the probability that any European war would quickly escalate and engulf Soviet and American territory. As Ambassador François de Rose argued:

> The truth is that from the moment when the anti-aircraft defense of the Warsaw Pact rendered the penetration of manned planes too onerous and hazardous, it was necessary, *even in the total absence of SS-20*, to have in Europe some American weapons capable of reaching at least the western regions of Russia. This threat of involvement of its territory would obligate the Kremlin to respond against American territory which would assure the "coupling" between the defense of Europe and the American strategic system.[118]

This perceived need for strengthened "coupling" did not arise from Soviet deployments of long-or short-range intermediate nuclear forces. It was a function of the Warsaw Pact's conventional superiority and American vulnerability to Soviet strategic attack.

When forced to choose between accepting the zero option to honor the public commitment made in 1983, or retaining INFs to avoid decoupling, the German coalition splintered. Foreign Minister Hans-Dietrich Genscher of the Free Democrats was an enthusiastic proponent of the zero option, but Franz Josef Strauss, leader of the Christian Social Union (CSU), argued for rejection despite NATO's 1979 dual-track decision and the rhetoric of 1983. Chancellor Helmut Kohl of the Christian Democrats perched on the fence. Like many in the CDU, he hoped the United States would replace a small number of Pershing 2 missiles with Pershing 1Bs (a shorter range version) to minimize "decoupling." But May 1987 state elections in Hamburg and the Rhineland-Palatinate served as quasi-referendums on this issue and demonstrated strong public support for the FDP's position. Thus domestic politics, and strong American pressure, eventually caused Chancellor Kohl to go even further and scrap Germany's seventy-two Pershing 1A missiles whose warheads were under U.S. control.[119]

The French reaction to double zero was less ambiguous but not without confusion. Most politicians criticized the possible "denuclearization" of Western Europe—especially Defense Minister André Giraud, who compared it to the 1938 Munich Conference. The skeptics included both past Socialist defense ministers (Charles Hernu and Paul Quilès) and prominent conservatives such as former prime minister Raymond Barre and former president Valéry Giscard d'Estaing. President Mitterrand was the significant exception, but he was constrained by his past advocacy of "Neither Pershing nor SS-20." Like the Bonn government, Mitterrand faced a credibility problem if he refused to take yes for an answer. Mitterrand was also reluctant to widen the gap between France and her European allies—especially the Federal Republic—on this crucial issue. Because Prime Minister Chirac wished to minimize dissension between the Matignon and the Elysée on defense policy issues during the period of *cohabitation*,[120] he was swayed by Mitterrand, and Paris muted its opposition.

AMERICA AND EUROPEAN DEFENSE COOPERATION

Europeans are beset by increasing doubts concerning both legs of America's European commitment. As Michael Strümer argued in the *Frankfurter Allgemeine Zeitung*, "coupling" is less a matter of military capabilities than of "U.S. resolve to make Europe's security America's own and of how the Soviet Union views this attitude."[121] But SDI, Reykjavik, and double zero convinced many Europeans that "Americans would dearly like to escape the consequences of the fact that European security requires the United States to throw its own security into the balance."[122] But to the Europeans, a second concern is even more frightening; as one West European ambassador expressed it to *The New York Times*, "I would find it altogether extraordinary if the United States still had 326,000 troops in Europe in the year 2000."[123] This belief is particularly distressing because most Europeans agree with former NATO Secretary General Lord Carrington that "Flesh and blood count for more than abstract deterrent concepts. The tangible manifestation of the American commitment to the defense of Europe is . . . the presence of 326,000 in-place troops and their dependents." [124]

One cannot measure the precise impact of the diminished confidence in the American commitments, but even British Foreign Secretary Sir Geoffrey Howe has cautioned Europeans "to be alert to trends in American thinking which might diminish our security—perhaps not today or tomorrow, but possibly in the longer term."[125] Certainly more Europeans are asking the question posed by French parliamentarian (and secretary of the Defense Committee) Jean-Pierre Bechter: "Do you think 320 million Europeans can continue forever to ask 240 million Americans to defend us against 280 million Soviets?"[126]

Later chapters of this text will describe how fears of American decoupling have stimulated interest in European defense cooperation, but a prior question asks whether European defense cooperation would invigorate or enervate the Atlantic Alliance. Sir Geoffrey Howe has written that "No better image has ever been found for the Atlantic Alliance than the arch supported by two pillars, one planted in North America, the other in Western Europe."[127] Although common, this imagery is quite deceptive, for the evolution of a true European pillar was forestalled by the collapse of the EDC initiative. Therefore, the United States has dominated the Western Alliance, and European-American relations would be profoundly transformed if European cooperation spawned a more balanced partnership.

NATO rhetoric has long extolled the alleged advantages of two equal pillars. For example, Stanley Sloan recalled Secretary of State Dean Acheson's view that "the European Defense Community and NATO are completely interconnected. Neither is complete without the other," and according to Sloan, "The NATO alliance remains incomplete without a more coherent European contribution to Western defense."[128] Most observers share this perception, including former French defense minister André Giraud, who asserted in 1987 that "The defense of Europe must remain first of all a European responsibility. It is also a condition for the deepening of their alliance with the United States. The state of dependency does not lead to the solidarity of destinies."[129] In June 1984 even Prime Minister Thatcher overcame her ambivalence and proclaimed that the United Kingdom was ready "to strengthen the European pillar of the Alliance."

There is also The Economist's editorial judgment that "A lopsided alliance has come to be a bad-tempered alliance."[130] Americans resent

Europe's failure to bear a larger share of the defense burden and the tendency to distance itself from controversial U.S. policies such as the 1986 Libyan bombings. Europe, by comparison, resents American domination but fears abandonment. That these frictions arise from inequality is no guarantee that "It will be healthier for Europe, as well as calming for America, if the military burden is better shared."[131] Until Europe unifies politically (still a distant aspiration), the European pillar will remain a conglomerate of separate and querulous European states, not a unitary state comparable to the United States. Such an arrangement is inherently less stable than either the current structure based on American leadership or an alliance composed of two approximately equal states which neither could dominate.

Europeans are distressed by their exclusion from critical discussions which affect their vital interests. For example, Giscard decried the absence of Western Europe's viewpoint at the Iceland summit as "a historic scandal," and he argued that a European president was needed to fulfill this role.[132] Many Europeans hope to remedy this shortcoming by a two stage decision-making process which starts with European consultations followed by a U.S.-European dialogue. In September 1987, Giscard recommended that once the double zero agreement was final, European leaders should meet in an appropriate forum "for example that of the Western European Union, to define a method to undertake the clarification of their strategic concepts before discussing them with our American allies within the European-Atlantic alliance."[133]

One weakness of this approach is that intra-European disputes often obstruct efforts to forge a common European position. Recently, this has been true of policies concerning the application of arms control to battlefield nuclear weapons, SDI, terrorism, and the Persian Gulf. Furthermore, Washington dislikes being confronted by European ultimatums. For example, while serving as the Reagan administration's assistant secretary of state for European affairs, Richard Burt sent a letter to the seven WEU members to discourage discussions of current arms control issues within the WEU.[134] This produced a British apology for improper discussions, and the FRG also agreed to refrain. Meanwhile, the French were annoyed by Burt's interference and interpreted the British and German responses as fresh evidence that London and Bonn were Washington's lap dogs.

This case demonstrate's Washington's distaste for "pre-cooked" positions taken in forums which exclude the United States. As a senior U.S. diplomat told *The New York Times*, "We've always told them to get their act together, but when they do, we tell them they're undermining NATO consultation."[135] It also illustrates European susceptibility to American influence, and both factors militate against a European pillar operating as the Europeans hope. French Ambassador François Puaux even concluded that "true European defense" was impossible because "the hostility of the United States to all projects of this type makes it vain at the start."[136] But more recently, *Le Monde* editorialized that America's "initial mistrust of the WEU has abated . . . " and that Washington has now given "the green light" to strengthening the European pillar.[137]

If the United States follows Henry Kissinger's advice to "abandon its historic reserve and welcome a European identity in defense,"[138] Americans should expect that a stronger European pillar will magnify expressions of divergent European and American interests. For example, French leaders believe that European independence requires a *balance* between the superpowers, and at times Paris has sought to constrain the dominance of *both* superpowers.[139] Although François Mitterrand tilted more overtly toward the United States than previous Fifth Republic presidents had done, he did not alter France's basic strategy. Instead, Mitterrand was responding to his own perception that the advantage had shifted too far toward Moscow which impelled France to shift further toward the United States. If the United States were once more on the ascendant, France would adjust its policy. Walter Schütze has even argued that Mitterrand feared SDI because if successful it could create a destabilizing U.S. superiority.[140]

Some analysts argue that the United States is now more acceptant of European consultation than the Burt letter would imply. Indeed, in a November 1987 broadcast beamed to Europe, President Reagan said that Americans "applaud what we see as a new willingness, even eagerness, on the part of some of our allies to increase the level of cooperation and coordination among themselves in European defense." The President then explicitly praised both Franco-German defense cooperation and the WEU's security platform and asserted that

> all too often the United States has been viewed as the senior partner of the Alliance. Well today, when the economic strength of Western Europe and the United States are fully comparable, the time has long since come when we will view ourselves as equal partners. And a more equal relationship should not diminish our bonds, but strengthen them.[141]

But old habits die hard. America has managed NATO policy throughout its history, and further discord between the old and new worlds is inevitable as Europeans pursue an increasingly independent path.

NOTES

1. See Lawrence Freedman, *Britain and Nuclear Weapons* (London: Macmillan, 1980), p. 4 and Wilfrid L. Kohl, *French Nuclear Diplomacy* (Princeton: Princeton University Press, 1971), pp. 179–80.
2. James R. Schlesinger, "An American Perspective," in Robert E. Hunter, ed., *NATO: The Next Generation* (Boulder: Westview Press, 1984), p. 39.
3. See *The Defence of Europe* (Washington, D.C.: U.S. Department of State, n.d.), p. 3.
4. Former German Chancellor Helmut Schmidt has said, "I absolutely do not consider the American soldiers present in Europe as hostages." Helmut Schmidt, "L'équation allemande: Entretien avec Helmut Schmidt," *Politique internationale* (Spring 1985): 149.
5. See William W. Kaufmann, "Nonnuclear Deterrence," in John D. Steinbruner and Leon V. Sigal, eds., *Alliance Security: NATO and the No-First-Use Question* (Washington, D.C.: Brookings Institution, 1983), p. 62 and James A. Thomson and Nanette C. Brown, "Theater Forces: U.S. Defense Policy in NATO," in George E. Hudson and Joseph Kruzel, eds., *American Defense Annual 1985–1986* (Lexington, MA: Lexington Books, 1985), pp. 97–113.
6. "Defence Expenditures of NATO Countries 1970–1986," *NATO Review* 35 (February 1987): 32.
7. Calculated from data in Caspar W. Weinberger, Secretary of Defense, *Report on Allied Contributions to the Common Defense: A Report to the United States Congress* (Washington, D.C.: U.S. Department of Defense, April 1987). For a similar analysis, see Leonard Sullivan, Jr., "The Defense Budget," in George E. Hudson and Joseph Kruzel, eds., *American Defense Annual 1985–1986* (Lexington, MA: Lexington Books, 1985), pp. 74–75.
8. See "Defence Expenditures of NATO Countries 1970–1986," *NATO Review* 35 (February 1987): 33.
9. See John C. Kimball, *Europe and North America: An Atlas/Almanac of Allies and Adversaries* (New York: Foreign Policy Association, 1986), p. 68 and Barry R. Posen and Stephen W. Van Evera, "Reagan Administration Defense Policy: Departure From Containment," in Kenneth A. Oye, Robert J. Lieber, and Donald Rothchild, eds., *Eagle Resurgent? The Reagan Era in American Foreign Policy* (Boston: Little Brown, 1987), p. 98. For France alone, Heisbourg estimated the cost as equal to 0.5 percent of GDP; see François Heisbourg, "Défense Française: L'impossible statu quo," *Politique internationale* (Summer 1987): 142.
10. Government of the Federal Republic of Germany, *The German Contribution to the Common Defense* (Bonn: Press and Information Offices of the

Federal Republic of Germany and the Federal Ministry of Defense, 1986), p. 21.

11. See Richard Halloran, "Two Studies Say Defense of Western Europe Is Biggest U.S. Military Cost," *The New York Times*, 20 July 1984. Also see Earl C. Ravenal, "Europe Without America," *Foreign Affairs* 63 (Summer 1985): 1029 and Jeffrey Record, *Revising U.S. Military Strategy: Tailoring Means to Ends* (McLean, VA: Pergamon-Brassey's, 1984), p. 55. The U.S. ambassador in London, Charles Price, gave a slightly lower figure. He stated that "We maintain a third of a million troops in Europe and this costs us over $120 billion a year, about 40 percent of our defence budget." Charles Price, "The risks for Europe in anti-American sentiment," *Manchester Guardian Weekly*, 22 March 1987. Congresswoman Schroeder estimates that "60 percent of our defense budget has gone to North Atlantic Treaty Organization defense commitments." Pat Schroeder, "The Burden-Sharing Numbers Racket," *The New York Times*, 6 April 1988.

12. See NATO Press Service, *Financial and Economic Data Relating to NATO Defence*, M-DPC-2(87)48 (Brussels: NATO, December 1, 1987), p. 4.

13. These calculations are very sensitive to exchange rate fluctuations. In 1985, when the dollar was stronger, U.S. per capita spending for European defense exceeded that for every NATO-European country. See Caspar W. Weinberger, Secretary of Defense, *Report on Allied Contributions to the Common Defense: A Report to the United States Congress* (Washington, D.C.: U.S. Department of Defense, April 1987), p. 90 and Gordon Adams and Eric Munz, *Fair Shares: Bearing the Burden of the NATO Alliance* (Washington, D.C.: Defense Budget Project, March 1988), pp. 67–68.

14. Caspar Weinberger, "Europe-Amérique: la sécurité indivisible," *Le Monde*, 11 September 1987. Or, as NATO's Defense Planning Committee expressed it,

> the defence of Europe and North America is indivisible. The commitment of United States nuclear forces in Europe remains indispensable for the security of the whole Alliance. The continued presence of . . . United States forces at existing levels in Europe plays an irreplaceable role in the defence of North America as well as Europe.

Press Communique M-DPC-1(87)23 (Brussels: NATO Press Service, May 27, 1987), p. 1.

15. See "U.S. Faces Up to Erosion of Economic Supremacy," *Washington Post*, 15 April 1987.

16. Quoted in Phil Williams, *The Senate and U.S. Troops in Europe* (London: Macmillan, 1985), p. 71. In 1966, President Eisenhower wrote a letter to Senator Henry Jackson and Representative Edna Kelly recalling

that U.S. troops were deployed "on the strict understanding that 'as soon as Europe could raise, train and deploy' an adequate ground force of its own the 'major portion' of the American contingent would be returned to the United States, leaving only air and naval units on permanent guard in Europe." Benjamin Welles, "Eisenhower Calls for a 'Drastic' Amendment of Nation's Atomic Laws," *The New York Times*, 22 May 1966.

17. Quoted in Williams, *The Senate and U.S. Troops*, p. 137. The author's discussion draws heavily upon Williams' analysis. Also see James Chace, "Ike Was Right," *The Atlantic Monthly* 260 (August 1987): 39.

18. See James M. Markham, "Europe Looks to '92 as Year Dreams of Union Come True," *The New York Times*, 16 July 1988.

19. See Daniel Charles, *Nuclear Planning in NATO: Pitfalls of First Use* (Cambridge, MA: Ballinger, 1987), p. 165.

20. See U.S. Secretary of Defense, *Report of the Secretary of Defense Caspar W. Weinberger to the Congress on the FY 1988/FY 1989 Budget and FY 1988–92 Defense Programs* (Washington, D.C.: U.S. Government Printing Office, January 12, 1987), p. 29.

21. Ibid., p. 30. Also see Secretary Alexander Haig, "Peace and Deterrence," *Current Policy*, No. 383 (Washington, D.C.: U.S. Department of State, April 6, 1982); *NATO and the Warsaw Pact: Force Comparisons* (Brussels: NATO Information Service, 1984); and *Can America Catch Up?* (Washington, D.C.: Committee on the Present Danger, 1984), pp. 53–55.

22. Horst Ehmke, "A Second Phase of Detente," *World Policy* 4 (Summer 1987): 376.

23. Jonathan Dean, *Watershed in Europe* (Lexington, MA: Lexington Books, 1986), p. 57. Also see William W. Kaufmann, "Nonnuclear Deterrence," pp. 43–90; John J. Mearsheimer, "Why the Soviets Can't Win Quickly in Central Europe," *International Security* 7 (Summer 1982): 3–39; Barry R. Posen, "Measuring the European Conventional Balance: Coping With Complexity in Threat Assessment," *International Security* 9 (Winter 1984–85): 47–88; Barry R. Posen and Stephen W. Van Evera, "Reagan Administration Defense Policy", pp. 83–85; and Admiral Antoine Sanguinetti (ret.), "L'équilibre militaire conventionnel des deux blocs," *Le Monde Diplomatique* 34 (October 1987): 14–15.

24. See Bernard E. Trainor, "U.S. Rates Non-Atom NATO Arms," *The New York Times*, 30 November 1987 and *Newsweek*, 19 October 1987.

25. For example, in May 1987 the NATO defense ministers "reaffirmed the aim of a 3% real increase in defence expenditure as a general guide. . . ." *Press Communique*, p. 2.

26. See for example Reimund Seidelman, "Europeanizing European Security? A Political Demythologicalization," in Robert J. Jackson, ed., *Continuity of Discord: Crises and Responses in the Atlantic Community* (New York: Praeger, 1985), pp. 143–44.

27. For example, Pierre Lellouche writes that "the French certainly support their deterrent, but as an instrument of *non-war* rather than of defense." Pierre Lellouche, *L'Avenir de la guerre* (Paris: Editions Mazarine, 1985), p. 21; also see pp. 50–53.

28. See James A. Thomson and Nanette C. Brown, "Theater Forces," p. 105.

29. See François Heisbourg, "Défense et sécurité extérieure: le changement dans la continuité," *Politique étrangère* 50 (Summer 1985): 378 and Robbin Laird, "France's Strategic Posture," *Defense and Foreign Affairs* (May 1986): 9–11.

30. See "Défense: plus de 177 milliards de francs," *Le Monde*, 25 July 1987; "M. Giraud donne la priorité à l'équipement des armées," *Le Monde*, 9 October 1987; and Pierre Servent, "Défense: quelques pierres dans le jardin de l'Elysée," *Le Monde*, 11 November 1987.

31. See *The Week in Germany*, 4 December 1987, p. 1; 9 July 1987, p. 5; and 15 July 1988, p. 1.

32. Based on data from *The Military Balance*, and using the Joint Chiefs of Staff estimate of Soviet defense spending ($295 billion), the 1984 comparison is NATO $303 billion and WTO $319 billion. However, this does not include Japanese expenditures nor does it adjust for those Soviet expenditure (estimated by the Central Intelligence Agency), as 12.5 to 20 percent) which are directed toward China. See *The Military Balance 1986–1987* (London: International Institute of Strategic Studies, 1986), p. 212; Barry R. Posen and Stephen W. Van Evera, "Reagan Administration Defense Policy," p. 80; and Franklyn D. Holzman, "What Defense-Spending Gap?" *The New York Times*, 3 March 1986. Holzman estimated that after appropriate adjustments, during the decade from 1971 to 1980 NATO defense expenditures exceeded those of the WTO by $740 billion.

33. Robin Beard, "NATO armaments co-operation: picking up the gauntlet," *NATO Review* 35 (February 1987): 12. It is symptomatic that Britain and France place approximately 80 percent of their defense contracts with their own industries. See "Open Market In Defence: IEPG report on arms collaboration by Nato countries," *Financial Times*, 10 February 1987. Also see Michael Heseltine, "The Defense of Europe: Europe's Interests, Europe's Choices," *RUSI: Journal of the Royal United Services Institute for Defence Studies* 129 (December 1984): 5.

34. Quoted in Jérôme Dumoulin and Elie Marcuse, "L'Europe sans défense?," *L'Express*, 2 October 1987.

35. Richard Burt, "America Needs Troops in Europe," *Manchester Guardian Weekly*, 29 March 1987.

36. For example, Europeans point out that 84 percent of recent immigrants to the U.S. come from Latin America and Asia, while during the 1960s 62 percent came from Europe. See Wolfgang Borgmann, "Americans and Germans: four points of view," *The German Tribune*, 27 September 1987

(translated from *Stuttgarter Zeitung*, 17 September 1987). The prestigious *Frankfurter Allgemeine Zeitung* wrote that

> Californians know little about their distant German partner in the heart of Europe. Events in Mexico or Korea arouse greater interest. The appreciation of the worries and interests of the Germans is less pronounced than on the east coast, where the social elite is more aware of its proximity to European traditions."

Michael Groth, "Americans wrestle with the problem of trying to understand Germany," *The German Tribune*, 23 August 1987 (translated from *Frankfurter Allgemeine Zeitung*, 13 August 1987).

37. Klaus Knorr, "Burden-Sharing in NATO: Aspects of U.S. Policy," *Orbis* 29 (Fall 1985): 532.

38. After analyzing voting for Mansfield's amendment, and Senator Charles Mathias' (R-Maryland) softer version, Phil Williams concluded that "there was a clear majority in favour of a reduction of the US military presence in Western Europe." Phil Williams, *The Senate and U.S. Troops*, p. 198.

39. The Jackson-Nunn amendment of late 1973, and the final offset agreement signed in early 1974, concluded the offset issue. The problem was resolved by the elimination of fixed exchange rates and the deluge of OPEC revenues which flowed into the United States following the oil increases of 1973–1974. See Joseph Steven Lepgold, "Hegemonic Decline and Adaptation in American Foreign Policy: The United States and European Defense, 1960–1980," Vol. II, Ph.D. dissertation, Stanford University, 1986, pp. 448–51.

40. U.S. Congress, Senate *Congressional Record*, 98th Congress, 2nd Sess., Vol. 130, No. 85, June 20, 1984. Also see "Nunn Loses Round on Burden-Sharing But Starts Serious Debate on the Issue," *Congressional Quarterly* 42 (June 23, 1984): 1480–81 and Phil Williams, "The Nunn Amendment, Burden-Sharing and U.S. Troops in Europe," *Survival* 27 (January/February 1985): 2–10.

41. See David C. Morrison, "Sharing NATO's Burden," *National Journal*, 30 May 1987.

42. Robert D. Hershey, Jr., "U.S. Trade Deficit Narrows Further As Exports Grow," *The New York Times*, 13 February 1988.

43. See Susan F. Rasky, "Trade Debate Takes a Role in Campaigns," *The New York Times*, 27 July 1987. In 1986, Representative Schroeder obtained ninety votes for an amendment to decrease U.S. troops in Europe by 50 percent.

44. Martin Tolchin, "Paradox of Reagan Budgets Hints Contradiction in Legacy," *The New York Times*, 16 February 1988.

45. See Leonard Silk, "Military Budget Under Pressure," *The New York Times*, 12 February 1988.

46. See Tolchin, "Paradox of Reagan Budgets."

47. Clyde H. Farnsworth, "Budget Outlook Called Brighter," *The New York Times*, 20 August 1988.

48. Peter G. Peterson, "The Morning After," *The Atlantic Monthly* 260 (October 1987): 67. Similarly, Jeffrey Garten, a Carter administration State Department official, argued that, "The major issue facing the next Administration is not whether to share financial, trade and security burdens more evenly, but how to do it—fast." Jeffrey E. Garten, "The Looming Crisis With Bonn and Tokyo," *The New York Times*, 8 November 1987. Also see Felix Rohatyn, "Restoring American Independence," *The New York Review of Books*, 18 February 1988.

49. See Lawrence J. Korb, "Spending Without Strategy: The FY 1988 Annual Defense Department Report," *International Security* 12 (Summer 1987): 166.

50. Bill Powell, "The Politics of Austerity," *Newsweek*, 23 November 1987. The survey interviewed 500 adults by telephone on November 13, 1987.

   In August 1987, the public opposed tax increases (80 to 16 percent) and cuts in social programs (76 to 21 percent), but accepted reduced military spending (58 to 35 percent). See "Military Outlay Cut Wins Favor in Poll As a Deficit Tactic," *The New York Times*, 13 August 1987. The survey was conducted by Gallup; the sample equaled 1,607 adults above the age of eighteen. In a *New York Times*/CBS News Poll (N = 1326) conducted between October 18–22, 1987, 18 percent of the respondents favored increased defense spending, 28 percent favored decreased defense spending, and 51 percent said it should be "kept about same." "Poll Finds Iowa Voters More Liberal Than Nation," *The New York Times*, 1 November 1987.

51. See François Heisbourg, "Can the Atlantic alliance last out the century?" *International Affairs* 63 (Summer 1987): 413–417. Heisbourg, who is director of the International Institute for International Studies, was formerly a French defense ministry official and vice-president of Thomson SA. He estimates that "Such recurrent costs can typically represent 10 per cent of the purchase price of the equipment each year." (p. 415).

52. From Defense Secretary Carlucci's confirmation testimony. John H. Cushman, Jr., "Carlucci Hints Budget Plan Portends Shrinking Military," *The New York Times*, 13 November 1987.

53. Richard Halloran, "Military Cutbacks Set For 5-Year Period in 90's," *The New York Times*, 9 December 1987.

54. See "Falling Dollar Leaves Pentagon Facing a Deficit on Overseas Pay," *The New York Times*, 16 November 1987.

55. Henry Kissinger, "A Plan to Reshape NATO," *Time*, 5 March 1984.

56. Zbigniew Brzezinski, *Game Plan: A Geostrategic Framework for the Conduct of the U.S.-Soviet Contest* (Boston: The Atlantic Monthly Press,

1986), p. 181. More recently, Brzezinski argued that "It is now inevitable that some reallocation of resources and forces will have to take place, especially since the U.S. defence budget will certainly shrink." Zbigniew Brzezinski, "Next pull out the tanks," *The Times* (London), 17 September 1987. Also see Eliot Cohen, "Do We Still Need Europe?," *Commentary* 81 (January 1986): 28–35.

57. See Irving Kristol, "Reconstructing NATO: A New Role for Europe," *The Wall Street Journal*, 12 August 1982; Irving Kristol, "What's Wrong With NATO," *The New York Times Magazine*, 25 September 1983; Irving Kristol, "NATO Edges Toward the Moment of Truth," *The Wall Street Journal*, 14 April 1987; and Melvyn Krauss, *How NATO Weakens the West* (New York: Simon & Schuster, 1986). Krauss's analysis is defended in Angelo Codevilla, "American Hostages in Europe: Hostages to Fortune," *The National Interest* (Summer 1987): 89–93.

58. See William Safire, "Winds of Change," *The New York Times*, 2 April 1984 and "Europe After NATO," *The New York Times*, 22 June 1987. Zuckerman is quoted in Gar Alperovitz, "Naked NATO," *The New Republic*, 29 September 1986.

59. Krauss, *NATO Weakens the West*, p. 70.

60. Ibid., p. 76.

61. See Chace, "Ike Was Right": 39–41; David P. Calleo, *Beyond American Hegemony: The Future of the Western Alliance* (New York: Basic Books, 1987) and "The Costs of Being All Things to All People," *The New York Times*, 10 August 1986; Gar Alperovitz, "Naked NATO," *The New Republic*, 29 September 1986; "No More Rich Uncle to Rich Allies," *The New York Times*, 21 February 1986; and "The Fattest Target," *Atlantic Community News*, April-May 1986 (excerpted from TRB, *The New Republic*, 31 March 1986).

62. See for example Adam Meyerson, "How NATO Strengthens the West," *Policy Review* (Spring 1987): 82–85; John W. Coffey, "American Soldiers in Europe: a Bulwark of Freedom," *The National Interest* (Summer 1987): 83–89; Burt, "America Needs Troops," Gregory F. Treverton, letter to the editor, *The New York Times*, 5 March 1986; and Morton H. Halperin, *Nuclear Fallacy* (Cambridge, MA: Ballinger, 1987), pp. 112–14 and "Keeping Our Troops in Europe," *The New York Times Magazine*, 17 October 1982.

63. Caspar W. Weinberger, "Europe-Amérique: la sécurité indivisible," *Le Monde*, 11 September 1987.

64. John E. Rielly, ed., *American Public Opinion and U.S. Foreign Policy 1987* (Chicago: Chicago Council on Foreign Relations, 1987), p. 32.

65. *Defining American Strength: Results of a Survey of American Voters Conducted for The World Policy Institute October 15 Through October*

20, 1987 (Washington, D.C.: Mellman & Lazarus Research, 1987), p. 14. The sample equaled 1,505 registered voters.

66. See E.J. Dionne, Jr., "U.S. Poll Stresses Economic Strength," *The New York Times*, 11 November 1987.

67. Rielly, *American Public Opinion*, p. 22.

68. See ibid., p. 22, p. 38.

69. Defense Secretary Weinberger said it would actually cost $5 billion more in additional transportation, housing and maintenance costs if 100,000 troops were redeployed from Europe but not demobilized. See Leo Wieland, "Weinberger puts case for keeping US troops in Europe, but debate heats up," *The German Tribune*, 8 March 1987 (translated from *Frankfurter Allgemeine Zeitung*, 26 February 1987).

70. "Europe's braver colours," *The Economist*, 11 July 1987. Also see the discussion by Labour M.P. David Clark, "NATO's Public Relations Problems," in John Cartwright, et al., *The State of the Alliance 1986–1987: North Atlantic Assembly Reports* (Boulder: Westview, 1987), pp. 41–44.

71. Christopher Thomas, "Reagan warns that he will not abandon SDI," *The Times* (London), 29 October 1987.

72. See Chace, "Ike Was Right": 39 and R.G. Livingston, "Reagan's Debt to West Germany's Chancellor," *The New York Times*, 19 September 1987.

73. See Richard Smoke, *National Security and the Nuclear Dilemma: An Introduction to the American Experience*, 2nd ed. (New York: Random House, 1987), pp. 66–83, 106–30.

74. Quoted in George Lichtheim, *The New Europe: Today and Tomorrow*, 2nd ed. (New York: Frederick A. Praeger, 1964), p. 31.

75. Robert S. McNamara, "The Military Role of Nuclear Weapons: Perceptions and Misperceptions," *Foreign Affairs* 62 (Fall 1983): 79.

76. Henry A. Kissinger, "NATO: The Next Thirty Years," in Christoph Bertram, ed., *Strategic Deterrence in a Changing Environment* (Montclair, NJ: Allenheld, Osmun, 1981), p. 109.

77. Sam Nunn, "NATO: Saving the Alliance," *Washington Quarterly* 5 (Summer 1982): 21.

78. Stansfield Turner, "Les Avanies d'un parapluie," *Etudes polémologiques* (troisième trimestre 1984); quoted in General Etienne Copel, *La puissance de la liberté: Les chances d'une défense de l'Europe* (Paris: Lieu Commun, 1985), p. 50 and p. 176.

79. Irving Kristol has written that when he persists in asking

> "But *will* the President press the red button?" they say, "Well, it is not certain that he won't."
> That is the official view—it is not certain that he won't. In my view, it is as certain as anything can be in the political universe that he won't. It strikes me

> as absurd to think that a President is going to risk the destruction of the United States by inaugurating a nuclear holocaust because Russian tanks have moved into West Germany and our conventional forces on the Continent have failed to stop them.

Irving Kristol, "What's Wrong With NATO?" *The New York Times Magazine*, 25 September 1983.

80. *The President's Strategic Defense Initiative* (Washington, D.C.: U.S. Government Printing Office, January 1985), p. 3. According to the administration,

> to achieve the benefits which advanced defensive technologies could offer, they must, at a minimum, be able to destroy a sufficient portion of an aggressor's attacking forces to deny him confidence in the outcome of an attack or deny an aggressor the ability to destroy a militarily significant portion of the target base he wishes to attack. (p. 5)

81. Quoted in Bernard Gwertzman, "Minimum Goals Set on Space Weapons," *The New York Times*, 21 February 1985.

82. As Defense Secretary Weinberger reported, "In 1960, the DoD spent as much on active defenses against Soviet strategic bombers as on our own offensive nuclear forces." U.S. Secretary of Defense, *Report*, p. 51.

83. Because of the ABM Treaty (1972), the Safeguard facility was mothballed following construction.

84. On several occasions since 1983, President Reagan reiterated his intention to share SDI technology with the Soviets. Despite these assertions, it is inconceivable that the United States would abandon its far-reaching efforts to keep relatively innocuous technology such as Digital minicomputers and equipment to produce quieter submarines from Soviet hands and instead offer them the nation's most sophisticated secrets. This would be especially dangerous, as access to the technology would substantially abet the Soviets' effort to overcome American defenses or to apply the technology to offensive weapons. See David E. Sanger, "Many Hesitant to Share 'Star Wars'," *The New York Times*, 24 November 1985.

    Nonetheless, in previous cases the Soviets have usually matched American technological developments without American assistance. When they have not, for example, strategic bombers, it was presumably because of an explicit choice to emphasize ballistic missiles. In the case of strategic defense, no one doubts that the Soviet Union would attempt to duplicate American achievements.

85. President Reagan wrote that ". . . SDI will be a crucial means by which both the United States and the Soviet Union can safely agree to very deep reductions, and eventually, even the elimination of ballistic missiles, and the nuclear weapons they carry." *President's Strategic Defense Initiative*, p. i. Also see U.S. Secretary of Defense, *Report*, p. 54.

86. Quoted in Ivo H. Daalder, *The SDI Challenge to Europe* (Cambridge, MA: Ballinger, 1987), p. 39. Also see Henry A. Kissinger, "The Political

Realities of the Transatlantic Relationship," in Frans Bletz and Rio Praaning, eds., *The Future of European Defence* (Dordrecht: Matinus Nijhoff, 1986), p. 97 and Albert Wohlstetter, "Swords Without Shields," *The National Interest* (Summer 1987): 36.

87. Consider, for example, the opinion of former French Defense Minister Paul Quilès in a December 1985 *Le Monde* interview:

> The space shield considered in the SDI project is adapted to long- and medium-range missiles. It should therefore be able to intercept SS-20s. On the other hand, it is ineffective against short-range ballistic missiles (SS-21s, SS-22s, SS-23s), not to mention aircraft and cruise missiles which remain in the atmosphere throughout their trajectories.
>
> Consequently, if a space shield is the perfect answer for protecting the United States from the threat of ICBMs, its contribution to the protection of Europe will be very limited and wholly dependent on the political authority controlling it.
>
> For Europe only a ground defence can be considered. But an inordinately large number of systems would be necessary to protect its people. The fact is, a system appropriate for Europe could only be aimed at defending military targets.

Jacques Isnard, "SDI's real purpose is to create a consensus in American society," *Le Monde* section, *Manchester Guardian Weekly*, 5 January 1986. Under the INF agreement, the Pershing 2 missiles that created the greatest defensive challenge to the USSR are being withdrawn.

88. See Charles Mohr, "'Star Wars' Director Urges Drive For Short-Range Missile Defense," *The New York Times*, 31 October 1985, and Ivo H. Daalder, *The SDI Challenge*, pp. 8–12.

89. See U.S. Congress, Office of Technology Assessment, *Ballistic Missile Defense Technologies*, OTA-ISC 254 (Washington, D.C.: U.S. Government Printing Office, September 1985), pp. 104–06, Charles Mohr, "Antimissile Shield Held to Raise Risk of a Nuclear War," *The New York Times*, 25 September 1985; and Bill Keller, "Pentagon Disputes Report on Missile Defense," *The New York Times*, 26 September 1985.

90. As Stanley Hoffmann has written:

> even partially effective defenses would narrow the range of limited nuclear strikes each side might be able to carry on against targets in the other country. The very thing the President seems to dread most—planning for all-out nuclear war—thus becomes more rather than less likely. The loss of the more limited options would hurt the US (which has envisaged them in case of a Soviet conventional attack on NATO) more than the Soviets, who seem to have no plans for limited nuclear strikes against the United States.

Stanley Hoffmann, "Fog Over the Summit," *The New York Review of Books* 32 (January 16, 1986): 24.

91. Military technology is dynamic, and eventually every defense is defeated. For example, the machine gun's role in World War I represents the apogee of defense in this century, but in 1939 and 1940 German panzer

tactics shifted the advantage to the offense. On this general point, see Walter C. Clemens, Jr., "Good Offense Beats a Good (Star Wars) Defense," *The Wall Street Journal*, 24 April 1985.

92. Walter Pincus, "Weinberger Urges Buildup Over Soviet 'Violations,'" *The Washington Post*, 18 November 1985.

93. Pierre Lellouche, "La France, la SDI et la sécurité de l'Europe," in Karl Kaiser and Pierre Lellouche, eds., *Le couple franco-allemand et la défense de l'Europe* (Paris: Economica, 1986), p. 264. Also see Daalder, *The SDI Challenge*, p. 25; John Fenske, "France and the Strategic Defense Initiative: speeding up or putting on the brakes?" *International Affairs* 62 (Spring 1986): 231–46 and "La Guerre des étoiles," *Le Monde: dossiers et documents* (April 1986): 1–4.

94. *Le Monde*, 25 October 1986.

95. There is relatively greater support for SDI on the right side of the political spectrum. See Christoph Bluth, "SDI: the challenge to West Germany," *International Affairs* 62 (Spring 1986): 249–50 and Hans Günter Brauch, "SDI, EUREKA and/or a European Defense Initiative," paper presented at International Studies Association Convention, Anaheim, CA, March 25–29, 1986.

96. Egon Bahr, "Joint Security in Europe," *Review of International Affairs* 38 (June 20, 1987): 1. Also see Manfred R. Hamm, "Strategic Defense and the West German Social Democrats,"*Strategic Review* 14 (Spring 1986): 23.

97. Albert Wohlstetter, "Swords Without Shields," *The National Interest* (Summer 1987): 40.

Christoph Bertram makes a related but more abstract argument concerning why "Europeans are profoundly convinced that their security rests on America's recognition of its **own** vulnerability. For Europeans, American-European solidarity is not just a matter of declared interests, but of shared fate." Christoph Bertram, "Strategic Defense and the Western Alliance," *Daedalus* 114 (Summer 1985): 282.

98. See Kai-Uwe von Hassel, "Implications for Western Security Policy," in J.L. Janssen van Raay, et al., *The European Defense Initiative EDI: Some Implications and Consequences* (Rotterdam: High Frontier Europa, December 1985), pp. 21–31; Werner Kaltefleiter, *The Strategic Defense Initiative: Some Implications for Europe* (London: Institute for European Defence, 1985); and Werner Kaltefleiter and Ulrike Schumacher, "Europas Interesse an SDI: Primat der Sicherheitspolitik," *Europäische Wehrkunde* 35 (1986) 323–26.

99. Elizabeth Pond, "The security debate in West Germany," *Survival* 27 (July/August 1986): 332. Also see Michael B. Froman, et al., "Strategic Implications of SDI for France and West Germany," *RUSI: Journal of*

the Royal United Services Institute for Defence Studies 132 (June 1987): 51.

There was stronger support among Christian Socialists including party leader Franz Josef Strauss. Some French analysts argued that SDI was attractive to Strauss and other German nationalists because the FRG is precluded from possessing nuclear weapons, and by shifting to a new form of military technology, Germany might rise to the first rank of European powers. See "Les Allemands et la 'guerre des étoiles,'" *Le Monde*, 6 April 1985.

100. See Christoph Bluth, "SDI": 247–64.
101. Federal Minister of Defense, *White Paper 1985: The Situation and the Development of the Federal Armed Forces* (Bonn: The Federal Minister of Defense, 1985), p. 32. See Karl Kaiser, "L'IDS et la politique allemande," in Karl Kaiser and Pierre Lellouche, eds., *Le couple franco-allemand et la défense de l'Europe* (Paris: Economica, 1986), p. 286.
102. See Daalder, *The SDI Challenge*, pp. 77–78.
103. Labour Party and SPD, *Joint Communiqué: Meeting of the Joint Commissions of the Labour Party and the SPD on Questions of Security and Foreign Policies* (Bonn: November 14, 1986), p. 3.
104. David Owen and David Steel, *The Time Has Come: Partnership for Progress* (London: Wiedenfeld & Nicolson, 1987), p. 124. For another discussion of Alliance, and Labour, criticisms, see Trevor Taylor, "Britain's Response to the Strategic Defense Initiative," *International Affairs* 62 (Spring 1986): 227–28.
105. Albert C. Pierce, "The Strategic Defense Initiative: European Perspectives," in Catherine M. Kelleher and Gale A. Mattox, eds., *Evolving European Defense Policies* (Lexington: Lexington Books, 1987), p. 161. Also see Nanette C. Brown, *The Strategic Defense Initiative and European Security: A Conference Report*, R-3366-FF (Santa Monica: Rand Corporation, January 1986), pp. 17–20.
106. Quoted in Trevor Taylor, "Britain's Response": 220.
107. Colonel J. Alford, "The Strategic Realities of the Atlantic Alliance: A European View," in Frans Bletz and Rio Praaning, eds., *The Future of European Defence* (Dordrecht: Matinus Nijhoff, 1986), p. 30.
108. "The Prime Minister's Visit to NATO," (New York: British Information Services, February 18, 1988).
109. Michael Evans, "Britain fails to gain SDI cash," *The Times* (London), 8 December 1987.
110. See Caspar W. Weinberger, "It's Time to get S.D.I. Off the Ground," *The New York Times*, 21 August 1987. National security adviser Frank Carlucci stated, "We've never made any bones about the Strategic Defense Initiative. We intend to develop it as rapidly as we can and deploy it

when it is ready." Quoted in Michael R. Gordon, "Senate Committee Threatens Delay of New Arms Pact," *The New York Times*, 21 September 1987.

111. In his March 15, 1985 speech to the Royal United Services Institute.

112. See Hella Pick, "Howe takes issue with Weinberger on SDI," *The Manchester Guardian Weekly*, 8 February 1987.

113. See Michael Mandelbaum and Strobe Talbott, "Reykjavik and Beyond," *Foreign Affairs* 65 (Winter 1986/87): 226.

114. Richard Perle, "Reykjavik as a Watershed in U.S.-Soviet Arms Control," *International Security* 12 (Summer 1987): 176.

115. See Arnold Kanter, "Thinking about the strategic defence initiative: an alliance perspective," *International Affairs* 61 (Summer 1985): 454–56 and Stanley R. Sloan, "Implications for NATO Strategy of a Zero-Outcome Intermediate-Range Nuclear Missile Accord," (Washington, D.C.: Congressional Research Service, Library of Congress, July 14, 1987), pp. 6–8.

116. Sir Michael Howard, "Friends, foes and fears for the Alliance," *The Daily Telegraph*, 2 December 1986. Horst Ehmke wrote of Reykjavik:

> On the one hand, West Europeans were quite understandably upset by how easily Reagan placed into question agreed upon principles of security with his proposal for the elimination of ballistic missiles. On the other hand, there was a widespread feeling that Reagan had missed a historic opportunity for disarmament because of his refusal to compromise on SDI.

Horst Ehmke, "A Second Phase of Detente," *World Policy* 4 (Summer 1987): 370. John Grigg wrote that ". . . President Reagan came very near to doing a bilateral deal with Mr. Gorbachov that would have had the gravest consequences for Western Europe; and he was prevented from it, not by any concern for its impact on his European allies, but merely because he was unwilling to give up his 'star wars' project." John Grigg, "Silly swipe at the General," *The Times* (London), 25 September 1987. Also see Philip Williams, "Western European Security After Reykjavik," *Washington Quarterly* 10 (Spring 1987): 46.

117. Richard Perle, "N'abusez pas du parapluie américain," *L'Express*, 2 October 1987.

118. François de Rose, "L'option zéro une erreur grave," *Le Figaro*, 9 March 1987; (emphasis added). As former French Prime Minister Raymond Barre stated, "The Pershing II missiles are not solely a response to the SS-20's, as was claimed some years ago. They are an indispensable link in the chain of deterrence that should continue to bind Europe and the United States, since they can reach Soviet territory directly from Western Europe." Raymond Barre, "1987 Alastair Buchan Memorial Lecture: Foundations for European Security and Cooperation," *Survival* 29

(July/August 1987): 295. Also see Richard M. Nixon and Henry A. Kissinger, "To Withdraw Missiles We Must Add Conditions," *Los Angeles Times*, 26 April 1987, and François Puaux, "<<Découplage>> et bon sens," *Le Monde*, 14 March 1987.

119. Henry Kissinger described, "enormous pressure put on the Federal Republic of Germany to accept the withdrawal not only of the American medium-range missiles on its soil but also of Pershing 1A's. . . ." Henry A. Kissinger, "A New Era for NATO," *Newsweek*, 12 October 1987.

120. During his spring 1987 visit to Washington, Chirac asserted that on issues of diplomacy and defense, "France has a single position, a single policy, and speaks with one voice." Jacques Amalric and Bernard Guetta, "M. Chirac insiste sur l'unité de la diplomatie française," *Le Monde*, 2 April 1987. However, on May 3, 1987, Prime Minister Chirac expressed the "very strong reservations of the French government" concerning the removal of short-range intermediate nuclear forces. Bernard Brigouleix, "M. Chirac exprime ses <<très fortes réserves>> sur des <<options zéro successives,>>" *Le Monde*, 5 May 1987. On the general French reaction, see D. Bruce Marshall, "France and the INF Negotiations: An 'American Munich'?" *Strategic Review* 15 (Summer 1987): 23–26.

121. Michael Stürmer, "The three rules of the game of global chess," *The German Tribune*, 9 August 1987 (translated from *Frankfurter Allgemeine Zeitung*, 25 July 1987).

122. Ibid. Even before Reykjavik, General Pierre Gallois described the INF deployments "as an aberrant point on the curve representing American nuclear disengagement." Pierre Gallois, *La guerre de cents secondes: Les Etats-Unis, l'Europe et la guerre des étoiles* (Paris: Fayard, 1985), p. 115. And as Michel Tatu argued of double zero's effect, "The American president will still be able to unleash the nuclear fire, but he will be still freer not to do it. And the risks that the Soviet chief of staff must weigh diminish equivalently." Michel Tatu, "L'insulaire et le continental," *Le Monde*, 15 September 1987. Also see François Heisbourg, "Défense Française: L'impossible statu quo," *Politique internationale* (Summer 1987): 139–40.

123. James M. Markham, "U.S. Resolve and Europe," *The New York Times*, 7 October 1987.

124. "NATO Chief Warns of 'Euphoria,'" *The New York Times*, 18 September 1987. In the Federal Republic alone, the U.S. maintains over 240,000 troops and 289,000 dependents.

125. Sir Geoffrey Howe, "The Atlantic Alliance and the security of Europe," *NATO Review* 35 (April 1987): 6.

126. Quoted in Edward Cody, "W. Europe Reevaluates Its Defense: Debate Follows Proposed Arms Cuts," Washington Post Foreign Service, 13 July 1987.

127. Sir Geoffrey Howe, "The European Pillar," *Foreign Affairs* 63 (Winter 1984/85): 330–43.

128. Stanley R. Sloan, *NATO's Future: Toward a New Transatlantic Bargain* (Washington, D.C.: National Defense University Press, 1985), p. 163.

129. Jacques Isnard, "M. Giraud propose une <<charte de sécurité>> européenne: Un entretien avec le ministre de la défense," *Le Monde*, 9 April 1987.

130. "Europe's braver colours," *The Economist*, July 11, 1987, p. 11.

131. Ibid.

132. See "<<Il faut un président pour l'Europe>>, souhaite M. Valéry Giscard d'Estaing," *Le Monde*, 28 October 1986.

133. Valéry Giscard d'Estaing, "Un bon accord, une chance pour l'Europe," *Le Monde*, 23 September 1987.

134. See Samuel F. Wells, Jr., "The United States and European Defence Cooperation," *Survival* 27 (July/August 1985): 166; Bridget Bloom, "U.S. objects to European moves on defence policies," *The Financial Times*, 2 April 1985; and "Washington s'inquiète des initiatives de l'Union de l'Europe occidentale," *Le Monde*, 3 April 1985.

135. James M. Markham, "The Alliance Enters the Age of Edgy Reassurance," *The New York Times*, 27 September 1987.

136. François Puaux, "La France, l'Allemagne et l'atome: Discorde improbable, accord impossible," *Défense nationale* 41 (December 1985): 16.

137. "Les Européens et leur défense," *Le Monde*, 29 October 1987.

138. Henry A. Kissinger, "A New Era for NATO," *Newsweek*, 12 October 1987.

139. For example, Boniface, et al. assert that "The objective of the French government is to increase cooperation between states to form a European pillar of the Alliance and thus to affirm the European personality in comparison to the superpowers." Pascal Boniface, et al., *L'année stratégique*, Institut National Supérieur d'études de Défense et de Désarmement/FEDN (Paris: Editions J.-C. Lattes, 1985), p. 17.

140. Walter Schütze, "Die Aussen- und Sicherheitspolitik Frankreichs vor den Parlamentswahlen vom März 1986," *Europa Archiv* 41 (1986): 33.

141. President Ronald Reagan, "Remarks by the President to Worldnet" (Washington, D.C.: Office of the White House Press Secretary, November 3, 1987), p. 5.

3 FRANCE AND GERMANY

François Mauriac's epigram, "I love Germany so much that I am happy there are two of them,"[1] precisely expressed French attitudes toward Germany in the 1940s and 1950s. In the debate preceding the French Parliament's rejection of the European Defense Community in August 1954, one deputy recalled that Germany had invaded France in 1792, 1814, 1815, 1870, 1914 and 1940.[2] Earlier, in December 1944, de Gaulle had signed in Moscow a twenty-year treaty of alliance and mutual assistance directed against Germany.[3] And an October 1950 survey of French attitudes toward nine countries ranked Britain and the United States first and second, and Germany last.[4]

Most Americans retain this outmoded image of Franco-German relations tinged by *Erbfeindschaft* (hereditary enmity),[5] but since 1945 these ancestral enemies have successfully forged the closest relationship among the principal nations of Western Europe. Their postwar security relationship has evolved through four stages: deep distrust from 1945 through the French rejection of the EDC; an initial period of cooperation in the late 1950s and early 1960s (especially under the leadership of Adenauer and de Gaulle), stagnation during the late 1960s through the 1970s; and renewed progress during the 1980s. Although further progress is impeded by the traditional sticking points—France's quest for autonomy and West Germany's dependence upon the U.S. defense commitment—recent events, including President Reagan's bargaining stance at Reykjavik and

51

the incipient removal of INFs from Europe have heightened Franco-German interest in European security cooperation.

Former SPD Chancellor Helmut Schmidt has repeatedly advocated a Franco-German defense community which would unite the two militaries (including the French nuclear deterrent force) under the French president.[6] Although this remains a distant goal, former CDU Defense Minister Manfred Wörner did foresee "the possibility that one day there would be a common army."[7]

GERMAN ALLIANCE VERSUS FRENCH INDEPENDENCE

To protect its exposed position, Germany has formulated a defense policy based upon three principles: alliance, forward defense, and nuclear deterrence. In addition to the 495,000 men of the Bundeswehr, more than 400,000 troops from six allied armies (the United States, United Kingdom, France, Netherlands, Belgium, and Canada) are based in the Federal Republic. The key foreign contribution is American: the United States contributes approximately one-quarter of the NATO forces on the Central Front and also extends a nuclear guarantee. According to the German Defense Ministry's 1985 White Paper, "The close integration of Western Europe with the United States is indispensable for the preservation and shaping of peace on the European continent. . . . Without the military protection of the United States, West European security cannot be guaranteed."[8]

In contrast to Germany's alliance strategy, France withdrew from NATO's integrated military structure in 1966 to pursue a policy of independent nuclear deterrence. According to French doctrine, the principal purpose of France's conventional forces (which absorb 80 percent of the defense budget) is to test the adversary's intentions to determine whether vital French interests are jeopardized. If vital interests are at stake, France will threaten nuclear attacks. According to the ultraorthodox position of influential strategist General Lucien Poirier, "This operation being only *the means to inform the chief of state*, it has nothing to do with a defensive battle delivered with the hope of stopping the assailant. . . . these forces pertain to deterrence: it is their only purpose. . . . "[9]

If the president concludes that vital French interests are threatened which would justify use of strategic nuclear arms, the French intend to signal their resolve by firing tactical nuclear weapons. In 1983, the Socialist government rechristened French tactical nuclear weapons "prestrategic" to emphasize that they were not battlefield weapons but the *l'ultime avertissement* (final warning) prior to the use of strategic forces.[10] Pluton is the principal ground-based prestrategic weapon with a maximum range of 120 kilometers.[11] Beginning in 1991, Pluton is scheduled for replacement by forty-five launchers capable of firing 180 Hadès missiles with a range from 80 to 480 kilometers.[12] It will then be possible to strike targets in East Germany and Czechoslovakia from French territory, which would reduce the likelihood that French use of prestrategic nuclear weapons would inevitably occur on West German territory.

FORWARD DEFENSE VERSUS NONBELLIGERENCY

The second principle of orthodox German thinking, forward defense, stipulates that the Federal Republic must be defended at the border. Domestic opinion precludes any plan to wage modern warfare on densely populated German territory. But Bonn justifies this policy in alliance terms by arguing that "Forward defence close to the border . . . is also in the interests of our allies. Vigorous defence from the very beginning will offer a reliable guarantee for the protection of their territories as well."[13] The SPD, while embracing the principle of forward defense, rejects the overall policy of Bonn's center-right ruling coalition. The Social Democrats seek an alternative defense which is non-nuclear, "non-provocative," and less costly.[14] However, the task of defining a plausible forward defense which fulfills these contradictory goals is sisyphean, and many SPD loyalists would be satisfied by a policy which was merely *less* nuclear and *less* provocative.

Deep and unresolved contradictions remain between France's autonomous nuclear defense of the Hexagon and the multilateral conventional defense of the Federal Republic. West German territory is extremely narrow, equal to only two stages of the Tour de France, as de Gaulle said, and French leaders acknowledge that any aggression against Germany would immediately threaten their security. Furthermore, France has deployed troops in the Federal Republic since the FRG became sovereign in 1955: there are 50,000 troops in three armored divisions, plus nearly 30,000 dependents and 10,000 civilian employees.

Contingency plans exist for French participation in the conventional defense of the Federal Republic, and since 1980 France and Germany have staged joint exercises to test these plans. In 1986, 3600 French troops participated in the first French military exercise east of the Main River. In September 1987 the much larger "Bold Sparrow" exercise near Augsburg in Bavaria demonstrated that 20,000 FAR troops equipped with 240 helicopters and 500 armored vehicles could intervene quickly to help defend the Federal Republic. Despite the achievements of this exercise, including the profound symbolism of French troops serving under a German commander, "Bold Sparrow" exposed Franco-German incompatibilities. These arose from language problems as well as the French army's unfamiliarity with NATO procedures.

According to the West German *White Paper*, "The stationing of the II French Corps with its three tank divisions and about 50,000 men clearly indicates that France will participate in the defense against an attack in Central Europe."[15] Bonn believes that although France refuses to rejoin NATO's integrated military structure, she will participate in the common defense. As Lothar Rühl, a Defense Ministry official responsible for Franco-German relations, has written:

> France's allies count, in truth, on the efficacious support of French forces which have the mission of operational reserves; they suppose that these forces would be available in case of need and are convinced that France will act in a realistic manner during an acute crisis in Europe, seeking its security with its allies without too much waiting for the evolution of the conflict.[16]

In the mid-1980s, Germans believed that French interests demanded rapid French intervention because any aggression against the Federal Republic had dire implications for French security, because French forces in Germany were hostages,[17] and because French forces were too weak to mount a credible defense at the Rhine. Therefore, German military officers asserted privately that they had "no doubt that France will participate as an operational reserve in the event of war" and called French involvement "definite."

Nonetheless, this view contrasted sharply with official French policy statements. As former defense minister Hernu had written, France's "engagement in Europe would not be automatic since it is not a question of reintegrating in the NATO military structure nor of occupying a sector in the 'forward battle'. . . . France, and France alone, will decide the moment when she will join her forces to those of her allies."[18] General Poirier pointed out that de Gaulle withdrew France from the integrated alliance structure precisely to avoid being "automatically involved in the struggle even though she had not wished it."[19] Even the 1987 *loi de programme militaire* asserted that

> France will honor her commitments according to modalities that, as in the past, she will freely determine. Her independent position does not permit her to integrate her means in advance within a mechanism over which she could not exercise her sovereign decision when the time comes. This preoccupation in no way affects France's determination to intervene in Europe alongside her allies. If the survival of the nation comes into play at the borders of the country, her security can come into play at her neighbors' borders with the president judging in light of the circumstances whether the country's vital interests are threatened.[20]

Therefore, even as the French became increasingly convinced that French and West German security interests were inseparable,[21] the option of nonbelligerency remained a central element of France's official policy. Of course, this did not prove that Bonn's expectation of French assistance was mistaken. French politicians may have been privately committed to forward defense but unwilling to publicly disavow autonomy, which was seen as a cornerstone of the French consensus. In fact, President Mitterrand raised the following rhetorical question in a 1986 book:

> What is the "forward battle" when less than two hundred kilometers separate the Rhine from the Thuringian salient which is three-quarters hour by air for an airmobile division and six minutes for a formation of planes? A theoretical dispute. . . . I have difficulty conceiving our troops encamped in the Federal Republic as they are today and, at the first alert, executing a half turn to return home.[22]

French strategists also justified their ambiguity by arguing that deterrence is actually strengthened by uncertainty. But the Germans were not convinced. General Franz-Joseph Schulze, former commander of NATO's Central European forces, forcefully critiqued the French contention that "uncertainty on the part of the adversary concerning the moment and extent of French intervention would constitute an essential element of deterrence. . . . " He argued that

> in reality, not responding to the question of if, when, and with what forces one wishes to react to aggression does not increase the adversary's uncertainty but that of one's own allies. . . . The most important and effective deterrent element is the potential aggressor's conviction that an absolute solidarity exists among all the allies. . . . what is necessary for us is the demonstration of the

French wish to participate as soon as possible in the common defense. It is this clear signal, and not an imprecise announcement of the type 'it is practically sure,' that the partner needs and that the potential enemy will not ignore.[23]

French conventional forces have two roles: to defend the FRG conventionally alongside the allies *if the president makes that determination*, but also to conduct the national deterrent maneuver (to test the enemy's intentions) prior to the use of prestrategic (*l'ultime avertissement*) weapons. Pierre Lellouche is among those who criticize "this ambiguous situation where the 1st Army sees itself entrusted with two missions which are difficult to reconcile. . . . "[24] General Poirier argued that the solution was "two systems of air and ground forces different enough in their nature so their respective functions are perceived as distinct at the same time by the adversary, by the allies, and by ourselves."[25] And he thought the FAR could provide the necessary intervention force in the second circle while the First Army was reserved for the national deterrent maneuver.[26] However, the Socialist government avoided drawing such a sharp distinction between the functions of the FAR and the First Army. In fact, then Defense Minister Hernu asserted that "the First Army will belong to the first circle or the second, depending on the mission that will be assigned to it."[27]

During 1987 this major obstacle to improved Franco-German security cooperation was largely resolved. On March 26, former French Prime Minister Raymond Barre presented a significant speech in London before the International Institute for Strategic Studies and asserted that, "all must be made aware that for France, the battle begins the very moment Western Europe, and primarily West Germany, suffers aggression."[28] In the words of *Express*, "For the first time a French politician broke openly with the ambiguity of an unquestioned Gaullist tradition"[29]

Then, in June, Chancellor Kohl proposed creating a mixed Franco-German brigade. Kohl's proposal responded to American nuclear policies and CDU parliamentary leader Alfred Dregger's more far-reaching proposal that France should lead a future European security community and extend its nuclear guarantee to the Federal Republic.[30] France's political elite responded quickly and positively to Kohl's suggestion, and a survey indicated that 60 percent of the French public supported the concept.[31] Dissent was limited to the Communists and dogmatic Gaullists such as Michel Debré who feared it would lead indirectly toward French reintegration into NATO.

Defense Minister Wörner declared that the brigade should be more than a symbolic gesture, but difficulties arose from Bonn's reluctance to remove forces from NATO's integrated command and Paris's refusal to place its forces within NATO. The solution was to draw the two German battalions from the 55th Brigade of the Territorial Army, which is under national rather than NATO command. The 4,000 member brigade consists of two infantry battalions, one armored battalion, and one battalion of artillery based at Böblingen south of Stuttgart. Initially, the rotating command was filled by General Jean-Pierre Sengeisen, a German-speaking French officer. The brigade's headquarters unit is mixed, but the two French and two German battalions are national units.

In the event of war, the two governments will exercise joint control over the brigade, which could be assigned to defend the rear of the battle area or used to reinforce a French or NATO unit. German officers point out that the brigade could then come under the orders of SACEUR. The brigade was further evidence of France's willingness to defend West Germany. As one French officer said, "In case of conflict, how could France not be automatically pulled in when a part of her forces would be organically joined to German forces?"[32]

On December 12, 1987, Prime Minister Chirac finally committed France unambiguously to automatic participation in the FRG's defense. According to Chirac, in a speech before the Institut des hautes études de défense nationale:

France now possesses means which permit the affirmation of the European dimension of her security. The maturation of our prestrategic nuclear forces, allows us more flexibility in using our air and ground forces. During the period when Pluton was the principal instrument of the nuclear warning, its use was the priority mission of our forces, and this situation impelled us to withhold these forces for a deterrent maneuver conducted as close as possible to our border. The deployment of ALCMs [air-launched cruise missiles] frees us from this constraint. Pluton's replacement in 1991 by much longer-range Hadès missiles will perfect this evolution.

Were West Germany to be the victim of an aggression, who can now doubt that France's commitment would be immediate and wholehearted? There cannot be a battle of Germany and a battle of France.[33]

President Mitterrand, in a subsequent *Nouvel Observateur* interview, confirmed that he had read an advance copy of the prime minister's speech.

The president added that Chirac's remarks were consistent with the views he himself expressed during his most recent visit to the Federal Republic.[34]

DILEMMAS OF EXTENDED NUCLEAR DETERRENCE

The third principle of German defense policy is the assumption that nuclear deterrence is indispensable to European security and that "Dependence of West European defense on the nuclear capabilities of the United States could be reduced, but not eliminated."[35] This is a complex issue for Germany as the "double zero" imbroglio illustrated. Between 1959 and 1983, a defense consensus prevailed in the Federal Republic which the SPD shattered by opposing the Pershing 2 and cruise missile deployments.[36] In 1987, the prospect of removing all superpower missiles in the range between 500 and 5,500 kilometers from Europe caused disarray within West Germany's ruling coalition.

Nuclear threats are double-edged: they reinforce deterrence but risk potentially catastrophic outcomes if deterrence fails. Throughout the postwar era, German governments have emphasized the positive effects of deterrence. For example, in January 1987 Defense Minister Manfred Wörner argued that

> there is no substitute for the nuclear strategy which has helped preserve the peace of America and Europe; and it makes no sense to take nuclear weapons, for instance, out of the compound system of the military instruments of that strategy in order to subject them, in isolation, to arms control, while the conventional forces would remain free from control and could again be used for war as a means of an aggressive policy.[37]

The Greens, and large parts of the SPD, reject this argument. They fear that the very nature of power politics between the superpowers, combined with the dynamics of arms races, makes it nearly inevitable that nuclear weapons will eventually be used. And when deterrence fails, they expect the annihilation of Germany. The German Left also believes that potential aggressors are not deterred by suicidal nuclear threats, so they have devised numerous proposals for non-nuclear defense.[38]

This profound German ambivalence toward nuclear weapons is not unique; as Richard Betts has argued, "For European populations as much as the American, the logic of extended deterrence is acceptable only when it is out of mind."[39] Even in France, a 1987 survey found that only 41 per-

Table 3–1. Attitudes Toward a German Nuclear Force (percent).

Question: Do you think it would be a good thing or a bad thing to authorize the Federal Republic of Germany to have its own nuclear weapons?

	France	UK	FRG
Good	30	25	10
Bad	52	56	74

Source: Jacques Fontaine, "A quoi rêvent les européens," *L'Expansion* (25 May–7 June 1984), p. 86. Opinion surveys under the general supervision of Sofres: France (N = 1,000) April 13–18, 1984; FRG (Infas, N = 1,219) March 19–April 8, 1984; UK (Gallup, N = 779) April 4–9, 1984.

cent of the public (compared to 48 percent opposed) favored using France's nuclear weapons "if the USSR invaded French territory."[40] But German *angst* is intensified by the knowledge that the country's fate rests so completely in foreign hands. At the 1986 SPD party congress, Bundestag member Andreas von Bülow revealed a secret defense ministry study that found despite NATO's first use policy, 35 percent of commissioned officers and 65 percent of non-commissioned officers thought there were no circumstances which could justify using nuclear weapons.[41] And when asked in September 1985, "Should NATO fall back upon the use of nuclear weapons if it is being threatened by a defeat in a conventional war?" only 11 percent of the German public agreed and 80 percent disagreed.[42] According to the prominent French Socialist Jean-Pierre Chevènement, an unidentified German politician told him that, "If a single atomic rocket happened to explode on Germany, we would not be more courageous than the Japanese in 1945: the white flag would go up immediately."[43]

Furthermore, although Germans frequently assert that it is allied (and Soviet) opposition which precludes the possibility of a West German nuclear deterrent force, the repudiation of German nuclear weapons is actually stronger within the Federal Republic than elsewhere in Western Europe.[44] As Table 3–1 indicates, a 1984 poll found that only 10 percent of Germans agreed that "it would be a good thing . . . to authorize the Federal Republic of Germany to have its own nuclear weapons" This compared to 30 percent of the French and 25 percent of the British respondents.[45]

Some allied acceptance of German nuclear weapons is also indicated by the signature in November 1957, barely a decade following World

War II, of a secret tripartite agreement among France, Germany, and Italy for the joint development of nuclear weapons. President de Gaulle later terminated this cooperation which, according to Italian Ambassador Giuseppe Walter Maccotta, was judged not to violate the prohibition on German manufacture of atomic weapons under Protocol III of the 1954 Paris Accords amending the Brussels Treaty, because "none of the three powers could have a monopoly of fabrication but the contribution of all was always indispensable."[46]

The German perception of nuclear weapons is schizophrenic. Although the majority believes that nuclear deterrence has maintained the peace since 1945, there is substantial questioning of NATO policy, and a sizable minority condemns all nuclear capabilities. This is understandable considering Germany's location at the center of East-West tension, residual feelings of guilt for Nazi policies, and dependence upon capricious foreign leaders for the very survival of the state.

When French policy focused on deterring attacks on the "national sanctuary," there was a consistent nuclear doctrine. Contradictions arose when France redefined her vital security interests to encompass territory beyond the Hexagon, for the "national deterrent maneuver" and the "final warning" could take place on West German territory, that is, within the territory of France's vital interests. Would France destroy Germany in order to save it?

French decisionmakers tried to resolve this contradiction between nuclear autonomy and Franco-German cohesion. There were two approaches, and both involved dividing French conventional, tactical nuclear, and strategic nuclear forces into two categories. President Mitterrand's approach differentiated conventional forces from *both* tactical and strategic nuclear forces. Prime Minister Chirac, former President Giscard d'Estaing, and Defense Minister Giraud packaged tactical nuclear forces and conventional forces together and treated strategic nuclear forces as a separate category.

According to Giscard, France must "put in place two distinct deterrent levels: the strategic level and the tactical level intended to destroy the invader's forces. . . . "[47] Tactical nuclear weapons could then be used to support conventional forces permitting what Chirac has called a coupling between the "maneuver of conventional forces and the threat of recourse to nuclear weapons."[48] On this point, the Socialist Mitterrand is more Gaullist than the General's political heirs, for he rejects any notion of flexible response and insists that prestrategic weapons are inseparable from the overall strategy and not "a simple extension of the conventional battle."[49] According to Mitterrand, it is not possible "to carve up the nuclear warning into small pieces."[50] His alternative envisions a conventional battle for Germany (using the FAR and the First Army) and a separate nuclear battle for France.

The approach of Chirac, Giscard, and Giraud is weak because it rejects extension of the strategic nuclear guarantee to the Federal Republic but contemplates a limited nuclear war on German territory; this feeds German anxieties rather than quelling them.[51] Mitterrand's position is flawed because it permits the Soviets to attack the Federal Republic with less fear of French nuclear reprisals.[52]

An essential step toward Franco-German agreement on nuclear issues was taken during the summit of February 28, 1986, when President Mitterrand pledged to Chancellor Kohl that "In the limits imposed by the extreme rapidity of such decisions. . . . " he would "consult the chancellor of the FRG on the eventual use of French prestrategic weapons on German territory."[53] But for Bonn genuine consultation involves more than a telephone link so, time permitting, the French president can announce his decision. Bonn wishes to know whether the First Army will be committed, if it will be equipped with Pluton, what targets have been selected, and how the ultimate decision will be made.

These subjects are under discussion, but apparently President Mitterrand rejected the proposal of François Fillon (RPR, chairman of the National Assembly's defense committee) and others that France's nuclear war plans be shared with Bonn.[54] Moreover, the director of France's Cours supérieur interarmées (CSI), which includes Bundeswehr officers, said that "You will easily understand that you do not discuss together the nuclear attack plans!"[55]

During his state visit to the Federal Republic in October 1987, Mitterrand attempted a further clarification of French policy. In a well-publicized declaration, Mitterrand affirmed that "Nothing allows one to say that France's final warning against the attacker would be delivered on German territory."[56] Apparently, the final warning prior to strategic nuclear attacks could take various forms. It could be nonnuclear and possibly even nonmilitary.[57] Alternatively, France could adopt Heisbourg's suggestion and offer the Federal Republic the option of deploying Hadès missiles in Germany, "if the Bonn government expressed the desire for it," which "would permit them to fire beyond East German territory."[58] However, Chancellor Kohl told *Le Monde* that "It is completely out of the question that we would demand a second key to use these [French nuclear] arms."[59] Mitterrand agreed; he told *Die Welt* "it is not conceivable that the Federal Republic, or any other country including the United States, could take part in the decision to use French nuclear weapons."[60]

A final possibility is to eliminate short-range tactical nuclear forces and transfer the final warning to longer-range delivery vehicles, such as the Mirage 2000 and Super-Etendard aircraft equipped with air-to-surface missiles. Mitterrand has always considered Pluton and Hadès mistakes, and their purpose has remained ambiguous: are they battlefield nuclear weapons intended to offset the WTO's conventional superiority, or logically inseparable from the strategic forces? Increasingly, French opinion conceives the final warning as a limited counterforce attack against the adversary's home territory, but even Hadès' longer range will be inadequate for that. Hadès could also fall victim to a "triple zero" option which would eliminate all ground-based missiles from Europe. And, as Charles Hernu observed, even equipped with "neutron" warheads, Hadès' use would entail nuclear warfighting. Therefore, Hernu proposed that Franco-German agreement on basic issues of European security could be facilitated by "sacrificing" Hadès and fulfilling the prestrategic mission with ALCMs.[61] However, in June 1988 the new Socialist defense minister, Jean-Pierre Chevènement, announced that Hadès would be maintained.

A major advantage of longer range airborne systems, compared to Pluton or Hadès, is the continued ability to threaten Soviet territory after the American INFs are withdrawn. Disadvantages include greater vulnerability to adverse weather conditions and enemy defenses. Reliance on attacks against Soviet territory also contradicts France's traditional strategy by blurring the distinction between prestrategic and strategic strikes. It also ignores the opinion of Jacques Chirac and André Giraud that land-based tactical nuclear weapons are needed to compensate for the Eastern Bloc's conventional superiority. As a result, Mitterrand's remarks left France with what L'Express called "a strategy too many."[62]

The taboo of nonbelligerency was shattered, but France still confronts the issue of extended nuclear deterrence. Former Socialist Prime Minister Laurent Fabius said that "It is now necessary to consider the extension of our strategic nuclear guarantee to German security."[63] Former U.S. ambassador to Paris Evan Galbraith echoed this possibility by urging France "to become the nuclear guarantor of Germany to compensate for the loss of the Pershings which were the only missiles in Europe capable of attacking the USSR."[64] At the 1988 Wehrkunde conference, Defense Minister Giraud obliquely implied a similar view by observing that France's deterrent was intended to protect vital interests and these are partially based upon France's political, economic, and cultural ties with her neighbors. "Thus, a threat can intervene in front of our borders, and likewise our own nuclear deterrent can be concerned in these same circumstances."[65] Moreover, 50 percent of the French public favors using French nuclear weapons to defend the Federal Republic.[66]

So far, however, official French thinking considers extended deterrence an American rather than a French responsibility. President Mitterrand not only refused to share the nuclear decision with Bonn, he also rebuffed the possibility of an explicit nuclear commitment. This, he said, was a question for the Atlantic Alliance rather than for France; however, the French president would remain the sole judge of whether France's vital interests were threatened by an attack against Germany.[67]

German reactions to this issue are also somewhat Delphic. Although Chancellor Kohl described the existence of France's deterrent force as reassuring to Germany, he added that "it is obvious that she cannot assume the weight of the defense of the Federal Republic and Western Europe."[68] Willy Brandt cautioned the FRG not to be too demanding: "It is for France to determine its own interests."[69]

FRANCO-GERMAN RELATIONS

Following World War II, many French and German citizens vowed to end the cycles of violence between their countries,[70] and efforts to erase historical animosities became increasingly successful following the EDC debacle.[71] The first of fourteen meetings between President Charles de Gaulle and Chancellor Konrad Adenauer was held in September 1958. In January 1963, they signed the Elysée Treaty whose preamble proclaims the conviction

> that the reconciliation of the German people and the French people, ending a centuries-old rivalry, constitutes a historic event which profoundly transforms the relations between the two peoples. . . . [and recognizes] that increased cooperation between the two countries constitutes an indispensable stage on the way to a united Europe, which is the aim of the two peoples. . . .

After the signing, the small existing network of Franco-German "sister cities" grew rapidly, and there are now approximately 1,200 relationships between French and German cities and more than 2,500 similar affiliations between schools.[72] There are also regularly scheduled meetings of the defense and foreign ministers every three months and semiannual summits. *L'Express* reported that Chancellor Kohl and President Mitterrand met some fifty times through October 1987. There were eleven meetings during 1985, and during 1986 Kohl met Mitterrand six times and Prime Minister Chirac five times.[73] At lower levels, meetings are even more frequent but also more dependent upon personal relationships. For example, when Roland Dumas originally served as French foreign minister, he met German Foreign Minister Genscher several times each month, and they spoke daily by telephone. When Jean-Bernard Raimond succeeded Dumas at the Quai d'Orsay, Genscher's contacts became less frequent.[74]

At their February 1986 summit, the two countries agreed to exchange diplomatic personnel for extended periods. And subsequently a French diplomat worked for nearly a year within the German foreign ministry and even represented the FRG officially at a CSCE (Conference on Security and Cooperation in Europe) meeting in Vienna.[75] There are also modest exchanges of military officers. In 1988, four German officers participated in the CSI at the Ecole militaire, with the number expected to triple by 1990, while three French officers attended the Führungsakademie in Hamburg.[76]

Other cooperative efforts were less fruitful. For nearly twenty years, the Elysée Treaty failed to harmonize Franco-German defense cooperation. De Gaulle sought to construct a European consensus independent from the superpowers, but in ratifying the treaty the Bundestag appended a preamble which confirmed the priority of the Federal Republic's American connection. This preamble referred not only to European unity but also to "a close partnership between Europe and the United States of America," "collective defense within the framework of the North Atlantic Alliance," and other goals irritating to France. As a result, the defense component of the treaty remained stillborn until 1982.

Moreover, there was no progress toward achieving the treaty's goal of Franco-German bilingualism. Although 85 percent of French youth and 79 percent of German youth have studied a foreign language, English is the overwhelmingly dominant foreign language in both countries. In France, 79 percent of the youth have studied English compared to 29 percent for German (and Spanish), and in West Germany 75 percent have studied English compared to 35 percent that have studied French. This situation has deteriorated in France during the last two decades as more French students select English rather than German as their first foreign language and Spanish rather than German as their second language. Between 1958–59 and 1985–86 the position of English as the first language of French students increased from 76 percent to 85 percent, while the German percentage fell from 21 percent to 13 percent. In the same period, Spanish rose as a second language from 30 percent to 47 percent while German declined from 33 percent to 27 percent.[77] In Germany, only 2.5 percent of students select French as their first language, half of these are in the Saarland where 90 percent of the students study French.[78]

Concerning their level of proficiency, 37 percent of the French youth report that they speak English fluently or well; only 10 percent say they speak German fluently or well. The comparable figures in Germany are 53 percent for English and 18 percent for French.[79] Not surprisingly, English frequently serves as the lingua franca of Franco-German relations. According to Professor François-Georges Dreyfus, "There aren't ten colonels in the French Army who speak decent German," so English is often used to communicate during Franco-German military exercises.[80]

Since 1963, nearly 5 million French and German youth have participated in Franco-German exchanges (130,000 in 1985),[81] but the level of personal contacts remains disappointing. In 1985, 73 percent of French youth (fifteen to twenty-four years) and 81 percent of German youth had visited a foreign country, but only 40 percent of German youth had visited France, fewer than had visited Austria (49 percent) or Italy (42 percent). Only 25 percent of the French youth had visited the FRG, compared to Spain (36 percent), Italy (28 percent), and Britain (28 percent).[82] The preferred foreign destinations for French youth (by rank) were: the United States, Greece, Italy, Britain, Spain, North Africa, Scandinavia, Austria, Switzerland, Ireland, the Netherlands, and then the FRG. For German young people, the United States, Greece, Britain, Italy, and Spain all ranked higher than France.[83]

There is also a psychological distance which separates France and Germany. Foreigners are frequently told, especially in the Federal Republic, that the two peoples are "very different," and wonder is expressed that the bilateral relationship works as well as it does. The French refer frequently to *les incertitudes allemandes*, and the German edition of Brigitte Sauzay's pessimistic study of contemporary Germany (*Le vertige allemand*) is titled *Die rätselhaften Deutschen* (The Mysterious Germans). Sauzay's analysis described Germany as tormented and enveloped by a "general malaise, a sort of existential anguish."[84] More recently, however, the French have agonized over scenarios of national decline while, according to Christoph Bertram, "The Germans have never had it so good."[85]

The countries are also separated by basic policy differences including French enthusiasm for nuclear weapons and nuclear power—which repulses the Germans—and German zeal for ecological causes, which the French dismiss.[86] It is probably true, as Goethe said, that Germans like French wines better than the French and that emotionally and culturally France tends to ignore the Federal Republic, which is perceived as an economic success but otherwise antiseptic and boring.[87]

Despite these differences, considerable progress was made in joint Franco-German weapons production during the 1960s and 1970s.[88] Projects included the Transall transport plane, the Alpha Jet combat plane, two anti-tank missiles (Milan and HOT), and an anti-aircraft missile (Roland). This cooperation faltered after the early 1970s, and more than fifteen years have now passed since a major new bilateral arms project was successfully completed. Meanwhile, several attempts at bilateral or multilateral weapons cooperation failed conspicuously. A joint tank project inaugurated in 1980 was abandoned in 1982, largely because France and the FRG preferred different production timetables.[89]

France was also disappointed when the Federal Republic declined to develop a Franco-German optical reconnaissance satellite (Helios) following discussions held during 1983–84. Bonn argued that the project's success was jeopardized by frequent cloud cover over Central Europe, but some French experts also cited Bonn's disinclination to annoy Washington by entering the satellite field, and wrangling in Bonn concerning which ministry would foot the bill.[90] As Jérôme Paolini has argued, the two countries' very different relationships to NATO led them to discordant conclusions. French military strategy is based on autonomous nuclear deterrence, and an independent intelligence capability was highly desirable, but the FRG follows an alliance strategy, and U.S. intelligence "responded to her operational needs, was politically acceptable, and financially rational."[91]

The superpower INF agreement intensified France's desire for an independent surveillance capability, and France is developing the Helios optical satellite with 1993 as the expected launch date. Italy and Spain have joined as junior partners to defray some of this project's estimated cost, which exceeds $1 billion; they will contribute 15 percent and 5 percent respectively.[92]

A third significant failure was France's withdrawal in 1985 from talks with Britain, Italy, Spain, and the Federal Republic concerning a European Fighter Aircraft (EFA). France now plans to build an *avion de combat européen* (ACE) based upon Dassault-Breguet's Rafale prototype while the other countries proceed with the EFA.[93]

The principal ongoing Franco-German project is the combat helicopter program. First contemplated more than ten years ago, an agreement was signed in May 1984 to produce an anti-tank helicopter for the Bundeswehr and anti-tank and anti-helicopter models for the French from a single base. The lack of commonality among the three versions led to substantial cost escalation, and there were deep conflicts concerning design specifications.[94] These controversies are now resolved, and at the fiftieth biannual summit in November 1987 the two countries agreed to proceed. France will acquire 215 helicopters and the FRG 212, with deployment to begin in 1992–93. The program's high cost, more than DM 9 billion for the FRG and approximately Fr 30 billion for France, made it vulnerable to political attack, but support for the project now appears firm as a symbol of Franco-German cooperation.[95] There are also new projects to produce a Franco-German tank recovery vehicle constructed on France's AMX-40 chassis and a pilotless battlefield surveillance system (CL-289) which will also include Canada.[96]

The armament markets of individual European countries are relatively small, making it difficult to compete successfully against much larger American firms. Advocates claim that armament cooperation can reduce unit costs through economies of scale, maintain technological independence and competitiveness vis-à-vis the United States (and increasingly Japan), and strengthen institutions for European unification. The Franco-German experience illustrates the difficulty of achieving these goals. Although François Heisbourg has argued that "The cost of the next generation of weapon systems means that European arms co-operation is not only desirable but an absolute necessity,"[97] cooperative arms programs are not always cost effective. During the EFA episode, French Defense Minister André Giraud claimed that joint programs often have *higher* costs and more delays than national programs;[98] this is plausible given the difficulty of coordinating the frequently incompatible needs, timetables, and doctrines of separate military organizations.

Because of export considerations and out-of-area responsibilities, France often prefers lighter and cheaper weapons than the FRG, whose concerns are limited to Central European contingencies. These considerations influenced France's withdrawal from the EFA consortium (which considered planes with sixteen possible weight and engine combinations) and also prompted French insistence that the Franco-German helicopter be able to weather sandstorms. The German constitution aggravates this conflict. Article 26 stipulates that "Weapons designed for warfare may be manufactured, transported or marketed only with the permission of the Federal Government," and German legislation prohibits arms exports to authoritarian regimes and to actual or potential war zones. In contrast, weapons have been a major French export. Until 1986, France was the third largest global arms exporter after the superpowers. France has now fallen to fifth position following the United States, a resurgent Britain, the Soviet Union, and China, and the French government is very concerned with declining arms exports.[99]

Project failures can also have negative political effects which may metastasize if politicians compensate by approving questionable projects merely to advance the political agenda. As National Assembly deputy Henri Louet wrote of the helicopter program:

> If the needs were very different, it would perhaps have been wiser to recognize it and to refrain. Far from this attitude, the defense minister, Charles Hernu, needed a success following the abandonment of the Franco-German tank project and that of the fighter plane which was already outlined on the horizon. . . . the wish to succeed was so strong on the French side . . . that the minister at the time was led to accept the unacceptable.[100]

Defense Minister Giraud criticized both autarkic approaches and efforts to produce every weapons system through multinational programs. He advocated a division of labor among the European countries and said each country should specialize in weapons technologies where it possessed particular expertise. For example, the Federal Republic might build tanks while France built aircraft. Giraud thought it absurd to seek a balance of national benefits from each individual program; instead, the equilibrium should be sought across a range of armament projects.[101] Elsewhere in Europe, and particularly in the FRG, there is substantial support for the logic of this argument, but the domestic clout of arms manufacturers, and the lack of agreement among military chiefs of staff, persist as major hindrances to more rational armaments production.

Although the helicopter program now appears assured, and France remains the FRG's principal partner for bilateral projects and second partner (after the United Kingdom) for multilateral projects,[102] prospects for future weapons cooperation remain clouded. The helicopter is proceeding for political reasons even though the purchase of American aircraft would be less expensive. Until the cooperative process is rationalized, armaments are unlikely to reassume their earlier status as a leading sector of Franco-German cooperation.

FUTURE RELATIONS

In just forty years, France and the Federal Republic have progressed from *Erbfeindschaft* to *"relations privilégiées"* with the German chancellor and the French president referring to a "community of destiny" between their countries and Chancellor Kohl declaring that "France and the Federal Republic can only master their future together."[103] This is a momentous achievement, and it is essentially true, as François Mitterrand has written, that "the only embryo of common European defense resides in the Franco-German Elysée Treaty."[104] Certainly the most probable scenario for European defense cooperation is the emergence of a Franco-German defense community, which would then enlarge to include the other members of the Western European Union (Great Britain, Italy, and Benelux), and perhaps Spain, Portugal, and others. This might occur as a "European pillar" within the Atlantic Alliance or as a substitute for NATO; in either case it would have profound importance.

But is a Franco-German community probable considering the obstacles on both sides? France has finally discarded the option of nonbelligerency, but French leaders remain reluctant to sacrifice their residual autonomy. France is still adamant that she will not rejoin NATO's integrated military structure, and the thorny issue of France's nuclear doctrine is unresolved.

The Germans value the French connection but remain much closer to and dependent upon the United States and the Alliance. Although France has become more tolerant of the close German-American tie,[105] the intimacy of this relationship remains an irritant between Bonn and Paris. It often seems to the French that the FRG accords more priority to the United States and the East (in that order) rather than to Western Europe.[106] There is also a deep divide separating French and German conceptions of European security.

The French are obsessed by fears of German neutralism and pacifism; these constitute the new French nightmare having replaced the old fear of German aggression.[107] Renata Fritsch-Bournazel has admonished that "To speak constantly of a German drift, of a nationalist-neutralist temptation, is surely not the best way to convince the Germans of the sincerity of the sentiments of solidarity that the French feel toward their closest neighbor."[108] But the French cannot help themselves; they are trapped by the logic of Napoleon's dictum that "The policy of a nation is in its geography." French fears are fed by the Greens' growing electoral strength (8.3 percent and forty-four seats in the January 1987 Bundestag election compared to 5.6 percent and twenty-seven seats in 1983),[109] the SPD's accommodationist defense policies, and survey results such as those from a secret government poll divulged in May 1987 by the newspaper *Bild* showing that 71 percent of the population favored reunification of a non-aligned Germany.[110] They are also unnerved when the FRG's most celebrated "hawk," Franz Josef Strauss, returns from his first trip to Moscow and says that "We no longer have to fear the aggressive intentions of the USSR." [111]

For this reason, France's commitment to European cooperation intensifies when the Federal Republic is perceived as drifting toward neutralism and pacifism. For example, in the early 1980s when West Germany confronted the contentious INF deployment decision, the long suspended defense component of the Elysée Treaty was implemented (February 1982), President Mitterrand supported the INF deployments before the Bundestag (January 1983), and the moribund Western European Union was reactivated by the Rome Declaration (November 1984). But as the INF crisis receded, and France became less fearful of German neutralism, the enthusiasm for new initiatives faded in both countries.[112]

American behavior is also a crucial variable, for Franco-German cooperation tends to flourish when the United States is perceived as a weaker or less dependable ally.[113] This is not surprising, for both countries have relied upon the American military commitment throughout the postwar era. It is the keystone of German defense but also fundamental to French policy, which depends upon America's contribution to overall European, and especially German, defense. Major changes in U.S. behavior significantly affect Franco-German security relations, and the events of late 1986 (Reykjavik) and 1987 (double zero) stimulated new interest in European defense cooperation.

The most significant recent accomplishment of Franco-German relations may prove to be the bilateral Defense and Security Council. Proposed by President Mitterrand in September 1987, and formally established in January 1988, the Defense Council includes the German chancellor, the president and prime minister of France, the foreign and defense ministers, and the army chiefs of staff. Mitterrand modeled his proposal on the French defense council, chaired by the president, which determines French military policy.

The mandate of the Franco-German council is similarly broad. It is intended to harmonize all aspects of defense policy including organization of the brigade, joint maneuvers, arms control, interoperability of weapons, and armament cooperation. The council has a secretariat in Paris under the leadership of the German Lothar Rühl and must meet at least semi-annually. A Franco-German Finance and Economic Council was also created to coordinate economic policies. Its members are the economics and finance ministers and the heads of the central banks, but its task is complicated by opposition from the independent Bundesbank.

France and Germany continue to be divided by many aspects of defense policy. These include different relationships to the Atlantic Alliance, substantially different attitudes toward arms control and overall East-West relations, the uncertain future of joint armament programs, and ambiguities in French nuclear policy, for example, the role of TNFs (theater nuclear forces), how the final warning would be delivered, and possible extension of France's nuclear umbrella to include the Federal Republic.

In themselves, these issues constitute a very full agenda for the Defense Council, but the two countries have also invited other countries to associate themselves with this initiative, and this possibility interests Spain particularly. If the bilateral council succeeds, it could lead to a Franco-German defense community as envisioned by Helmut Schmidt. Even more futuristically, a multilateral defense council might constitute the nucleus for a European defense community.

NOTES

1. Quoted in Phillipe Moreau Defarges, "La France et l'Europe: le rêve ambigu ou la mesure du rang," *Politique étrangère* 51 (Spring 1986): 203.
2. Alfred Grosser, "Germany and France: A Confrontation," in Daniel Lerner and Raymond Aron, eds., *France Defeats EDC* (New York: Frederick A. Praeger, 1957), p. 67. For analyses of the EDC, see Maurice Delarue, "1954, vie et mort d'une armée européenne," *Le Monde*, 24 September 1987; Edward Fursdon, *The European Defence Community: A*

History (London: The Macmillan Press, 1980); Alfred Grosser, *Affaires extérieures: La politique de la France 1944–1984* (Paris: Flammarion, 1984), pp. 106–12; and F. Roy Willis, *France, Germany, and the New Europe: 1945–1967*, revised and expanded edition (Stanford: Stanford University Press, 1968), pp. 130–84.

3. See Adalbert Korff, *Le revirement de la politique française à l'égard de l'Allemagne entre 1945 et 1950* (Ambilly-Annemasse: Imprimerie Franco-Suisse, 1965), p. 40.

4. See Jean Stoetzel, "The Evolution of French Opinion," in Daniel Lerner and Raymond Aron, eds., *France Defeats EDC* (New York: Frederick A. Praeger, 1957), p. 74.

5. For example, a recent *New York Times* editorial (9 September 1987) discussed the issue of German reunification in terms of "the same German bellicosity, in war after war, that has frightened the French. . . ."

6. See Helmut Schmidt, "Europa Muss sich selbst behaupten," *Die Zeit* (November 21, 1986): 3 (translated in *The German Tribune*, 30 November 1986, and 7 December 1986); "L'Equation Allemande: Entretien avec Helmut Schmidt," *Politique internationale* (Spring 1985): 147–59; Helmut Schmidt, "La France, l'Allemagne et la défense européenne," *Commentaire* (1984): 411–17.

7. Quoted in James M. Markham, "Paris and Bonn Set Up Military Link," *The New York Times*, 23 January 1988.

8. Federal Minister of Defense, *White Paper 1985: The Situation and the Development of the Federal Armed Forces* (Bonn: The Federal Minister of Defense, 1985), pp. 8, and 17.

9. Lucien Poirier, "Le deuxième cercle: La défense égoïste de la citadelle et la grande aventure au-delà de la contrescarpe," in Lucien Poirier, *Essais de stratégie théorique* (Paris: Fondation pour les Etudes de Défense Nationale, *Collection les sept épées*, No. 22, premier trimestre 1982), p. 308. Also see Lucien Poirier, "La Greffe," *Défense nationale* 39 (April 1983): 12.

10. Chirac's defense minister, André Giraud, preferred the label "theater weapons." See "Le ministre de la défense: concentrer les moyens," *L'Express*, 6 June 1986. However, the label prestrategic was retained in the latest military planning law. See Assemblée Nationale, *Projet de loi de programme relatif à l'équipement militaire pour les années 1987–1991*, (Paris: huitième session ordinaire de 1986–87), No. 432, p. 14.

11. There is disagreement concerning the number of Plutons, but apparently it exceeds one hundred. See David S. Yost, *France's Deterrent Posture and Security in Europe: Part I: Capabilities and Doctrine*, Adelphi Paper Number 194 (London: International Institute for Strategic Studies, Winter 1984/5), p. 49.

12. Jacques Isnard, "Le missile Hadès aurait une portée accrue," *Le Monde*, 22 January 1988.

13. Federal Minister, *White Paper 1985*, p. 35; also see p. 76 and Geoffrey Manners, "Forward defence 'indispensable' CINCENT tells Allies," *Jane's Defence Weekly* 3 (May 4, 1986): 746–47.

14. Specifically, the party supports a reduction in military spending to the level of the last SPD defense budget in 1982.

15. Federal Minister, *White Paper 1985*, p. 120.

16. Lothar Rühl, "1982: La relance de la coopération franco-allemande," in Karl Kaiser and Pierre Lellouche, eds., *Le couple franco-allemand et la défense de l'Europe* (Paris: Economica, 1986), p. 42.

17. This opinion is sometimes echoed in France. Ambassador François Puaux has written that "Their presence . . . is a physical and human token infinitely superior to all the guarantees that we could give." "La France, l'Allemagne et l'atome: Discorde improbable, accord impossible," *Défense nationale* 41 (December 1985): 14.

18. Charles Hernu, *Défendre la paix* (Paris: Editions J.-C. Lattès, 1985), p. 59. François Gorand (pseud.) of the Foreign Ministry has written that "There is nevertheless one point on which the German consensus is not in doubt: it is the hostility to nonautomatic intervention by France in case of conflict. Now it is a point which, in principle at least, is not negotiable for us." "La politique de sécurité européenne de la France de 1981 à 1985 et après," *Commentaire* (Spring 1986): 14.

19. Charles de Gaulle, Declaration of February 21, 1966; quoted in Poirier, "Le deuxième cercle," p. 297. Ambassador François de Rose presented a contrasting view. He wrote of the NATO withdrawal: "Its goal was never to permit us to shirk these commitments from the moment one of our allies was the victim of aggression." François de Rose, "Lettre ouverte au futur président de la République," *L'Express*, 11 December 1987.

20. Assemblée Nationale, *Projet de loi*, pp. 9–10.
    Poirier sees "nothing contradictory or ambiguous in this position . . . [France] retains the possibility of choosing the moment, the place, and the means of our military engagement according to the attitude of the allies and also according to our interests involved in the crisis." Poirier, "Le deuxième cercle," p. 298.

21. For example, Pierre Lellouche argued that "The only way to transmit this signal is to redeploy the whole of our system no longer on the Rhine but precisely on the Elbe." Pierre Lellouche, *l'Avenir de la guerre* (Paris: Editions Mazarine, 1985), p. 281. François Heisbourg called for "the political affirmation at the highest level of the automaticity of the engagement of our forces in case of aggression in Europe." François Heisbourg, "Défense Française: L'impossible statu quo," *Politique inter-*

nationale (Summer 1987): 150. Also see Henri Froment-Meurice, "L'Allemagne n'est pas notre glacis," *Le Monde*, 30 April 1985 and Christian Megrelis, "Pour une confédération franco-allemande," *Le Monde*, 5 February 1986.

22. François Mitterrand, *Reflexions sur la politique extérieure de la France: Introduction à vingt-cinq discours (1981–1985)* (Paris: Fayard, 1986), pp. 98–99. During the Bold Sparrow maneuvers, Mitterrand said that "in a conflict, when there was an immediate peril, the duty of France would be to come to the aide of those who are her allies and to Germany." Jacques Isnard, "M. Mitterrand a lancé le projet d'un conseil de défense commun," *Le Monde*, 27–28 September 1987.

23. Franz-Joseph Schulze, "La nécessité d'une réaction de défense immédiate et commune," in Karl Kaiser and Pierre Lellouche, eds., *Le couple franco-allemand et la défense de l'Europe* (Paris: Economica, 1986), pp. 161, 168.

24. Lellouche, *L'Avenir*, p. 269.

25. Poirier, "La Greffe," p. 22.

26. According to Poirier:

    If the policy and the circumstances of the crisis demand it, the rapid action and assistance force must be able to be engaged, indeed consumed, without affecting the credibility of our deterrent; but simultaneously the chief of state must permanently possess, as a reserve disengaged from all assumptions, some conventional forces necessary for the national deterrent maneuver in the event that the enemy wins the battle for the glacis.

    Ibid., p. 25.

27. Cited in David S. Yost, *France and Conventional Defense in Central Europe* (Boulder: Westview Press, 1985), p. 89; see pp. 87–103 for a very useful discussion of the FAR.

28. Raymond Barre, "1987 Alastair Buchan Memorial Lecture: Foundations for European Security and Cooperation," *Survival* 29 (July/August 1987): 298. Also see Barre's July 4, 1987 speech at La Rochelle on France's world role, *Le Monde*, 7 July 1987.

29. Jérôme Dumoulin, "Les nouvelles armes de Barre," *L'Express*, 3 April 1987.

30. Alfred Dregger was a longtime supporter of close German-American ties, but press reports indicated that, "In his party's private councils, Mr. Dregger has been bitterly saying that the United States betrayed and abandoned West Germany." James M. Markham, "Paris and Bonn Start to Think of a Special Alliance," *The New York Times*, 24 June 1987. Also see Henri de Bresson, "Le chancelier Kohl propose de créer une brigade franco-allemande," *Le Monde*, 21–22 June 1987.

31. See "M. Chirac: tout ce qui renforce les liens entre les deux pays va dans le bon sens," *Le Monde*, 25 June 1987; Jacques Isnard, "Paris est

favorable à l'idée d'une brigade franco-allemande," *Le Monde*, 23 June 1987; Daniel Vernet, "Paradoxes franco-allemands," *Le Monde*, 25 June 1987; and Thankmar von Münchhausen, "Schmidt idea about joint Franco-German force gathers rapid momentum," *The German Tribune*, 5 July 1987 (translated from *Frankfurter Allgemeine Zeitung*, 25 June 1987).

32. See Jérôme Dumoulin and Dominique de Montvalon, "Europe: la brigade du Rhin," *L'Express*, 3 July 1987.

33. "<<L'engagement de la France serait immédiat et sans réserve dans l'hypothèse d'une agression contre l'Allemagne fédéral>>," *Le Monde*, 13–14 December 1987.

34. See François Mitterrand, "La stratégie de la France," *Le Nouvel observateur*, 18–24 December 1987.

35. Federal Minister, *White Paper 1985*, p. 36.

36. See Karl Kaiser, "L'IDS et la politique allemande," in Karl Kaiser and Pierre Lellouche, eds., *Le couple franco-allemand et la défense de l'Europe* (Paris: Economica, 1986), p. 282; Catherine McArdle Kelleher, *Germany and the Politics of Nuclear Weapons* (New York: Columbia University Press, 1975), pp. 115–16; and Philip Windsor, "The Role of Germany," in Stan Windas, ed., *Avoiding Nuclear War: Common Security as a Strategy for the Defence of the West* (London: Brassey's Defence Publishers, 1985), pp. 87–98.

37. Manfred Wörner, "Security Policy Perspectives and Tasks of the North Atlantic Alliance in the Light of Changing West-East Relations," Munich, 24th International Wehrkunde Meeting, January 31, 1987 (Bonn: Defense Ministry mimeo), p. 12. Emphasis in original.

38. See Horst Afheldt, *Pour une défense non suicidaire en Europe* (Paris: Editions La Découverte, 1985); German title: *Defensive Verteidigung* (Reinbeck bei Hamburg: Rowohlt Taschenbuch Verlag, 1983); Andreas von Bülow, "Vorschlag für eine Bundeswehrstruktur der 90er Jahre. Einstieg in die strukturelle Nichtangriffsfähigkeit," *Europäische Wehrkunde* 35 (1986): 636–46; Hans Günter Brauch, "West German Approaches to Alternative Defense," Paper presented at International Studies Association Convention, Washington, D.C., April 14–18, 1987; and David Gates, "Area defence concepts: The West German debate," *Survival* 29 (July/August 1987): 301–17.

39. Richard K. Betts, "Nuclear Weapons," in Joseph S. Nye, Jr., ed., *The Making of America's Soviet Policy* (New Haven: Yale University Press, 1984), p. 108.

40. Source: Sofres survey conducted November 21–25, 1987; N = 1,000. Michel Colomès, "Sommet Reagan-Gorbatchev: l'esprit de défense des Français," *Le Point*, 7 December 1987. Earlier but similar findings are cited by Lellouche, *l'Avenir*, p. 20.

41. Jonathan Steele, "SPD plans direct talks with Moscow," *Manchester Guardian Weekly*, 7 September 1986.

42. *Newsweek* (international edition), 7 October 1985. This compared to 29 percent and 27 percent who answered yes in France and the United Kingdom (negative 62 percent and 66 percent). The poll was conducted by Gallup between September 18–23, 1985. The sample size exceeded 500 in each country.

43. Jacques Amalric and Jean-Louis Andréani, "M. Chevènement: il faut une volonté politique franco-allemande," *Le Monde*, 24 September 1987.

44. For example, former Chancellor Willy Brandt recently said, erroneously, that "no one in France has ever wished nuclear weapons for Germany." Quoted in "Willy Brandt: ni pacifistes ni neutralistes," *L'Express*, 29 January 1988.

45. In 1985, a French survey indicated that a majority of the French public approved a German nuclear deterrent (32 percent) or had no opinion (26 percent). See Claire Tréan, "Un sondage IFOP pour <<Le Monde>> et RTL: La France doit garantir la sécurité de la RFA estime une majorité de Français," *Le Monde*, 28 June 1985.

46. See Giuseppe Walter Maccotta, "Alcune considerazioni sulla Force de Frappe," *Rivista Marittima* (April 1982); quoted in François Puaux, "La France, l'Allemagne et l'atome: Discorde improbable, accord impossible," *Défense nationale* 41 (December 1985). Also see Kelleher, *Politics of Nuclear Weapons*, pp. 149–51 and Wilfrid L. Kohl, *French Nuclear Diplomacy* (Princeton: Princeton University Press, 1971), pp. 54–61.

47. Quoted in Frédéric Tiberghien, "Puissance et rôle de l'armement préstratégique français," *Le Monde diplomatique* 34 (February 1987): 14.

48. Jacques Chirac, "La politique de défense de la France: Allocution du premier ministre le septembre 1986, lors de la séance d'ouverture de la 39e session de l'Institut des hautes études de défense nationale," *Défense nationale* 42 (November 1986): 12.

49. Quoted in Pierre Lellouche, "Défense: division française," *Le Point*, 3 November 1986.

50. Claire Tréan, "M. Genscher salue <<un puissant encouragement à l'Europe>>," *Le Monde*, 24 October 1987.

51. See Tiberghien, "Puissance et rôle," p. 14.

52. This assumes added significance in the context of double zero. See Lellouche, "Défense," and Yost, *France and Conventional Defense*, p. 95.

53. Mitterrand also stated that he and Kohl had agreed to establish technical means for immediate consultation during crises. *Le Monde*, 2–3 March 1986.

54. See Claire Tréan, "l'affaire du président," *Le Monde*, 23 January 1988.

55. Quoted in Elie Marcuse, "Défense: Paris va de l'avant," *L'Express*, 22 January 1988.

56. See Claire Tréan and Luc Rosenzweig, "<<La stratégie nucléaire de la France s'adresse à l'agresseur et à lui seul>>, affirme le président de la République," *Le Monde*, 21 October 1987.

57. See Kosta Christitch, "Mitterrand en RFA: ambiguïté stratégique," *Le Point*, October 26, 1987, p. 41.

58. Heisbourg, "Défense Française," p. 147. A similar proposal was made by Charles Hernu, who later retracted it, and Pierre Messmer. See François Schlosser, "Paris-Bonn: le malentendu nucléaire," *Le Nouvel observateur*, 16–22 October 1987.

59. Luc Rosenzweig and Daniel Vernet, "Le chancelier Kohl expose au <<Monde>> sa conception de la sécurité européenne," *Le Monde*, 20 January 1988.

60. "<<Même alliance, même Europe et, je l'espère, même avenir>>," *Le Monde*, 19 January 1988.

61. Jacques Isnard, "M. Hernu propose de sacrifier le missile Hadès au nom de la coopération franco-allemande," *Le Monde*, 24 December 1987.

62. Elie Marcuse, "Défense: une stratégie de trop," *L'Express*, 30 October 1987.

63. "M. Fabius propose d'étendre à la RFA la <<garantie nucléaire>> de la France," *Le Monde*, 17 June 1987. A similar but less explicit proposal is contained in Laurent Fabius, "La défense de la France à l'aube du XXIe siècle," *Défense nationale* 43 (November 1987): 22.

64. Quoted in Jean Schmitt, "Chaban met la Défense en avant," *L'Express*, 17 January 1988.

65. Quoted in "Washington met en garde l'Europe contre une dénucléarisation totale," *Le Monde*, 9 February 1988.

66. See "Un Français sur deux est partisan d'une garantie nucléaire à l'Allemagne fédérale," *Le Monde*, 9 February 1988. The survey (N = 1,000) was conducted January 11–20, 1988 by IPSOS for *le Journal du dimanche*.

67. See Mitterrand, "La stratégie."

68. Rosenzweig and Vernet, "Le chancelier Kohl."

69. Quoted in "Willy Brandt," *L'Express*.

70. Indeed, the Bureau International de Liaison et de Documentation (BILD) was formed in 1945; it was followed by the Comité Français d'Echanges avec l'Allemagne Nouvelle as well as the Deutsch-Französisches Institut in 1948. See F. Roy Willis, *France, Germany, and the New Europe: 1945–1967*, revised and expanded edition (Stanford: Stanford University Press, 1968); John E. Farquharson and Stephen C. Holt, *Europe From Below: an assessment of Franco-German popular contacts* (London:

George Allen and Unwin, 1975); and Caroline Bray, "Cultural and Information Policy: Bilateral Relations," in Roger Morgan and Caroline Bray, eds., *Partnership and Rivals in Western Europe: Britain, France and Germany* (Brookfield, VT: Gower Publishing Company, 1986), pp. 93–96.

71. See Nicole Gnesotto, "Le dialogue franco-allemand depuis 1954: patience et longueur de temps . . ." in Karl Kaiser and Pierre Lellouche, eds., *Le couple franco-allemand et la défense de l'Europe* (Paris: Economica, 1986), pp. 11–30.

72. See "L'intérêt de l'un pour l'autre," *Le Monde*, 21 January 1988, and *The Franco-German Youth Office* (Paris and Bad Honnef: Office franco-allemand pour la Jeunesse and Deutsch-Französisches Jugendwerk, n.d.), p. 30.

73. Marcuse, "Défense." The figure for 1985 is from "Interview with M. Roland Dumas, Minister for External Relations, Broadcast, on West German Radio (Sudwestfunk) (March 2, 1986)," Ambassade de France à Londres, March 14, 1986. The 1986 data are contained in a letter from Chancellor Kohl's office; they include neither the Tokyo Economic Summit nor the summits of European leaders.

74. See Tréan, "L'affaire."

75. See Rosenzweig, "Quand un Français représente la RFA dans les réunions internationales," *Le Monde*, 21 January 1988.

76. See Marcuse, "Défense."

77. See Philippe Bernard, "Le rendez-vous européen d'Expolangues," *Le Monde*, 26 March 1987.

78. See Michel Candelier, "Tous faibles en thème," *L'Express*, 22 January 1988.

79. *Die 15–24 jährigen und der deutsch-französische jugendaustausch/Les 15–24 ans et les échanges franco-allemands de jeunes* (Paris and Bad Honnef: Office franco-allemand pour la Jeunesse and Deutsch-Französisches Jugendwerk, October 1985), pp. 46–49.

80. Quoted in James M. Markham, "Too German for France, Too French for Germany," *The New York Times*, 30 December 1987. Also see Jonathan Steele, "If the Yanks go home: The end of the de Gaulle era," *The Guardian*, 21 October 1986 and Luc Rosenzweig, "Une double épreuve de vérité," *Le Monde*, 26–27 October 1986.

81. See "L'intérêt," *Le Monde*.

82. *Die 15–24 jährigen*, pp. 14–19.

83. Ibid., pp. 36–37.

84. Brigitte Sauzay, *Le vertige allemand* (Paris: Editions Olivier Orban, 1985), p. 21. Similarly, in October 1986 a reporter for the French newspaper *Libération* described browsing through a German bookstore as a

"descent into the vale of tears: almost all book-titles refer to mistrust and fear of natural sciences, of politics and of the future of this planet." Quoted in Josef Joffe, "The ambivalent relationship: France and the 'mysterious Germans,'" *The German Tribune*, 9 November 1986 (translated from *Süddeutsche Zeitung*, October 29, 1986).

85. Christoph Bertram, "Bonn—and Europe—owe much to Franco-German ties," *The German Tribune*, 31 January 1988 (translated from *Die Zeit*, January 22, 1988). Also see *L'Express* cover story, "Germany: The Takeoff of a Superpower," 30 January 1987.

86. See "Cavalier French attitude on conservation starts to grate on German nerves," *The German Tribune*, 10 August 1986 (translated from *Wirtschaftswoche*, 18 July 1986).

87. Sauzay, *Le vertige*, p. 10.

88. See Lars Benecke, Ulrich Krafft, and Friedhelm Meyer Zu Natrup, "France-West German Technological Co-operation," *Survival* 28 (May/June 1986): 195–207; Gustav Bittner, "La coopération franco-allemande en matière d'armement classique," in Karl Kaiser and Pierre Lellouche, eds., *Le couple franco-allemand et la défense de l'Europe* (Paris: Economica, 1986), pp. 131–49; André Brigot, "Une coopération franco-allemande en matière de sécurité est-elle possible?" in Groupe d'études sur les Conflits et les Stratégies en Europe, *Sécurité et Défense de l'Europe: Le Dossier Allemand*, (Paris: Fondation pour les études de Défense Nationale, *Collection les sept épées*, No. 36, troisième trimestre 1985), pp. 149–227; Pierre Dussauge, *L'industrie française de l'armement: Intervention de l'Etat et stratégies des entreprises dans un secteur à technologie de pointe* (Paris: Economica, 1985), pp. 83–91; William Wallace, "Defence: the Defence of Sovereignty, or the Defence of Germany?" in Roger Morgan and Caroline Bray, eds., *Partnership and Rivals in Western Europe: Britain, France and Germany* (Brookfield, VT: Gower Publishing Company, 1986), pp. 230–37.

89. However, France is now planning a new tank (Leclerc) which will use the same ammunition as the German Leopard.

90. See François Heisbourg, "Coopération en matière d'armements: rien n'est jamais acquis..." in Karl Kaiser and Pierre Lellouche, eds., *Le couple franco-allemand et la défense de l'Europe* (Paris: Economica, 1986), p. 122.

91. Jérôme Paolini, "Politique spatiale militaire française et coopération européenne," *Politique étrangère* 52 (Summer 1987): 443.

92. See "L'Italie et l'Espagne participeront à la construction du satellite Helios," *Le Monde*, 10 April 1987 and Jacques Isnard, "Le satellite militaire français Helios pourra espionner des radars adverses," *Le Monde*, 25 March 1987.

93. The French appear somewhat chastened by this experience, which may make France more cooperative in the future. See Henri de Bresson, "Les différends industriels pèsent sur la rentrée franco-allemande," *Le Monde*, 9 September 1986.

94. These included whether the crewmen would sit side by side or in line; whether an existing American targeting system would be used or a new system developed; and whether the aircraft's sights would be placed in the nose, on the roof, or on a strut above the roof. For a detailed analysis of these issues from a conservative French parliamentary perspective, see Henri Louet, "Commission de la Défense Nationale et des Forces Armées," *La coopération industrielle franco-allemande en matière d'hélicoptères de combat* (Paris: Assemblée Nationale, troisième session extraordinaire de 1985–86), No. 249.

95. See Serge Schmemann, "France and West Germany to Set Up Joint Councils," *The New York Times*, 14 November 1987; Jacques Isnard, "Paris et Bonn s'engagent à construire en commun un hélicoptère de combat," *Le Monde*, 18 July 1987; "Un hélicoptère franco-allemand," *Le Monde*, 18 July 1987; "Determination to press on with anti-tank helicopter," *The German Tribune*, 26 July 1987 (translated from *Süddeutsche Zeitung*, 16 July 1987); and "Défense: l'hélico vole trop haut," *Le Point*, 27 July 1987.

96. See "La France et la RFA reprennent leur collaboration en matière d'armement terrestre," *Le Monde*, 29 August 1987 and Martine Jacot, "La France, le Canada et la RFA produiront un système de surveillance du champ de bataille," *Le Monde*, 28 November 1987.

97. Quoted in Diana Geddes, "Defence: more a liaison than a marriage," *The Times* (London), 27 September 1986.

98. Quoted in Philippe Lemaitre, "Les membres européens de l'alliance atlantique pour une politique aéronautique à long terme," *Le Monde*, 2 May 1986.

99. Sales dropped from Fr 62 billion in 1984 to Fr 25.5 billion in 1986 and continued to sag during 1987. See "French arms merchants on the defensive," *The Economist*, 24 October 1987 and "Britain overtakes arms sales rivals," *The Times* (London), 13 July 1987.

100. Louet, "Commission de la Défense Nationale," pp. 23, 66.

101. See Jacques Isnard, "M. Giraud propose une <<charte de sécurité>> européenne," *Le Monde*, 9 April 1987 and "Le ministre de la Défense: concentrer les moyens," *L'Express*, 6 June 1986.

102. According to German Defense Ministry official Lothar Rühl in a *Le Point* interview. See, "<<Une unité intégrée franco-allemande>>," *Le Point*, 29 June 1987.

103. Quoted in François Mitterrand, *Réflexions sur la politique extérieure de*

la France: Introduction à vingt-cinq discours (1981–1985) (Paris: Fayard, 1986), p. 104.

104. Ibid., p. 101.

105. Many French specialists have advised their government to respect the link between Bonn and Washington. For example, foreign ministry official François Gorand (pseud.) has argued that "France must avoid exaggerating her influence upon Germany!" "La politique de sécurité," p. 13, and Pascal Boniface and François Heisbourg advised Paris to avoid making Bonn choose between Paris and Washington—in part because Washington will always be chosen; see *La puce, les hommes et la bombe: l'Europe face aux nouveaux défis technologiques et militaires* (Paris: Hachette, 1986), p. 254.

106. See Gorand (pseud.), "La politique de sécurité," pp. 13–14.

107. For example, François-Georges Dreyfus, speaks of "pacifist, neutralist, anti-nuclear propaganda. . . ." François-Georges Dreyfus, "Les Allemagnes et le national-neutralisme," *Revue des deux mondes* (February 1987): 356.

108. Renata Fritsch-Bournazel, "Interrogations stratégiques et quête d'identité," in Groupe d'études sur les Conflits et les Stratégies en Europe, *Sécurité et Défense de l'Europe: Le Dossier Allemand* (Paris: Fondation pour les études de Défense Nationale, *Collection les sept épées*, No. 36, troisième trimestre 1985), p. 142.

109. In September 1987 a special conference of the Greens approved a resolution condemning NATO as "aggressive and offensive" and calling for West Germany's withdrawal; see *The Week in Germany*, 25 September 1987. But this is one of several issues which divides Green "realists" and "fundamentalists." For example, Otto Schily said, "The slogan 'Out of NATO' is nonsense. I'm in favor of dissolving both military blocs, but it's not feasible now." Serge Schmemann, "For Germany's Greens Movement, Conventional Success Breeds a Schism," *The New York Times*, 11 October 1987.

110. See "Rumeurs à Bonn à propos de la réunification," *Le Monde*, 14 May 1987.

111. Quoted in Yves Cuau, "Mars et Mercure," *L'Express*, 5 February 1988.

112. As Peter Schmidt has written of the WEU, "Much of the motivation for the relaunching sprang from the specific political situation in the context of the debate on the two-track decision and was thus of a limited nature." Peter Schmidt, "The WEU—A Union Without Perspective?" *Aussen Politik* 37 (1986): 399.

113. See Karl Kaiser and Pierre Lellouche, "Le couple franco-allemand et la sécurité de l'Europe: synthèses et recommandations," in Karl Kaiser and Pierre Lellouche, eds., *Le couple franco-allemand et la défense de l'Europe* (Paris: Economica, 1986), p. 313.

4 BRITAIN BETWEEN EUROPE AND AMERICA

Chapter 1 referred to the widespread opinion that economic constraints will require the sacrifice of one of Britain's four traditional military missions: the independent nuclear deterrent, conventional defense of the British Isles, the continental commitment, or the naval mission. Britain covered past fiscal shortfalls by across-the-board reductions, but many skeptics contend that that alternative is no longer viable. Resources are extremely tight, and there is no more "fat," so in the words of a *RUSI* editorial, "something's got to give."[1] The question is, what?

The most controversial British defense program has been modernization of the nuclear deterrent with new submarines and Trident 2 missiles. But the Conservative's victory in the 1987 general election resolved that issue. When the Tory mandate expires in 1992, more than one-half of Trident's total cost will be expended, or at least contracted, erasing the economic rationale for cancelling the program. Consequently, even a SDP party document acknowledged that "we are therefore faced with the extremely unpleasant fact that, as far as the future of our deterrent is concerned, it is Trident or nothing. . . ."[2]

Trident will cost approximately £9 billion over twenty years and absorb 6 percent of the defense budget and 11 percent of the equipment budget in 1989–90. Moreover, this price is fixed and cannot be underfunded.[3] As home defenses are already neglected, any cuts must trim either continental or naval missions.[4]

Britain pledged in 1954 to maintain until 1998 "on the mainland of Europe, including Germany . . . four divisions and the Second Tactical Air Force, or such other forces as the Supreme Allied Commander, Europe, regards as having equivalent fighting capacity."[5] There are now approximately 55,000 men in the British Army of the Rhine (BAOR) and over 10,000 British airmen in the FRG. By comparison, France maintains 50,000 men in the 2nd Corps of the First Army headquartered at Baden-Baden. As the size of Britain's military contracted, the deployment in Germany became an increasingly large portion of British capabilities. During the mid-1950s, 14 percent of the British Army was stationed in Germany, but as Britain's regular army shrank to 153,000 men, this proportion rose to 39 percent.[6]

Britain's acceptance of permanent troop deployments on the European mainland marked a major reversal of traditional policy. Nevertheless, military historian Sir Michael Howard argued that Britain is "unlikely ever again to have statesmen . . . who maintain that the security of the United Kingdom can be considered in isolation from that of our Continental neighbors east as well as west of the Rhine."[7] The continental commitment is perceived as vital to British security, and official statements regularly describe "the forward defense of the FRG as the forward defense of Great Britain itself."[8]

Nonetheless, skeptics observe that Britain spends more for defense than either France or Germany despite having a smaller economy. They consider it incongruous that 36 percent of Britain's defense spending goes to defend the Federal Republic whose GDP (Gross Domestic Product) per capita is 50 percent higher than Britain's.[9] Many critics concede the wisdom of NATO membership but argue that Britain's traditional naval role should retain first claim on scarce resources. For example, Keith Speed (Margaret Thatcher's minister of state for the Navy until his dismissal in May 1981) argued that shifting resources from the BAOR to the Navy

> does not mean the scrapping of the British Army of the Rhine to pay for a huge new Navy—far from it. But neither does it mean cutting the Navy's surface ships, their manpower, their logistic support to dangerous levels in order to preserve, apparently for ever, 55,000 soldiers in Northern Germany . . . because these numbers appeared sensible in the early 1950s.[10]

Speed and others observe that the Navy receives only 25 percent of Britain's defense budget but furnishes 70 percent of NATO's readily available naval forces in the Eastern Atlantic and the Channel. By comparison, despite an expenditure of 36 percent of the defense budget, Britain supplies only 10 percent of the forces in the Central Region, comprised of the FRG and Benelux.[11] Withdrawing British land forces would affect NATO's conventional deterrent in the Central Region much less adversely than a further reduction in Britain's naval fleet whose size has declined 75 percent in fifty years. Some argue that there could be considerable savings, and little loss of combat effectiveness, if the BAOR were reduced in size and augmented with a capability for rapid reinforcement from the United Kingdom.[12]

Michael Chichester and John Wilkinson have tabled a similar proposal. They assume that nuclear deterrence should be the principal military priority of Britain and France. They also argue that the Soviet threat to the North Atlantic area has become more geographically diffuse: the threat on the Central Front has diminished, but the naval threat from the Soviet's Northern Fleet has intensified. Therefore, Britain's conventional military missions should emphasize maritime, air, rapid deployment forces, and homeland defense while retaining "a tactical air force and a reduced land force in the Federal Republic for as long as political considerations rendered their presence necessary."[13]

Chichester and Wilkinson propose that Bonn should assume more responsibility for Germany's conventional defense, including command of the Northern Army Group, supported by the United States, France, Belgium, the Netherlands, and a much reduced British Army deployment of approximately 15,000 men. This would free British resources for a larger maritime role in the airspace and waters surrounding Western Europe in an arc from North Cape to Gibraltar which, according to Chichester and Wilkinson, are vital to NATO's forward defense.[14]

These arguments are rebutted by former Defence Secretary Sir John Nott. He contends that "nothing is more vital for British foreign policy than the interests of continental Europe. It dwarfs every other interest." According to Nott, the central rationale for the continental presence is more political than military: it is essential glue which holds the Western Alliance together. Furthermore, although it is "perfectly conceivable that U.S. ground and air forces could be withdrawn from Germany—the U.K.'s own front line . . . it is inconceivable that the U.S. Navy would ever withdraw from the Atlantic, which is the front line of the United States."[15] Therefore, the Royal Navy's contribution to Western defense in the Channel and Eastern Atlantic is valuable, but not vital. The first priority of British defense policy must be home defense of Britain. In a worst-case scenario, the British Isles could provide an essential base from which to reinforce the Central Front or to launch a counterattack if Europe were overwhelmed. Therefore, the United Kingdom should reluctantly sacrifice its naval missions to specialize on home defense and the Central Front.

Generalizing from the events of 1939, postwar British decisionmakers assumed that British security was principally threatened by an adversary's control of the European mainland. Thus, a prudent policy should seek to avert the piecemeal conquest of Western Europe by uniting with allies to resist aggression from the outset. If these assumptions are valid, it is not altruistic for Britain to devote a large portion of its military budget to defend the FRG. By defending Germany, Britain also defends its home territory and diminishes the risk of war on British soil.

Alternatively, Britain's status as an island nation, equipped with a nuclear deterrent, might permit a policy of armed neutrality.[16] If deterrence fails, NATO membership subjects Britain to a high likelihood of annihilation, but a neutral Britain could probably remain a noncombatant. And if the Soviets or Americans *did* attempt to occupy the United Kingdom during a war, they would probably attempt to limit destruction in order to capture British resources intact.[17] According to a neutralist perspective, NATO does not safeguard British security; it imperils it. Although there is little organized political support for the neutralist position, in late 1981 a neutral policy was supported by 46 percent of the British public.[18]

If Britain reduced the BAOR, it would strongly reinforce its Anglocentric reputation elsewhere in Europe.[19] Whether the reduction occurred to strengthen the Navy, or to pursue a neutral policy, it would create serious difficulties for Britain's continental allies. Germany's demographic shortfall would probably preclude the FRG from replacing British forces, and Christopher Coker maintains that it is "no secret that the Belgians, rather than serve under a German commander, would pull out entirely if the British relinquished overall command."[20] (This may be true, but in fact a German officer already serves as overall commander of the Central Region.)

Schemes to pare Britain's military obligations usually emphasize reducing either nuclear forces, for example Labour's defense program, or naval missions. If savings in the nuclear arena are precluded by the Conservative government's commitment to Trident, then further naval decrements are probably the most politically palatable alternative to reduce defense commitments.[21] Former Defense Secretary John Nott's 1981 defense review is illustrative; it mandated thinning naval assets in the Eastern Atlantic by reducing Britain's fleet of destroyers and frigates from fifty-nine to forty-two.[22] The immensely popular Falklands War (1982) blunted these cuts and the fleet was maintained at fifty. But even following the Falklands War, the Central Region continued to receive higher priority,[23] and skepticism has risen concerning the government's fidelity to the repeated pledge to maintain "around fifty" frigates and destroyers. Type 23 frigates to replace older Leander models are being ordered at a slow pace. The government abandoned the goal of ordering three new frigates each year: one was ordered in 1984, two in 1985, and three in 1986 and 1988, but none in 1987. Meanwhile, the service of older ships is being extended, but some Conservative backbenchers predict that the Navy will be reduced to forty frigates by 1991.[24] In contrast, the BAOR will probably be shielded from the largest cuts, although there may be delays in replacing obsolescent Chieftain tanks.[25]

THE "SPECIAL" RELATIONSHIP

Postwar British foreign policy, and especially defense policy, is often described as "obsessed by the idea of a special relationship with the United States."[26] This portrayal depicts Britain as attracted toward both Europe and America, with the pull from America usually prevailing. The French are notorious for this perspective; de Gaulle's fulminations against the "Anglo-Saxons" are legendary, and this perception of Anglo-American collusion survives in France. For example, Charles Hernu recently characterized Britain as "a tributary of the United States for its security and the American forward base in Europe."[27]

Other analysts emphasize Britain's grudging and incremental adaptation to her sharply diminished global status following World War II. They argue that the British failed to behave as "good" Europeans more from pretensions to national independence than from Anglo-Saxon affinities. As the late David Watt wrote, "the fundamental British illusion has had much more to do with the old vision of Britain as a major independent actor on the world stage than with any very profound belief in the combined destinies of the English-speaking peoples."[28] Anthony Eden, who served as both prime minister and foreign secretary during the 1950s, epitomized this outlook: opposed to European unity, resentful of American hegemony, and unwilling to adapt to the substantial diminution of British power.[29]

Although defense spending was as high as 10 percent of GNP in 1951, these delusions of postwar grandeur gradually eroded under sustained pressure from a series of setbacks: Britain was forced to withdraw from Palestine, then from all her important colonies, and finally from east of Suez. The United States assumed Britain's earlier role in Greece and Turkey in 1947, and Suez administered the *coup de grâce* to many British pretensions. Meanwhile, Britain's economic position deteriorated. In 1950, Britain's economy nearly matched that of France and the Federal Republic combined, and Britain retained the world's second largest economy as late as 1959. By 1970 Britain's economy was smaller than Germany's and level with France's; now it is smaller than Italy's.[30] Between 1971 and 1985, the growth in Britain's GDP (28 percent) lagged behind the NATO average (45 percent).[31]

Unquestionably, as Britain adjusted to decline, the Anglo-American congruences of language, history, and culture facilitated close relations. But these were less important than Britain's conviction, shared by the Federal Republic, that European security required a prominent American presence. To insure that presence, British leaders opposed any semblance of a European cabal which "could make the United States feel either not wanted or not needed in Europe."[32]

Unlike France with its Fouchet Plan, Britain never considered European cooperation as a possible substitute for the American anchor. Instead, Britain pursued European cooperation precisely to retain the U.S. engagement in Europe. For example, when the Korean War prompted the United States to demand German rearmament, Britain played a vital role by agreeing to retain ground and air forces on the continent. This commitment assuaged French fears of German militarism and facilitated the FRG's integration into the Western Alliance.

Thus, having opted out of the stillborn EDC, Britain participated in the WEU to preserve the American commitment. In his memoirs, former Prime Minister Harold Macmillan revealed his resentment of subsequent French ingratitude:

It has certainly been a bitter pill for us to swallow when, in later years, we are repelled by the French Government which was almost a suppliant for our guarantees against their fears of a revived Germany. That we have adhered to our undertakings in completely changed circumstances is forgotten, as is our succour of France after her tragic collapse in 1940. If it now has happily been possible for the French to forget the injuries which they suffered at Germany's hands, for the benefits that they have received from Britain it seems impossible for them to extend any sincere forgiveness.[33]

Therefore, just as the Federal Republic prevented the Elysée Treaty from overshadowing NATO, Britain was mindful that European initiatives such as the WEU should reinforce rather than eclipse the Atlantic Alliance.

Like other Europeans, the British are now less confident of the American guarantee. Their current priorities are to deepen the European defense commitment, but not by sacrificing U.S.-European relations.[34] Furthermore, although the other European leaders regret Margaret Thatcher's lukewarm support for European goals, they acknowledge and appreciate her unique ability to present Europe's positions to Washington on issues such as SDI and arms control.[35] Her Camp David meeting with President Reagan in November 1986 following the Reykjavik summit was illustrative: she managed to obtain the president's assurance that the Iceland meeting did not jeopardize the Anglo-American Trident agreement plus his agreement to a set of arms control priorities favored by the Europeans: INF, a 50 percent reduction of superpower strategic weapons within five years, and a chemical weapons ban.[36]

Anglo-American relations have blended close emotional ties with what David Watt called "the strong currents of anti-Americanism that have flowed on the left and right wings of British politics since 1945. . . ."[37] Even in 1980, 35 percent of British respondents believed that the United States posed a military threat to the United Kingdom.[38] Recently, a larger percentage of the British public believed that "the Russians genuinely want to stop the arms race," (35 percent yes and 52 percent no) than believed that "the Americans genuinely want to stop the arms race" (31 percent yes and 57 percent no).[39] Americans are hardpressed to distinguish this "equidistant" attitude from outright anti-Americanism. American ambassador (to London) Charles Price said of anti-Americanism, "I can't define it, but I sure can recognize it when I see it. And nowadays, I see a lot of it, in Britain and in Europe."[40]

BRITAIN AND EUROPE

Among the French and Germans, there is a widespread perception that "Great Britain hardly has the European fiber."[41] Moreover, findings from an April 1984 survey (Table 4–1) indicate that even the British share this perception. Unlike both the French and German respondents, who perceive their home countries as most committed to European values, British respondents agree that their country is least committed.

Table 4–1.   Commitment to Europe (percent).

Question: Which country is, according to you, most committed to the construction of Europe?			
	FRG	*France*	*UK*
French Opinion	19	49	2
German Opinion	75	8	2
British Opinion	32	24	9

Source: Jacques Fontaine, "A quoi rêvent les européens," *L'Expansion* (May 25–June 7, 1984): 83. Opinion surveys under the general supervision of SOFRES: France (N = 1,000) April 13–18, 1984; FRG (Infas, N = 1,219) March 19–April 8, 1984; United Kingdom (Gallup, N = 779) April 4–9, 1984.

There are several explanations for this perception. One is Britain's general demeanor toward the continent, which the late Italian journalist Luigi Barzini vividly captured:

Still today, when one asks a Briton, any Briton, pointblank, "Are you European?" the answer is always, "European? Did you say European? Er, er"—a long thoughtful pause in which all other continents are mentally evoked and regretfully discarded—"Yes, of course, I'm European." This admission is pronounced without pride and with resignation.[42]

Beyond this prevalent orientation toward Europe, there are specific historical actions which reinforced this impression: abstention from the proposed European Defense Community in the early 1950s, initial rejection of the Treaty of Rome, noninvolvement in the European Monetary System, and Britain's apparent preference for a "special" Anglo-American relationship.[43] Similarly, Margaret Thatcher's government manifests only tepid enthusiasm for European unity and, as *The Economist* noted, "she invariably describes" the other European Community members as "'them' rather than 'our partners' or even 'the others'. . . ."[44]

There are also cultural distinctions. As was mentioned in the previous chapter, nearly all French and German students study English. And considerable attention is devoted in these countries to the language's role as the dominant international language and to the fact that knowing English improves career prospects. By comparison, Britain is relatively monolingual. Although approximately 80 percent of students study a foreign language (usually French) between the ages of eleven and thirteen, only 40 percent study a foreign language beyond age fourteen.[45] By 1976, the percentage of secondary students who studied French at the more advanced 'A' level had diminished to 4.5 percent (from 7 percent in 1966). German fared even worse, declining to 1.5 percent.[46] Among Inner London Education Authority schools, "Entries for French and German 'O' levels fell by 42 per cent between 1977 and 1983," and in 1985 only 69 students (of 25,000) passed 'A' level German.[47]

The British media are also more insular. The author's strong, albeit subjective, judgment is that Le Monde's coverage of Britain (and especially the FRG) is more complete than any British paper's coverage of either France or the Federal Republic. And in 1986, "there were no resident British television correspondents anywhere on the European continent. . . ."[48] In contrast, approximately seventy German correspondents (including four television) work in France, and there are twenty French correspondents (two television) in Germany.[49]

Trade is also an important indicator of Britain's detachment from Europe. Since entering the EC (European Community), Britain's trade with European states has increased, and intra-EC exports now equal 50 percent of the British market, up from one-third previously. However, Britain retains a relatively close economic relationship with Anglophone countries—especially the United States and Canada—and in 1985 Ireland was the only EC country for whom Britain was the principal trading partner. That year, British trade equaled 8 percent of total trade for both France and the Federal Republic. By comparison, Franco-German trade equaled 16 percent of total French trade and 11 percent of total German trade.[50]

Nonetheless, a very significant shift in British attitudes toward European unity has occurred during the last two decades. The percentage of the British public favoring a "United States of Europe" has risen from 30 percent (48 percent opposed) in 1970 to 52 percent favorable (37 percent opposed) in 1987.[51] This level remains substantially below that in the six original EC member countries, including France and Germany, but it does indicate movement toward a more positive assessment of European integration. There are also larger number of British politicians who agree with Michael Heseltine, former secretary of state for defence, that Britain's "future cannot lie only in ourselves. We have a European destiny."[52] And there is some recognition of change on the continent. For example, Peter Hort wrote in the *Frankfurter Allgemeine Zeitung* that "Today everything is different. The British are regarded as being just as good Europeans as the French or the Germans, and are represented in Brussels by first-class diplomats and officials."[53]

ANGLO-FRENCH RELATIONS

Anglo-French relations remained prickly in the postwar era. This is not surprising considering what Dorothy Pickles described two decades ago as "the cumulative effect of a long history of misunderstandings."[54] Or, as de Gaulle once told the British ambassador, "Our two countries have always been at war except when they were allied against a common enemy."

Suspicion has seeped deeply into bilateral cultural relations. More British citizens have visited France than any other foreign country, at least one-third compared to fewer than one-quarter that have visited the FRG, but "only 2% say they admire the French. . . ."[55] And, expressions of mistrust infiltrate the reportage and scholarly literatures of both countries. Commenting from a British perspective, William Wallace wrote that "reporting in *Le Monde* and other newspapers has demonstrated a degree of underlying hostility undiminished by the recent improvement in intergovernmental relations."[56] But he also cited *The Sun*'s "Hop it, Frogs" campaign in 1984 which encouraged British newspaper readers to submit anti-French jokes.[57]

Survey research findings confirm these generalizations. For example, a British survey in October 1980 examined trust in other nations. Seventy percent of the respondents judged the United States either "very trustworthy" or "fairly trustworthy" (compared to 18 percent who responded "not particularly" or "not at all trustworthy"). The Germans also fared well, 60 percent trustworthy and 25 percent untrustworthy, but the French were considered more untrustworthy (53 percent) than trustworthy (32 percent).[58]

In 1984, residents of Britain, France, and Germany were asked whether they would accept a foreign prime minister if there were a united European government. Two conclusions from the results are apparent from Table 4–2. First, the French are most willing to accept a foreign leader, and the British are least acceptant. Second, a German prime minister would be more palatable than either a French or British leader, because Anglo-French animosity makes both the British (26 percent to 65

Table 4–2. Acceptance of Foreign Leader (percent).

Question: If there were a true European government, would you accept

		Yes	No
To French:	A German prime minister	69	19
	A British prime minister	39	50
To Germans:	A French prime minister	51	31
	A British prime minister	38	42
To British:	A French prime minister	26	65
	A German prime minister	49	41

Source: Jacques Fontaine, "A quoi rêvent les européens," *L'Expansion* (May 25–June 7, 1984): 88. Opinion surveys under the general supervision of SOFRES: France (N = 1,000) April 13–18, 1984; FRG (Infas, N = 1,219) March 19–April 8, 1984; United Kingdom (Gallup, N = 779) April 4–9, 1984.

percent) and the French (39 percent to 50 percent) opposed to a leader from the other country.

A related issue concerns which allies would be most dependable in case of war, and once again British suspicion of France is striking. A seven-country Gallup poll conducted between December 1983 and January 1984 asked, "In case of conflict, could we count on each of the following countries?" The French had equal confidence in the United Kingdom (57 percent) and the FRG (53 percent) as did the Germans in the French (41 percent) and the British (37 percent). But the British were much less confident in the French (13 percent) than in the Germans (39 percent).[59]

Similarly, a 1985 survey asked, "Which country would you say is Britain's best friend on the Continent of Europe?" The Federal Republic (with 24 percent) led by a wide margin over France (12 percent) and Holland (8 percent).[60] In France, a 1987 survey asked, "On the whole, do you have sympathy, antipathy, or neither sympathy nor antipathy for the following countries?" When the net level of sympathy is calculated (by subtracting the percentage of "antipathetic" responses from the percentage of "sympathetic" responses) Britain ranked last among the NATO countries included: Belgium (72 percent), Canada (71 percent), Luxembourg (66 percent), Netherlands (62 percent), Italy (59 percent), Spain (58 percent), Sweden (58 percent), Denmark (57 percent), Greece (55 percent), West Germany (51 percent), United States (50 percent), and Great Britain (47 percent). However, Britain was not far behind either Germany or the

United States.[61] As Diana Geddes of *The Times* pointed out in *Le Point*, however,

> Relations between France and Great Britain have rarely been better. . . . Britain is still distrusted and ranks in only fifth place among 'the most reliable friends of France,' behind Belgium, Canada, the United States, and West Germany. Despite unequaled support during two world wars, evidently the French have still not forgotten 'perfidious Albion.'[62]

A chronic problem is London's suspicion that Paris wants to dominate Europe, and French suspicion that British loyalties are more "Atlantic" than "European." Their mutual competition to influence the FRG, with France more often succeeding, further aggravates the relationship.[63] For example, the *Daily Telegraph* reported in 1985 that General Sir Nigel Bagnall (commander in chief of the BAOR) "cautioned yesterday against too close Franco-German defence co-operation at the expense of Britain." Citing the fact that Britain was discouraged from joining the Franco-German helicopter project, Bagnall implicitly chided French policy by stating that "Britain would be obliged to look elsewhere for collaborative ventures with the danger of a resulting polarisation of defence co-operation among those nations *which actually subscribe forces to forward defences.*"[64]

President de Gaulle's veto in 1963 of Britain's application to enter the European Community was the nadir of postwar Franco-British cooperation. By comparison, the recurrent efforts to improve Franco-British relations were less dramatic. The most comprehensive, and quixotic, was Prime Minister Guy Mollet's personal and informal proposal in 1956 to Anthony Eden that, building on proposals which Churchill supported before the fall of France in 1940, France and Britain should form a political union. When Britain rejected that suggestion, Mollet countered by proposing that France should join the Commonwealth, but the British also rebuffed that alternative.[65]

Prospects for Anglo-French cooperation dimmed after de Gaulle returned to power in 1958. However, in 1962 de Gaulle and Macmillan met at Rambouillet, and later there were the so-called de Gaulle-Soames conversations of 1969. Neither succeeded in dissipating the mutual distrust. In 1971–72, there was more success between Edward Heath (the most overtly "European" postwar prime minister) and Georges Pompidou. According to William Wallace, in this period it appeared that France might "place more weight on the Anglo-French relationship than on the Franco-

German, or at least to balance the Franco-German relationship by parallel ties with Britain."[66] This did not occur, however, and later Giscard d'Etaing was much more oriented toward Germany and his close relationship with Helmut Schmidt, while Wilson and Callaghan leaned more toward the United States than the continent.

Recent cooperative efforts have been more fruitful. One example is the Eurotunnel project. Since 1802, there have been twenty-seven proposals to connect France and Britain by bridge or tunnel, and there was even construction work as recently as 1975 which Britain's Labour government subsequently cancelled. But now a £6 billion railroad tunnel is finally being constructed, which will open in 1993 and allow travel between the center of London and Paris in three hours. Not surprisingly, there was greater French enthusiasm for the project: three-quarters of the French public supported it, but in Britain a 1986 Gallup survey showed that 51 percent of respondents were doubtful.[67] The French are generally predisposed toward both European cooperation and large public works projects, and the British also feared the defense implications of a permanent link with the continent. Nonetheless, Margaret Thatcher became increasingly enthusiastic, and in early 1988 she even described the "Chunnel" as probably "the most historic initiative since the Treaty of Rome. . . ."[68]

There are also initial efforts to increase weapons cooperation. Historically, both countries have pursued relatively autarkic procurement policies: Britain produces 80 percent of its equipment domestically and only 15 percent collaboratively.[69] By comparison, 70 percent of West Germany's arms spending "has involved at least another European partner."[70] Nonetheless, there was collaboration during the 1960s on several aircraft programs: the Jaguar strike/trainer and three military helicopters: Lynx, Puma, and Gazelle. But this cooperation eventually withered, and both countries turned more toward Germany as an arms partner. As a result, Anglo-French weapons sales became negligible.

Despite this unpromising background, beginning with the British-French decision in 1986 to improve their bargaining position by coordinating orders for AWACS (airborne warning and control system) planes from Boeing, they have begun to remove barriers to free trade. Because their national markets are relatively small, and research and development equals 25 to 30 percent of armament costs, a common market in weapons seems rational.[71] In September 1987, this issue was addressed by a two-day London conference attended by one hundred British and French government officials and businessmen. The initial meeting focused on army procurement, but a subsequent meeting in March 1988 addressed naval systems, and a third conference covering air systems was scheduled for later in the year. Concrete results of the first meeting included creation of an Anglo-French committee to promote bilateral military procurement and agreement to publish jointly a regular bulletin to solicit bids on upcoming army contracts.[72] In 1987, there was also agreement that Panhard (France) and Alvis (United Kingdom) would manufacture an armored car for the British Army.[73]

Nuclear weapons policy is a potentially more significant sphere for cooperation. The French often assert that Britain precluded nuclear cooperation when Kennedy and Macmillan signed the Nassau agreement (1962) which Boniface and Heisbourg describe as "irreparably subordinating Britain's nuclear future to Anglo-American cooperation. . . ."[74] Thereafter, the periodic discussions were unfruitful.[75] The British briefly considered the option of Franco-British cooperation when they began to seek a Polaris replacement, but questions were raised about both the costs and sophistication of French technology.[76]

In September 1986, David Owen and David Steel (then leaders of the Social Democratic and Liberal parties) revived this idea by meeting in Paris with French leaders, including President François Mitterrand, Prime Minister Jacques Chirac, former prime ministers Raymond Barre and Laurent Fabius, Socialist politician Michel Rocard, Defense Minister André Giraud, and Foreign Minister Jean-Bernard Raimond. Although British comics joked about a Inspector Clouseauian "Euro-beurmbe," SDP defense spokesman John Cartwright described the meetings in very positive terms: "In no case was the concept of greater Anglo-French cooperation rejected. The responses varied from cautious acceptance to enthusiastic endorsement."[77] And the Liberal/SDP Alliance contested the 1987 election on a policy of Franco-British nuclear cooperation "as a means of cutting costs and reducing arms . . . and insurance against the wekening or withdrawal of the U.S. guarantee."[78]

By the time of these meetings, French leaders doubtlessly realized that the Alliance could not win the 1987 election outright and was not even likely to govern in coalition. So their positive responses to the Owen-Steel visit were probably intended to signal to Margaret Thatcher that Paris would welcome a closer nuclear relationship. The most feasible forms of nuclear cooperation include coordinated patrols and refittings of nuclear missile submarines to maximize forces on station and joint efforts to counter Soviet anti-submarine warfare. It may also be possible to overcome French reluctance to joint targeting policy. In the longer run, the two might develop nuclear weapons jointly, including a possible air-to-surface stand-off missile. Michael Heseltine is among those who advocate Anglo-French cooperation to develop and produce the next generation of strategic nuclear weapons.[79]

In France, former prime ministers Raymond Barre and Laurent Fabius both advocated Anglo-French coordination of their nuclear submarine fleets and joint development of nuclear weapons. According to Barre, "It all depends upon the British will to participate in this effort of solidarity."[80] In addition, François Fillon (RPR, chair of the National Assembly's defense committee) authored a legislative report that foresaw development of Anglo-French cruise missiles.

Prospects for all forms of defense cooperation improved as a result of frequent and cordial meetings between the two defense ministers, André Giraud and George Younger. In late 1987, there was even public mention of possible monthly meetings of the defense ministers to discuss these issues.[81] In response to the scheduled withdrawal of American Pershing 2 and cruise missiles, they discussed potential joint development of a new medium-range nuclear missile and an air-launched cruise missile with a range of 300 miles, derived from France's ASMP (air-sol à moyenne portée). Deployed on Tornado, the ALCM would replace Britain's WE-177 gravity bombs around the year 2000.[82] There was also agreement for French nuclear submarines to visit British ports, for joint maneuvers, and serious discussions on joint patrolling.[83] Overall prospects for Anglo-French nuclear cooperation have improved markedly.

Unfortunately, serious obstacles to cooperation are raised by the dissimilar histories of the two nuclear programs. Britain's program originated with Anglo-American cooperation during World War II and evolved in that context following the war, despite interruption by the McMahon Act in 1946.[84] As a result, American restrictions on sharing highly classified data hinder British cooperation with any third country, including France.

In the case of Trident, the Anglo-American relationship is so intimate that British critics contend that Trident is not actually "independent." Labour Party leader Neil Kinnock called it "about as independent as my big toe is from me." This issue reemerged in October 1987 when it became clear that Britain would not be purchasing specific missiles; instead, both countries will draw from a common pool of British and American D-5 missiles. After seven or eight years of use, missiles will be returned to

King's Bay, Georgia for "deep servicing." This involves disassembling the missile to replace some components while overhauling others. But as Ministry of Defence officials told *The Times*, "the missile that goes in one end of the system is not the one that will come out the other end for loading into a Royal Navy submarine."[85] This caused a furor over whether Britain was actually purchasing Trident missiles, or merely renting them.

The Soviet Union immediately suggested that as American missiles, Trident should be addressed in superpower arms talks. The British government, however, forcefully declared that both the submarines and, much more significantly, the warheads would be owned outright by the United Kingdom.[86] This disclosure also raised questions concerning Trident's viability as a British deterrent if it was eliminated from the American arsenal as part of a Soviet-American arms control agreement. It is assumed that Britain could then purchase D-5 missiles, but it would be necessary to construct a very expensive missile processing depot in Britain—probably by rebuilding the Polaris facility at Coulport in Scotland.

There has been close Anglo-American intelligence cooperation throughout the postwar era.[87] This also has special relevance because Trident's guidance system will employ NAVSTAR, the U.S. global positioning system, which will eventually consist of eighteen navigation satellites.[88] Again, critics question whether Trident is sufficiently independent to function without access to American intelligence. The answer seems to be yes, but only by sacrificing the very precise accuracy which gives Trident 2 its counterforce capability against hardened targets.[89]

The French nuclear experience is markedly different. During the 1960s, Secretary of Defense McNamara feared that the use, or threatened use, of nuclear weapons by a European ally against the USSR could unleash a Soviet attack against the United States. Therefore, the United States opposed the proliferation of nuclear weapons to NATO-European allies—especially to France and the Federal Republic. And, as Paul-Marie de La Gorce has written, "the United States opposed keenly and with all the means it possessed the choice that France was making."[90] Therefore, France developed its nuclear force separately from the United States.

France is also largely detached from the American intelligence network. According to the French, their countercity nuclear policy is less dependent on intelligence data than the superpowers' counterforce strategies. Nonetheless, the French do fear that the United States might deny them tactical warning of nuclear attack.[91] This is one reason to build the Helios military reconnaissance satellite, which will combine capabilities for signals, optical, and infrared data collection.[92] In fact, for similar reasons, Britain considered deploying a satellite (ZIRCON) to gather signals intelligence and reduce British dependence upon the United States during a crisis.[93]

American attitudes toward French nuclear forces have changed since the 1960s. NATO's Ottawa Declaration of 1974 officially acknowledged that the British and French nuclear deterrents were capable of "contributing to the overall strengthening of the deterrence of the Alliance . . .."[94] And recently, General John Galvin (SACEUR) wrote of the French deterrent, "Let us not forget . . . the contribution to deterrence from France's *autonomous* nuclear forces which . . . create additional uncertainties for Soviet planners."[95] Furthermore, the importance of the French and British deterrents will rise as American INFs are removed.[96] Indeed, the United States presented a parallel argument to Spain in that country's unsuccessful effort to retain nuclear-armed F-16 jet fighters at Torrejón air base near Madrid, saying that the INF treaty increased the need to retain other nuclear capabilities in Europe. Following the double zero agreement, the U.S. government is more aware that nuclear cooperation among two of Washington's most influential European allies advances American interests. A policy of encouraging rather than impeding Anglo-French nuclear cooperation should include a full sharing of intelligence data with *both* countries.

Persistent mistrust is a second barrier to Anglo-French nuclear cooperation. Some former high British officials reportedly say, "take it from us, you can't trust the French," and Whitehall responded to Owen and Steel's quest for Anglo-French nuclear cooperation by enumerating past failures to coordinate French and British policies. Military opposition is particularly strong, and David Owen (a former Labour defence minister) has noted, "the traditional naval preference for American rather than European cooperation."[97]

Despite these difficulties, important progress is being made. It is increasingly common for British observers to write, as John Grigg did recently in *The Times*, that

Despite the linguistic and other differences, France is our natural ally, because it is a country of roughly the same size, with many shared interests and values, and separated from us by only 30 miles. The United States is not, to the same degree, our natural ally, despite the linguistic, legal and other affinities, because it is a vast continental superpower 3,000 miles away.[98]

And more Frenchman now concur with Jean-Paul Pigasse's sentiment that

> Thank God, the United Kingdom is governed today by a woman whose character is of tempered steel. Therefore, more than with the Germans, it is with the British that we should build the system of defense which is indispensable to our security. Doubtless this partner is not very accommodating, but at least Britain has demonstrated many times the same concept of liberty and independence as we. One could not find a better ally in these times.[99]

ANGLO-GERMAN RELATIONS

The rhythms of Anglo-German relations are somewhat asymmetrical. Since the war, German respect for Great Britain has eroded while British admiration for the Federal Republic has increased.[100] There is much evidence that the British feel more rapport with Germany than France, but conversely Germans empathize more with France than Britain. Germans are, as was mentioned, more favorable toward a French than a British prime minister for a united Europe. Opinion surveys between December 1983 and November 1986 show that Germans overwhelmingly favored better relations with France, Britain, and the United States. But averaging across thirty-one separate surveys, the mean support for improved Franco-German relations was 91 percent, compared to 84 percent for Anglo-German and 83 percent for German-American relations.[101] A German official summarized this difference by describing "his government's partnership with Britain as a business relationship, and with France as a marriage."[102]

Following a 1983–84 review, Bonn and London proclaimed the basic health of their bilateral relationship, and in 1985 they appointed part-time coordinators to oversee bilateral relations.[103] However, the relationship has lacked a close personal rapport between the leaders. Apparently, Margaret Thatcher considers Chancellor Kohl "a 'waffler' fond of empty phrases." And, "He was equally unhappy with her for being too business-like, too fond of laying down the law, and too nationalistic."[104] Whereas Thatcher held semiannual day-long meetings with Kohl's predecessor, SPD Chancellor Helmut Schmidt, which included foreign and defense ministers, a British official described Thatcher and Kohl as having "one full meeting a year at most."[105] During all of 1987 there were no full meetings and only three brief encounters. It appears that both Thatcher and Kohl were more comfortable with François Mitterrand.

Anglo-German relations turn upon the NATO security dimension and economic ties within the European Community. The United States is the principal external guarantor of West German security. But since 1954, when Britain made its continental commitment, and especially following French withdrawal from NATO's military structure in 1966, the United Kingdom has been Germany's principal European security partner. Not only do Britain and Germany share NATO doctrine, but their cooperative weapons programs far surpass those connecting France and Britain and even overshadow individual Franco-German weapons programs.

To date, Germany and Britain's largest joint venture is the Tornado aircraft program which combines Britain and Germany with Italy. Germany has ordered more than 360 Tornadoes, Italy 115, and Britain 385 (at a price exceeding the expected cost of the Trident program). If exports are added, the total program equals nearly 1,000 planes.[106] The European Fighter Aircraft program will involve these partners, plus Spain. Estimated British costs exceed £8 billion for 250 aircraft to replace the Phantom interceptor and Jaguar ground attack plane; German costs are estimated at DM 20 billion.[107] Although it would be cheaper for Britain to purchase the American F-18, it is expected to procure the EFA and also to proceed with the NATO Frigate (NFR 90) project which combines Britain, Germany, France, the United States, Italy, Spain, the Netherlands, and Canada to replace the Royal Navy's Type 42 destroyer in the late 1990s.[108] Defense Minister George Younger believes that collaborative programs like the EFA and the NFR 90 are desirable for both political reasons and to standardize NATO equipment. As Michael Evans wrote in *The Times*:

> Although Mrs. Thatcher and a number of other ministers are not enthusiastic supporters of European collaborative programmes, it is considered politically important for Britain to be seen to be playing a role in joint European defence projects.[109]

Without question, the keystone of Anglo-German security is the 140,000 servicemen and dependents that Britain maintains in the FRG. This, however, is not an entirely felicitous relationship. For example, some British fear that an element of divided loyalty is introduced because approximately 10 percent of British Army soldiers now have German spouses.[110] In addition, the British military is sometimes described as behaving quite imperiously in the Federal Republic. William Wallace cited a German staff officer who "remarked a little unkindly that BAOR behaves in Federal Germany rather as the British army must have behaved in India, with the intense camaraderie and introversion of a foreign posting rather than as a natural part of a common European defence on European soil." But Wallace conceded that

> The pride with which British officials and military officers pointed to the new policy that all BAOR brigade commanders and above should be proficient in German, after thirty years in which British army officers had been spending up to a third of their career service in Federal Germany, suggests that his remark was not entirely inaccurate.[111]

A German foreign affairs expert characterized British behavior in similar terms, as an opportunity to prolong Britain's imperial role by "keeping the Germans under control." He described Britain as quite "ruthless" in exercising its prerogatives, for example, destroying a Berlin forest for airfield construction and conducting damaging military exercises.

Concerning the always controversial issue of German control over nuclear weapons, British attitudes have shifted somewhat. As late as the mid-1960s, it was possible to write that "The 'nth-country problem' in Great Britain means first of all 'the German problem'. . . ."[112] Twenty years later, general opposition to nuclear weapons proliferation remains strong, and a large minority in Britain favors unilateral renunciation of their own nuclear capability. Under these circumstances, there is scant enthusiasm for a German deterrent force, but the specifically anti-German component has faded. As was mentioned in the previous chapter, by 1984, 25 percent of the British public thought it a "good thing" for the FRG to have its own nuclear capability. Even granting that the Federal Republic has no interest in acquiring a national deterrent force, these responses do suggest a growing British acceptance for German participation in a European nuclear deterrent capability which might someday replace the American nuclear commitment.

In both the security and economic spheres, a crucial question concerns the depth of Britain's commitment to European goals. In the economic arena, this is highlighted by Britain's failure to participate in the European Monetary System (EMS), the hard-fought (and ultimately successful) campaign to redefine the financial terms for British membership in the EC, and Britain's continuing role as *demandeur* of fiscal prudence in European organizations such as the EC and the European Space Agency (ESA).

In all these contexts, not only the French, but also Britain's other partners, distrust Britain's dedication to European values. This prompted Helmut Schmidt to argue that French leadership was the essential foundation for European security cooperation because

Britain today would hardly be inclined to assume the leadership because British mentality and tradition repeatedly make Britons feel maintaining their special relationship with the Americans is more important than their reluctantly accepted identity of interest with the continent.[113]

Therefore, although Britain has slowly moved toward greater cohesion with the continent, and increasingly sees its destiny in European terms, Britain is unlikely to take the lead in either realm: security or economic. The author has argued that Franco-German behavior is largely reactive to American initiatives, but Britain is even more reactive to Washington. The United Kingdom participates in European ventures without enthusiasm to avoid being left on the sidelines, to avoid repeating the Treaty of Rome debacle when Britain "missed the bus." Nonetheless, Britain remains a significant actor because of her size and her historically pivotal role in European security questions. But on these questions, London is now less central than Bonn, Paris—or Washington.

NOTES

1. "Something's got to give?" *RUSI: Journal of the Royal United Services Institute for Defence Studies* 131 (March 1986): 1–2. Also see "The best form of defence . . ." *The Independent*, 8 October 1986; David Watt, "Defence: the great retreat," *The Times* (London), 16 May 1986.
2. Simon Head, "Britain's defence in a European setting," in *Looking Forward: Issues for 1991* (London: SDP, 1987), p. 59.
3. See Nicholas Wood, "Trident project saves £376m," *The Times* (London), 22 January 1988; Michael Evans, "Trident plan moves ahead costing £50m every month," *The Times* (London), 4 June 1987; and E.R. Hooton, "The United Kingdom Trident Programme," *Military Technology* (January 1986): 26.
4. According to *Statement on the Defence Estimates 1987*, Vol. 1 (London: Her Majesty's Stationery Office, 1987), p. 54, only 21 percent of the military budget is devoted to homeland defense.
5. See "Protocol II on Forces of Western European Union," Ruth C. Lawson, ed., *International Regional Organizations: Constitutional Foundations* (New York: Praeger, 1962), pp. 160–61. Also see Edward Fursdon,

The European Defence Community: A History (London: The Macmillan Press Ltd, 1980), p. 325; Harold Macmillan, *Tides of Fortune: 1945–1955* (New York: Harper & Row, 1969), pp. 41–43; Roger Morgan "The Historical Background: 1955–85," in Roger Morgan and Caroline Bray, eds., *Partnership and Rivals in Western Europe: Britain, France and Germany* (Brookfield, VT: Gower Publishing Company, 1986), p. 8; and John Baylis, "Britain, the Brussels Pact and the Continental Commitment," *International Affairs* 60 (Autumn 1984): 615–29.

6. For a discussion of British ground and air forces in the FRG, see Hugh Beach, "British Forces in Germany, 1945–85," in Martin Edmonds, ed., *The Defence Equation: British Military Systems—Policy, Planning and Performance* (London: Brassey's Defence Publishers, 1986), pp. 157–73.

7. Michael Howard, *The Continental Commitment: The Dilemmas of British Defence Policy in the Era of Two World Wars* (London: Temple Smith, 1972), p. 146.

8. See, for example, Sir Geoffrey Howe, "The Atlantic Alliance and the security of Europe," *NATO Review* 35 (April 1987): 3. But according to one well-informed British observer, this rhetoric is primarily intended to keep the Federal Republic in NATO.

9. Calculated from data in *Defence Estimates 1987*, p. 54. In 1985, Britain's GDP per capita equalled only 91 percent of the EEC average while the FRG's was 138 percent; *The Economist*, 20 June 1987.

10. Keith Speed, *Sea Change: The Battle for the Falklands and the Future of Britain's Navy* (Bath: Ashgrove Press, 1982), pp. 158–59.

11. See *Defence Estimates 1987*, pp. 25 and 54; and George Richey, *Britain's Strategic Role in NATO* (London: Macmillan, 1986), especially pp. 90–91. Richey advocates a double shift in Britain's NATO role: maritime rather than continental, and Northern Region rather than Central Region.

12. See, for example, James Adams and John Witherow, "Message to the New Defense Secretary: Think Small," *The Sunday Times*, 12 January 1986.

13. Michael Chichester and John Wilkinson, *British Defence: A Blueprint for Reform* (London: Brassey's Defence Publishers, 1987), p. 107. But Christopher Coker argues that given the Northern Fleet's superiority over the Royal Navy, no British government is likely to support this British variant of the Reagan administration's "maritime strategy." See Christopher Coker, *British Defence Policy in the 1990s: A Guide to the Defence Debate* (London: Brassey's Defence Publishers, 1987), pp. 14–16.

14. See Chichester and Wilkinson, *British Defence*, p. 110.

15. John Nott, "Strategy begins at home," *The Times* (London), 6 October 1987.

16. See Peter Johnson, *Neutrality: A Policy for Britain* (London: Temple

Smith, 1985), pp. 93–96; however, Johnson rejects British retention of strategic nuclear weapons.

17.   Peter Johnson argues that:

the chances that a neutral Britain would be attacked in a super-power war are low. On the second level, if she *were* so attacked, the objective would be the use of her facilities and the quality of destruction might be lower than that expected in alliance, when she would enter a war as an ally and host to the forces of a main combatant.

Johnson, *Neutrality*, pp. 82, 79–82. Also see John Burton, A.J.R. Groom, Margot Light, C.R. Mitchell, Dennis J.D. Sandole, *Britain Between East and West: A Concerned Independence* (Brookfield, VT: Gower Publishing, 1984) and Dan Smith, *The Defence of the Realm in the 1980s* (London: Croom Helm, 1980), pp. 233–37.

18.   See David Capitanchik and Richard C. Eichenberg, *Defence and Public Opinion,* Chatham House Papers 20 (London: Routledge & Kegan Paul, 1983), p. 25.

When asked in mid-1985, "Do you think it is important for this country to try to be a leading power, or would you like to see us be more like Sweden or Switzerland?" there was substantial British public support for using neutral countries as models:

Be a world power	37%
More like Sweden, Switzerland	55%
Don't know	8%

Gordon Heald and Robert J. Wybrow, *The Gallup Survey of Britain* (London: Croom Helm, 1986), p. 276.

19.   See William Wallace, "Shifts in British Defence Policy," in John Roper, ed., *The Future of British Defence Policy* (Brookfield, VT: Gower, 1985), pp. 105–08.

20.   Christopher Coker, *A Nation in Retreat: Britain's Defence Commitment* (London: Brassey's Defence Publishers, 1986), pp. 58–59.

21.   See, for example, "The best form of defence..." *The Independent*, 8 October 1986 (editorial). For a discussion of the Royal Navy's travail since 1945, see Eric Grove, "The Royal Navy: the Fleet Comes Home," in Martin Edmonds, ed., *The Defence Equation: British Military Systems—Policy, Planning and Performance* (London: Brassey's Defence Publishers, 1986), pp. 79–113.

22.   See John Baylis, "British Defense Policy," in John Baylis, et al., *Contemporary Strategy*, 2nd ed., Vol. II (New York: Holmes and Meier, 1987), p. 153.

23. Some observers fear that after 1989–90, when the cost of defending the Falklands will be absorbed into the overall defense budget, funding for the Falklands will be adversely affected by overall budget pressure. Therefore, a 1987 report of the parliamentary Defence Select Committee stated that "force levels should be determined by operational need rather than by financial considerations." Martin Fletcher, "Cut Falklands budget at peril, warn MPs," *The Times* (London), 10 July 1987. However, the cost of the Falklands garrison is steadily declining from £397 million in 1985–86 to £140 million in 1987–88." See "Falklands helped by airfield," *The Times* (London), 10 December 1986.

24. See Martin Fletcher, "Government abandons target for warships," *The Times* (London), 22 October 1987 and Michael Evans, "Senior Tories fear new Navy cuts," *The Times* (London), 11 January 1988.

25. According to David Robertson:

> the British defense budget will come under impossible strain in the next decade. If there is no defense review, the consequence will be that all of the tasks of the services will be so underfunded as to reduce efficiency very seriously, and quite possibly to damage the confidence that the rest of NATO . . . has in Britain.

David Robertson, "British Defense Policy in the Late 1980s," in Carol Edler Baumann, ed., *Europe in NATO: Deterrence, Defense, and Arms Control* (New York: Praeger, 1987), p. 171.

26. John Grigg, "The defenders Europe needs," *The Times* (London), 5 June 1987. Also see William Wallace, *Britain's Bilateral Links Within Western Europe*, Chatham House Papers 23 (London: Routledge & Kegan Paul, 1984), p. 10.

27. Quoted in Jacques Isnard, "M. Hernu dénonce l'absence d'une Europe de la défense," *Le Monde*, 17 March 1987.

28. David Watt, "Introduction: The Anglo-American Relationship," in William Roger Louis and Hedley Bull, eds., *The 'Special Relationship': Anglo-American Relations Since 1945* (New York: Oxford University Press, 1986), p. 10. Bernard Porter argues that the key factors which supported this illusion in the early postwar period were the survival of the empire and the acquisition of nuclear weapons. See Bernard Porter, *Britain, Europe and the World, 1850–1982* (London: Allen & Unwin, 1983), pp. 117–23. Also see David Calleo, "Early American Views of NATO: Then and Now," in Lawrence Freedman, ed., *The Troubled Alliance: Atlantic Relations in the 1980s* (London: Heinemann, 1983), p. 15.

29. See David Cannadine, "The Next Best Man," *The New York Review of Books*, 22 October 1987.

30. See Ernest R. May and Gregory F. Treverton, "Defence Relationships: American Perspectives," in William Roger Louis and Hedley Bull, eds., *The 'Special Relationship': Anglo-American Relations Since 1945* (New York: Oxford University Press, 1986), p. 172.

31. Caspar W. Weinberger, Secretary of Defense, *Report on Allied Contributions to the Common Defense: A Report to the United States Congress* (Washington, D.C.: U.S. Department of Defense, April 1987), p. 87.
32. Trevor Taylor, "Britain and European Defense Cooperation," in Lothar Brock and Mathias Jopp, eds., *Sicherheitspolitische Zusammenarbeit und Kooperation der Rüstungswirtschaft in Westeuropa* (Baden-Baden: Nomos Verlagsgesellschaft, 1986), p. 148.
33. Macmillan, *Tides of Fortune*, p. 483.
34. See, for example, Kenneth Hunt, "Comments on Chapters 2 and 3," in John Roper, ed., *The Future of British Defence Policy* (Aldershot: Gower, 1985), p. 70.
35. See Francis Cornu, "Mme Thatcher estime avoir aussi plaidé pour la France auprès de M. Reagan," *Le Monde*, 11 November 1986 and Steven Erlanger, "Mrs Thatcher under European Eyes," *New Statesman*, 26 June 1987.
36. See Lionel Barber and Peter Riddell, "Thatcher wins Reagan promise on modernizing UK deterrent," *The Financial Times*, 17 November 1986.
37. Watt, "The Anglo-American Relationship," p. 8.
38. See Ivor Crewe, "Britain: Two and a Half Cheers for the Atlantic Alliance," in Gregory Flynn and Hans Rattinger, eds., *The Public and Atlantic Defense* (Totowa, NJ: Rowman & Allenheld, 1985), p. 19; Table 2.3, "Perception of the threats posed to Britain and other European countries by the USSR and the United States (Gallup 1/80)." The question asked, "Does the USSR/US pose a threat in the: military field? political field? scientific field? economic field?"
39. David Fairhall, "Europe wary of American nuclear stance," *The Manchester Guardian Weekly*, 22 February 1987. The British sample equaled 1,463; the survey was conducted by Marplan sometime between November 1986 and January 1987.
40. Charles Price, "The risks for Europe in anti-American sentiment," *Manchester Guardian Weekly*, 22 March 1987.
41. Pascal Boniface, et al., *L'année stratégique*, Institut National Supérieur d'études de Défense et de Désarmement/FEDN (Paris: Editions J.-C. Lattès, 1985), p. 17.
42. Luigi Barzini, *The Europeans* (New York: Penguin Books, 1984), pp. 64–65.
43. As William Wallace has written:
   The history of Britain's reluctant approach to European collaboration is less well remembered in Britain than on the continent. Indeed one of the underlying obstacles to the successful pursuit of British interests through collaboration with other West European governments is the different set of images and recollections about Britain's relationship with the Continent which prevail in Britain from elsewhere.

   Wallace, *Britain's Bilateral Links*, p. 9.

44. "Europe disagrees to do nothing," *The Economist*, 4 July 1987.

45. See Sarah Thompson, "Languages 'should be taught to all under 16,'" *The Times* (London), 27 March 1987.

46. G.R. Potter, "Reviving School Language Studies—The Resource Implications," in Headquarters' Conference, *The Teaching of Modern Language: A View for the 1980's* (London: Headquarters' Conference, 1980), p. 13.

47. Simon Heffer, "The case for a better class of school," *The Daily Telegraph*, 22 December 1986.

48. Caroline Bray, "National Images, the Media and Public Opinion," in Roger Morgan and Caroline Bray, eds., *Partnership and Rivals in Western Europe: Britain, France and Germany* (Brookfield, VT: Gower Publishing Company, 1986), p. 63.

49. See "L'intérêt de l'un pour l'autre," *Le Monde*, 21 January 1988.

50. Calculated from data in the Organization for Economic Cooperation and Development (OECD), *Monthly Statistics of Foreign Trade*, Series A (Paris: OECD, December 1986), pp. 58–91. Also see Geoffrey Shepherd, "A Comparison of the Three Economies," in Roger Morgan and Caroline Bray, eds., *Partnership and Rivals in Western Europe: Britain, France and Germany* (Brookfield, VT: Gower Publishing Company, 1986), pp. 36–37.

51. The question asked "Are you personally for or against the European Community developing towards becoming a 'United States of Europe'?" The survey was conducted January 9–13, 1987 by Social Surveys (Gallup Poll); N = 1,048. Source: *Eurobarometer* (Brussels: Commission of the European Communities, March 1987), p. 28.

52. Michael Heseltine, "Little Britain ignores its space destiny," *The Times* (London), 19 October 1987.

53. Peter Hort, "Britain's turn in Brussels a chance for pragmatism," *The German Tribune*, 17 August 1986 (translated from *Frankfurter Allgemeine Zeitung*, 2 August 1986).

54. Dorothy Pickles, *The Uneasy Entente: French Foreign Policy and Franco-British Misunderstandings* (London: Oxford University Press, 1966), p. 1.

55. Theodore Zeldin, *The French* (New York: Vintage Books, 1983), p. 5. A British survey conducted between November 5–10, 1985 by Market and Opinion Research International (MORI), with a sample of 2,000 adults, aged fifteen years or older, found that 23 percent of the respondents had visited West Germany. The results were published (London: Embassy of the Federal Republic of Germany, 3 December 1985), mimeo.

56. Wallace, *Britain's Bilateral Links*, p. 29.

57. Also see Bray, "National Images," p. 64.

    In 1987, *Le Monde*'s satirist Claude Sarraute and *The Guardian*'s Richard Boston engaged in similar mockery. See "Frank phobia," *The Manchester Guardian Weekly*, 8 November 1987.

58. See Crewe, "Britain: Two and a Half Cheers," p. 41.

59. See *L'Express*, 3 February 1984. The polls were conducted by Gallup International between December 9, 1983 and January 4, 1984; the aggregate sample size for the seven countries equaled 5,742.

60. Survey was between November 5–10, 1985 by Market and Opinion Research International (MORI); the sample comprised 2,000 adults, aged fifteen years or older. The results were published (London: Embassy of the Federal Republic of Germany, December 3, 1985), mimeo.

61. The survey was conducted by Sofres between June 8–11, 1987. The sample consisted of 1,000 French residents aged eighteen or older. "Le hit-parade des chefs d'Etat étrangers," *Le Point*, 22 June 1987.

62. Diana Geddes, "Peu aimée, mais admirée: Margaret Thatcher," *Le Point*, 22 June 1987. A 1987 survey by BVA/*Paris Match* asked which country "France can count on the most in the case of international tensions." The United States was the resounding leader (47 percent), followed by the FRG (16 percent), and the United Kingdom (7 percent). See *News from France*, 15 June 1987.

63. See Philippe Ducros, "Grande-Bretagne: Politique de défense et relations internationales," *Défense nationale* 42 (October 1986): 89–90.

64. Michael Farr, "Allies cautioned," *Daily Telegraph*, 16 March 1985 (emphasis added).

65. See John Zametica, "France tried to join the Commonwealth," *The Sunday Times*, 6 September 1987, and Michel Kajman, "Quand Guy Mollet proposait l'adhésion de la France au Commonwealth," *Le Monde*, 9 September 1987.

66. Wallace, *Britain's Bilateral Links*, p. 26.

67. See Alain Faujas, "Le pas de Calais à pied sec," *Le Monde*, 30 July 1987; Francis Cornu, "<<La reyne le veult>>, mais ses sujets?" *Le Monde*, 30 July 1987; and Rodney Cowton, "Two big steps for the Channel tunnel," *The Times* (London), 23 July 1987.

68. Quoted in "Thatcher: la défense de l'Europe, c'est d'abord l'OTAN," *L'Express*, 5 February 1988.

69. See *Defence Estimates 1987*, p. 52.

70. Coker, *British Defence Policy*, p. 73.

71. See Michael Evans, "Britain and France pool arms research," *The Times* (London), 19 September 1987.

72. See Dominique Dhombres, "Londres souhaite développer avec la France

des achats croisés d'armes conventionnelles," *Le Monde*, 20–21 September 1987, and Michael Evans, "Anglo-French defence accords sought," *The Times* (London), 21 December 1987.

73. See *News from France*, 15 October 1987 and "French arms merchants on the defensive," *The Economist*, 24 October 1987.

74. Pascal Boniface and François Heisbourg, *La puce, les hommes et la bombe: l'Europe face aux nouveaux défis technologiques et militaires* (Paris: Hachette, 1986), p. 237.

75. See Jean Klein, "Le débat en France sur la défense de l'Europe," *Stratégique* (quatrième trimestre 1984): 13; Colin McInnes, *Trident: The Only Option?* (London: Brassey's Defence Publishers, 1986), pp. 175–87; and William Wallace, "European Defence Co-operation: The Reopening Debate," *Survival* 26 (November/December 1984): 254.

76. See Hooton, "Trident Programme," p. 19.

77. John Cartwright, "The Alliance fights for European defence," *The Guardian*, September 12, 1986.

78. David Owen and David Steel, *The Time Has Come: Partnership for Progress* (London: Wiedenfeld & Nicolson, 1987), p. 125.

79. See Robin Oakley, "Heseltine calls for link with France on nuclear weapons," *The Times* (London), 25 September 1987. Also see François Heisbourg, "Défense Française: L'impossible statu quo," *Politique internationale* (Summer 1987): 145–46.

80. "La France et l'Allemagne fédérale doivent étudier l'organisation d'un espace stratégique commun suggère M. Raymond Barre," *Le Monde*, 10 November 1987. Also see Laurent Fabius, "La défense de la France à l'aube du XXIe siècle," *Défense nationale* 43 (November 1987): 21.

81. Michael Evans, "Britain vows to keep up momentum over planned nuclear ties," *The Times* (London), 2 October 1987.

82. See *News from France*, 15 October 1987) and Michael Evans, "France may join UK over missile," *The Times* (London), 1 December 1987.

83. See Dominique Dhombres, "Paris et Londres veulent construire un missile nucléaire," *Le Monde*, 16 December 1987; "Nuclear Franglais," *The Times* (London), 16 December 1987; and Howell Raines, "Britain and France Stay at Odds on Economic and Defense Policy," *The New York Times*, 30 January 1988.

84. See John Simpson, *The Independent Nuclear State: The United States, Britain, and the Military Atom*, 2nd edition (London: Macmillan, 1986); Lawrence Freedman, "British Nuclear Targeting," in Desmond Ball and Jeffrey Richelson, eds., *Strategic Nuclear Targeting* (Ithaca: Cornell University Press, 1986), pp. 109–26; and Margaret Gowing, "Nuclear Weapons and the 'Special Relationship,'" in William Roger Louis and

Hedley Bull, eds., *The 'Special Relationship': Anglo-American Relations Since 1945* (New York: Oxford University Press, 1986), pp. 117–28.

85. Michael Evans, "Trident will depend on U.S. base staying open," *The Times* (London), 23 October 1987.

86. "Trident in Kremlin's firing line," *The Times* (London), 24 October 1987. However, Britain is obtaining plutonium from the United States, and the warheads are tested in Nevada. See Coker, *British Defence Policy*, p. 143.

87. See Jeffrey T. Richelson and Desmond Ball, *The Ties That Bind: Intelligence Cooperation Between the UKUSA Countries* (Boston: Allen and Unwin, 1985).

88. See Kosta Tsipis, *Arsenal: Understanding Weapons in a Nuclear Age* (New York: Simon & Schuster, 1983), pp. 126–28 and David Wessel, "Satellites Add More Accuracy to Locating Objects on Earth," *The Wall Street Journal*, 21 March 1986.

89. See Coker, *British Defence Policy*, p. 142.

90. Paul-Marie de La Gorce, *La Guerre et l'atome* (Paris: Plon, 1985), p. 93.

91. See Jérôme Paolini, "Politique spatiale militaire française et coopération européenne," *Politique étrangère* 52 (Summer 1987): 439–43 and General André Dubroca, *La France sans défense: Demain un nouveau mai 40?* (Paris: Plon, 1986), pp. 90–93. Also see William Wallace, "What price independence? Sovereignty and independence in British politics," *International Affairs* 62 (Summer 1986): 377. David Yost described "lack of a satellite mapping capability for cruise missile guidance systems" as an important constraint on French nuclear policy making. David S. Yost, *France's Deterrent Posture and Security in Europe: Part I: Capabilities and Doctrine*, Adelphi Paper Number 194 (London: International Institute for Strategic Studies, Winter 1984/5), pp. 20–21.

92. See Jacques Isnard, "Le satellite militaire français Helios pourra espionner des radars adverses," *Le Monde*, 25 March 1987.

93. This development was strongly supported by Chichester and Wilkinson, *British Defence*, pp. 86–88, but "it was reported in the press that the Ministry of Defence would not after all proceed to develop the rumoured Project Zircon. . . ." James Eberle and Helen Wallace, *British Space Policy and International Collaboration*, Chatham House Papers 42 (London: Routledge & Kegan Paul, 1987), p. 7. Also see David Fairhall, "Why Britain wants its own spy satellite," *The Manchester Guardian Weekly*, 1 February 1987.

94. Quoted in John Cartwright, "Nuclear Strategy and Arms Control," in John Cartwright et al., *The State of the Alliance 1986–1987: North Atlantic Assembly Reports* (Boulder: Westview, 1987), p. 305.

95. John Galvin, "Non à une Europe dénucléarisée," *L'Express*, 2 October 1987. Or, as François de Rose has written:

> the existence in Europe of two independent centres able to decide on use of these weapons necessarily introduces elements of uncertainty into the calculations of any aggressor through the danger they present of the extension, inside his frontiers, of any conflict from which he might wish to exclude his territory and that of the other superpower.

François de Rose, *European Security and France* (Urbana: University of Illinois Press, 1985), p. 90.

96. For example, Michael Stürmer wrote: "the British and French nuclear weapons . . . will become increasingly significant in the coming decade both in qualitative and quantitative terms." "Political implications after the missiles deal," *The German Tribune*, 25 October 1987 (translated from *Frankfurter Allgemeine Zeitung*, 14 October 1987).

97. David Owen, letter to *The Guardian*, 3 October 1986.

98. John Grigg, "The defenders Europe needs," *The Times* (London), 5 June 1987.

99. Jean-Paul Pigasse, "Libres propos," *L'Express*, 30 October 1987.

100. See Caroline Bray, "Cultural and Information Policy in Bilateral Relations," in Roger Morgan and Caroline Bray, eds., *Partnership and Rivals in Western Europe: Britain, France and Germany* (Brookfield, VT: Gower Publishing Company, 1986), pp. 85.

101. Computed from data in *Aktueller Politischer Dienst* (Bielefeld: EMNID–Institut, November 1986), p. 19.

102. Wallace, *Britain's Bilateral Links*, p. 29.

103. See Roger Morgan, "The Historical Background: 1955–85," in Roger Morgan and Caroline Bray, eds., *Partnership and Rivals in Western Europe: Britain, France and Germany* (Brookfield, VT: Gower Publishing Company, 1986), p. 21.

104. Andrew McEwen, "Thatcher and Kohl wage their own 'cold war'," *The Times* (London), 15 January 1988.

105. Ibid.

106. See Michael Evans, "Tornado sales may be boosted by Luftwaffe," *The Times* (London), 12 June 1987.

107. See Michael Evans, "£2bn take-off for new fighter," *The Times* (London), 7 November 1987 and Hans-Anton Papendieck, "Generals not happy at tight rein on spending," *The German Tribune*, 26 July 1987 (translated from *Hannoversche Allgemeine*, 13 July 1987).

108. As of early 1988, all eight partners had signed memorandums of understanding for the Project Definition Phase of the NATO Frigate program.

109. Michael Evans, "Defence spending splits Government," *The Times* (London), 22 September 1988. For a full list of Britain's collaborative projects see *Statement on the Defence Estimates 1988*, Vol. 1 (London: Her Majesty's Stationery Office, 1988), p. 42.

110. According to Hugo Beach, approximately one-third of the marriages in-
volving British military personnel in the FRG are to German women.
Hugh Beach, "British Forces in Germany, 1945–85," in Martin Edmonds,
ed., *The Defence Equation: British Military Systems—Policy, Planning
and Performance* (London: Brassey's Defence Publishers, 1986), p. 172.

111. William Wallace, "Shifts in British Defence Policy: How Would the
European Allies React?" in John Roper, ed., *The Future of British
Defence Policy* (Aldershot: Gower, 1985), p. 107.

112. Anthony Hartley, "The British Bomb," *Survival* 6 (July/August 1964):
175.

113. Helmut Schmidt, "European leadership changes had pivotal role in
changed relationship with US," *The German Tribune*, 7 December 1986
(translated from *Die Zeit*, November 21, 1986). Also see Bray, "National
Images," p. 58.

5 MULTILATERAL COOPERATION

Previous chapters examined bilateral relations between Britain, France, and the Federal Republic; this chapter looks at multilateral European security cooperation. The most prominent institutions are the Western European Union (WEU) and the Independent European Programme Group (IEPG), but other important organizations include the European Community (EC), EUREKA, and the European Space Agency (ESA).

The European Defense Community (EDC) was the first postwar attempt to establish multilateral defense cooperation. Because the EDC evolved from a French proposal (the Pleven Plan), it seems odd that its *coup de grâce* was delivered by France's National Assembly after the other signatories (Belgium, Germany, Italy, Luxembourg, and the Netherlands) had ratified the treaty, or were about to ratify the treaty. To understand this paradox, one should recall Raymond Aron's description of the EDC as "a compromise between the hostility of the French government and Parliament towards the remilitarization of Germany and the external pressure (mainly American) for it."[1]

Believing that German rearmament was unavoidable, the French devised the plan for a European army as the least distasteful way to swallow an unpleasant reality. The slogan of French EDC supporters, "EDC or Wehrmacht," reflected this viewpoint. Unfortunately, many parliamentarians mistakenly believed that by defeating the EDC they could prevent not only the European army but German rearmament as well. This ignored the fact that German remilitarization was inevitable and France's choices were limited to NATO or the EDC as the framework within which it would occur.

WESTERN EUROPEAN UNION

Within two months following the EDC's failure, the same countries, plus Britain, joined the Western European Union. On paper, the WEU had broad scope; for example, Article 5 of the WEU treaty included a more explicit collective security obligation than that contained in the North Atlantic Treaty:

> Article 5. If any of the High Contracting Parties should be the object of an armed attack in Europe, the other High Contracting Parties will, in accordance with the provisions of Article 51 of the Charter of the United Nations, afford the Party so attacked all the military and other aid and assistance in their power.[2]

But in truth, the WEU was clearly intended to serve NATO's purpose, as Article 4 made explicitly clear.[3] Therefore, the WEU languished in NATO's shadow for more than thirty years, and even *after* the WEU's recent reactivation, it has continued to pass resolutions reaffirming its subordinate status.

Under de Gaulle, France proposed a more European approach to European unification: a political confederation of the six EEC (European Economic Community) countries, the so-called Fouchet Plan. In October of 1961, with the principal objective of creating a common foreign and defense policy, Christian Fouchet proposed uniting the six EEC states under a council of heads of state or government which would make decisions by unanimity. De Gaulle hoped to achieve a fine balance: sufficient cohesion among the European states to avoid U.S. domination, while avoiding supranationalism, which would constrain French independence. The initiative failed because the Netherlands and Belgium feared Franco-German domination and a loosening of the Atlantic tie. Philippe de Schoutheete observed that because of these two countries' geographical position and their historical experience, the "golden rule of their diplomacy must be to hold the balance among their three large neighbors and to always find allies against the hegemonic tendencies of one or the other."[4] Consequently, they would accept an organization that excluded Britain only if it were supranational. Adenauer's insistence that a

European union should reinforce NATO was a further obstacle, for de Gaulle rejected any reference to the Atlantic Alliance.[5] France tried again in 1973 when Foreign Minister Michel Jobert attempted unsuccessfully to energize the WEU as an alternative to NATO's Eurogroup. But again the Federal Republic, and others, feared that a larger role for the WEU could devalue the Atlantic Alliance.

In the late sixties and early seventies, after France withdrew from NATO's integrated command but before Britain entered the European Community, the WEU provided a context for meetings among the principal European states. And in the late 1960s the Labour government tried to use the organization to discuss foreign policy and to keep its EEC application alive, but this provoked a French boycott of the WEU.[6] When Britain joined the EC this function evaporated and the WEU became moribund. Although the Assembly (composed of parliamentarians from the member states) continued to meet, between 1973 and 1984 ministers rarely attended WEU Council meetings, and the WEU was essentially vestigial.[7]

After years of quiescence, the possibility of European defense cooperation resurfaced in the 1980s. The INF controversy and fears of U.S. decoupling were catalysts, and once more France was a prominent initiator. France broached the possibility of trilateral security discussions to the FRG and Britain, but Italy protested her exclusion. When the possibility was raised that the WEU might be an appropriate venue, Belgium and Luxembourg were amenable, but Bonn hesitated. The WEU's restrictions on German armaments symbolized the FRG's second-class status and were resented, even though they never precluded any options that Bonn wished to exercise.[8] Bonn insisted that the last remaining constraints on German conventional arms, which banned German manufacture of long-range missiles and strategic bombers, be rescinded. This was done in 1985.[9] Germany remains committed "not to manufacture in its territory atomic, biological, and chemical weapons," but the nuclear restraint was effectively superceded when Bonn ratified the Non-Proliferation Treaty.

Britain and the Netherlands viewed WEU revitalization even more skeptically. Britain's first loyalty was to NATO, and even among European security organizations London preferred the IEPG to the WEU. According to Christopher Coker, the British assented reluctantly, "in the hope of restoring something of their European image which had been tarnished, if not permanently damaged, by years of acrimonious debate over Britain's budget rebates in the European Community."[10] Finally, with all members agreeing, in October 1984 the WEU Council met at the level of defense and foreign ministers for the first time in many years. Moreover, they agreed to semi-annual meetings at the foreign ministerial level. Alfred Cahan, former political director of the Belgian foreign ministry, was appointed in 1985 to a five-year term as Secretary-General, and he has worked to raise the WEU's public visibility.

At first, the WEU revival failed to create high expectations. As Pascal Boniface wrote, "In the minds of French leaders it is not a question of making the WEU an embryonic EDC. It is simply a matter of using an existing organization, for better political and military cooperation."[11] When the INF deployment controversy cooled, which diminished French fears of German neutralism, interest in the WEU receded further, and Charles Hernu dismissed it as a *café du commerce*, or "talking shop."[12] But then the Reykjavik summit, the double zero option, and renewed fears of U.S. decoupling traumatized European capitals. Suddenly, many Europeans lamented the absence of a European voice on security issues. This was especially true in France, where various top political leaders decried the absence of a European defense consensus. Jacques Chirac divided European cooperation into three parts—the economy, civilized values, and security—and assigned responsibility for them to the EC, the Council of Europe, and the WEU, respectively.[13]

London's interest in the WEU also rekindled. In March 1987, British Foreign Secretary Sir Geoffrey Howe presented an important speech to the Royal Institute of International Relations (Brussels) which traced the revitalization of the WEU to "a growing perception that a European forum *was* needed in which we Europeans could consult one another about our common fundamental security needs." Sir Geoffrey also observed that events like Reykjavik and double zero "underline the need for the European countries to consult more closely among themselves about their defence interests as well as with the Americans."[14] According to him, "A better European defence effort, galvanised perhaps through the WEU, can lead to a more substantial European pillar of the Alliance."[15]

Later that year, two members of the Conservative Party's Bow Group called upon the WEU "to take up the challenge it was created for, namely to be an embryo European Defence Community."[16] They also recommended that a "WEU European Corps" could evolve from the Franco-German brigade to align France more closely to NATO's integrated structure without violating French *amour-propre*.[17]

The WEU has taken two particularly significant steps since its revival. It managed to loosely coordinate a European naval response to attacks upon Persian Gulf oil tankers because of the Iran-Iraq war. This was a landmark: the first successful coordination of a nonregional security policy issue. During 1987, Belgium, Britain, France, Italy, and the Netherlands deployed military vessels to the Gulf. This included all of the WEU members except Luxembourg, which has no navy, and the Federal Republic, which interprets its Basic Law as prohibiting military operations outside the North Atlantic area.[18] However, for the first time, Bonn did reassign ships to NATO's standby force in the Mediterranean and called this "a contribution to support those allies who are protecting shipping in the gulf region. . . . "[19] In January 1988, Britain, Belgium, and the Netherlands agreed to form a single command for their minesweepers; France and Italy did not join this initiative, but they did coordinate their Gulf fleets bilaterally.[20]

The second initiative may eventually prove even more significant. In October 1987 the WEU approved a common "Platform on European Security Interests." In the aftermath of the Reykjavik summit, Prime Minister Jacques Chirac observed that the superpowers were making decisions affecting vital European interests without any Western European participation. According to Chirac, Europe's voice would only be heard when its position was elaborated and articulated, so a "charter" was needed to define a common European position on principal security questions.

The approved platform included the following major points:

1. European integration will remain incomplete until a security dimension is added.
2. Because Europe is divided, and exposed to the Warsaw Pact's superior conventional, chemical, and nuclear forces, Western European security "can only be ensured in close association with our North American allies." American conventional and nuclear forces "play an irreplaceable part in the defense of Europe."
3. A credible European defense policy must combine conventional and nuclear capabilities, for ". . . only the nuclear element can confront a potential aggressor with an unacceptable risk."[21]
4. Arms control and disarmament policy are integral parts of overall Western security policy.
5. WEU member states intend to reinforce the European pillar of the Alliance, enlarge their defense cooperation by all practical measures, improve their conventional forces, and pursue European integration (including security). Britain and France will maintain the credibility of their nuclear forces.

Each major European state could be gratified by some aspect of this formulation. For the French, the essence was affirmation that nuclear deterrence was central to European security. Both France and Britain were pleased by specific recognition that their nuclear forces "contribute to overall deterrence and security"[22] and the implicit endorsement of their nuclear modernization programs. The Federal Republic appreciated both the pledge that members would defend an ally "at its borders" and explicit recognition that détente, especially arms control, complements rather than contradicts Western security. The Germans and British applauded explicit references to America's indispensable role.

Italy was the most outspoken critic of the platform. Rome resented the more prominent status accorded to Britain and France because they were nuclear powers, was concerned that nuclear deterrence should not be embraced too fervently during a period of flux in East-West relations, and feared that the document might inflame American isolationism. The Dutch shared some of Italy's reservations, but eventually both countries concurred with the majority.[23]

Another important WEU initiative began in 1988, when France hosted a two week session at IHEDN (Institut des hautes études de défense nationale) for military officers, civil servants, managers of defense industries, and journalists from the member states. Similar joint meetings are planned in other countries, and a European college for security studies is under consideration.[24] These efforts are intended to foster more consensus on security issues among West Europeans.

The WEU Assembly is now based in Paris, while the secretariat is headquartered in London. It might be possible to strengthen the organization by consolidation in one city, and France proposed moving the secretariat to Paris. Prime Minister Thatcher suggested Brussels, saying, "It would help if WEU were transferred to Brussels so it is quite clear that it is NATO which is the shield and defence of freedom and justice and we must do absolutely everything to improve that."[25] But the French insist that the WEU remain distinct from both NATO and the European Community. Foreign Minister Raimond said it was necessary "to avoid any risk of confusion with the Atlantic Alliance or the European Political Cooperation (EPC)."[26]

Following the WEU's revival, several additional states wished to join. Portugal and Spain are formal applicants; Norway and Turkey are clearly interested, Greece made diplomatic inquiries, and Danish Foreign Minister Ellemann-Jensen opined that "Denmark must seek admission to the WEU if a true policy of European security cooperation begins in that forum."[27] But the current members were not agreed that expansion was advisable. Italy supported enlargement, but Britain argued that membership should be limited to countries that were "serious" about defense, which could exclude Denmark and possibly Spain, following the Torrejón controversy. London also maintained that the WEU needed a period of consolidation before expansion was considered.[28] The French attitude was equivocal: Paris seemed more reticent than Rome, but France did support the Spanish and Portuguese applications.[29] And Luxembourg's foreign minister wrote that "Countries such as Spain and Portugal . . . must not be kept waiting too long."[30]

Spain pursued its candidacy with particular vigor. The Spanish public is hostile toward the United States, but there is considerable popular backing for closer European relationships. Spain maintains bilateral military agreements with seven EC countries, and President Felipe González discussed European security issues with President Mitterrand in August 1987 and in September of that same year with Chancellor Kohl at the fifth German-Spanish summit. Until recently, Madrid's efforts to join the WEU were frustrated. An early obstacle was the impending referendum on Spain's continued NATO membership. That issue was successfully resolved, but WEU membership remained blocked, and Madrid suspected that the longstanding Gibraltar conflict prejudiced London's attitude. Finally, in April 1988, both Spain and Portugal were invited to open negotiations that might lead to membership, and these negotiations began the following month.

Despite these developments, in the near future Spanish participation in European security is likely to stress a close alignment with Franco-German initiatives.[31] This would build on existing relations, especially Spain's close ties to France. For example, in October 1987 the seventh Franco-Spanish interministerial seminar convened ten French and Spanish ministers for two days of meetings; there is also a Franco-Spanish committee co-chaired by the directors of political affairs of the foreign ministries, and there is armaments and space cooperation. In addition, Spain (and also the Netherlands) wishes to participate in the Franco-German brigade.[32]

It will probably enhance the WEU's prospects for long-term success if Britain's advice is followed and the organization remains relatively small and homogeneous. The EC followed a different path, and its expansion from six relatively cohesive and homogeneous members to twelve states with more diverse economies and cultures led to deepening decision-making paralysis. As the debate over the WEU's common security platform illustrated, it is difficult to resolve divergent military doctrines, or weapons requirements, even among the seven current members. It would be substantially more difficult if the membership included Denmark, Greece, Norway, Portugal, Spain, and Turkey. Gradualism is more likely to succeed than a too-rapid expansion.

The WEU seeks to strengthen European security cooperation but must confront the issue of Europe's proper relationship to the United States. Most members share the late Alois Mertes' concerns that Europe not see the WEU as "the instrument of a possible distancing from the United States" and that the United States not see the WEU as "an argument justifying neo-isolationism, the Americans thinking that the Europeans are following a 'do it yourself' policy which permits them to withdraw."[33] This apprehension was the principal obstacle to the Fouchet and Jobert initiatives, and it arose again when the common platform was debated. It remains a chronic concern which divides France from her European partners.

INDEPENDENT EUROPEAN PROGRAMME GROUP

The WEU's mandate includes arms collaboration, but in practice it defers to the IEPG in this field. The seven members of the WEU are handicapped in efforts to convince nonmembers to purchase military equipment from them rather than from American defense contractors. By comparison, the IEPG joins thirteen NATO-European states, which provides a more fertile context for coordinating European weapons procurement.[34]

According to General Philippe Morillon of the French DGA (Délégation générale pour l'armement), only 20 percent of European military hardware is cooperatively produced.[35] The level is higher for the Federal Republic, which "buys 15–20% of its weapons from foreigners, and another 60% or so from German companies collaborating with foreign ones."[36] As Chapter 2 indicated, inadequate arms collaboration creates two principal problems for NATO: insufficient standardization and interoperability on the battlefield, and inefficient utilization of scare alliance resources. Lack of cooperation also undermines Europe's technological competitiveness vis-à-vis the United States, both in the weapons field and in overall technological competitiveness.

According to the 1987 British *White Paper*:

a more cohesive European effort will strengthen the Alliance in a number of important ways: *politically*, by demonstrating our ability to work closely together; *militarily*, by reducing the inefficiency that comes from having different and incompatible versions of the same equipment on the battlefield; and *industrially*, by helping to produce a more competitive European industrial base.[37]

The *White Paper* particularly emphasized IEPG efforts to harmonize the weapons requirements of the member countries, to promote collaborative research projects, and to improve competitiveness by removing obstacles to free trade and industrial cooperation among European countries.

The IEPG's objectives were defined by the Rome Resolution (1976). They are to strengthen European identity, and the industrial and technological foundation for Western defense, by promoting standardization, interoperability, and efficient use of resources for weapons design and procurement.[38] Until 1984, the Group's work was relegated to the members' armament directors; during those years the organization was relatively inconspicuous and torpid. But as the WEU revived, states such as Denmark, Norway, and Spain, which were excluded from the WEU, sought to energize the IEPG as well. Thus, with strong support from British Defense Minister Michael Heseltine, an ardent advocate of European armaments cooperation, the IEPG convened its first annual defense ministerial meeting in November 1984.

IEPG efforts assume that collaborative ventures are more cost effective than national weapons programs. Under ideal conditions this would clearly be true. Both R & D (research and development) and production costs would be minimized if European states jointly defined specifications for a common weapon to satisfy their individual needs, and if the weapon was constructed by the most efficient prime contractor and suppliers. This would eliminate duplicative research programs, inefficient production runs, and sourcing from noncompetitive domestic suppliers.

But in the real world, cooperative ventures deviate from this ideal, and they may cost even more than national projects. Shaun St. John has described several chronic "diseconomies" that bedevil collaborative programs.[39] These include the failure to define a single set of operational needs. Gaps between differing national requirements are often "fudged" by building multiple versions, for example the Franco-German helicopter program, or by "goldplating" to produce a more sophisticated and expensive weapon than any individual partner would order.

Savings from research and development efficiencies are a second consideration. These are the most common savings from cooperative programs. For example, a recent (1987) IEPG report, *Towards a Stronger Europe*, used questionnaires to study the cost effectiveness of four multilateral programs: Tornado Fighter Aircraft, FH 70 Towed Howitzer, Tripartite Minehunter, and RITA Battlefield Communication System. All except RITA reported reduced development costs as a result of collaboration. In the case of the Anglo-German-Italian Tornado aircraft program,

> studies have shown that, for production, the additional costs of collaboration (for example the need for several assembly lines, sets of test equipment and rigs) are more or less balanced by the benefits in terms of reduced unit price through increased production runs. . . . The major savings however is in development costs, where even taking into account some extra costs due to collaboration, total national bills have been reduced.[40]

Unfortunately, development savings are rarely optimized because partners are reluctant to forego competence in technical fields that might be essential to future projects or could yield valuable commercial spinoffs.

Three, because collaborations involve *temporary* alliances among competitive producers, firms are often reluctant to share technology which may undermine their future competitive position. Four, production costs rise when prestige or domestic economic considerations compel redundant assembly lines or multiple sourcing of components. Five, there are increased transportation costs, particularly if sourcing of components and final assembly is divided among geographically distant partners; the magnitude of these costs is suggested by estimates that border controls alone add 8 percent to consumer prices in the EEC.[41] Six, multiple partners and duplicative bureaucracies boost program management costs. Seven, export sales suffer if partners disagree concerning criteria for admissible customers, or if overly sophisticated and costly designs are less competitive in foreign markets.

Because of these considerations, a rule of thumb predicts that unit costs for a given production run will increase by the square root of the number of partners: 40 percent more for two partners and 100 percent higher for four partners. Joint ventures are more cost effective only if economies of scale from larger production runs, and research and development savings are sufficient to offset these diseconomies. But St. John cites estimates by Britain's defense ministry that "the cost of collaborative aircraft programmes in the late 1970s suggested that national solutions could actually be cheaper in certain circumstances than collaborative procurement."[42]

These diseconomies are particularly intractable because weapons collaboration affects core national interests: national security and economic welfare (particularly employment and technology). Governments are loath to compromise the perceived requirements of their military forces, to forego technological self-sufficiency, or to export jobs, for the purpose of advancing some abstract concept of Europe's collective welfare. As the IEPG report concluded, "the fundamental issues are political and . . . can be resolved only by political courage and leadership."[43]

Despite these obstacles to an integrated European defense structure, or even a common agency for military procurement, a more modest goal may be attainable. IEPG objectives could be advanced by establishing free trade in armaments, that is, by extending the common market principle to weaponry. Currently, work on collaborative projects is apportioned among the partners in roughly the same proportion as their financial contributions. With a free trade approach, contracts would be awarded to the most efficient producers; this change would lengthen production runs, lower unit costs, and might reduce some duplication of R & D. Unfortunately, there is widespread reluctance to accept the IEPG report's advice that "governments should be more prepared to see *juste retour* organised on a broader base, but restricted to the military equipment field, and over a longer period than hitherto, which would make possible more efficient arrangements."[44]

Like the WEU, the IEPG's relationship with NATO and the United States is schizophrenic. The IEPG is *independent* because France insisted on separation from NATO,[45] and many Europeans agree that "it is vital that on the European side of the ocean we should speak with a single voice, representing the whole IEPG, as has already begun to happen. . . ."[46] Nonetheless, close contacts exist between the IEPG and NATO: the IEPG's Staff Group is based in Brussels, the armament directors attend both IEPG meetings and NATO's Conference of National Armaments Directors (CNAD), and there are cooperative arms programs among NATO countries. Some of these projects are part of the initiative sponsored by Chairman Nunn, with Senators Roth and Warner, to strengthen NATO's efficiency through cooperative research and development projects. Two hundred million dollars was budgeted for collaborative R & D projects, plus an additional $50 million to finance side-by-side testing of American and European systems.[47] Senator Dan Quayle sponsored other legislation, which permits European firms to compete on an equal footing with U.S. defense contractors for American military con-

tracts. The DoD also increased its interest in promoting collaborative programs; between 1987 and 1992, the Pentagon plans to invest nearly $3
billion in joint weapons development with NATO countries.[48]

The IEPG is Janus-faced. Transatlantic cooperation is one face; the
second face is improved European competitiveness *against* American
defense contractors, a U.S. armaments market two and a half times larger
than Western Europe's, and research and development spending approximately five times greater than Europe's.[49] In 1985, total European spending for military R & D equaled £5.1 billion (United Kingdom, £2.4
billion; France £1.8 billion; and the FRG, £.7 billion).[50] Viewed from this
perspective, some Europeans fear that the Nunn initiative could undermine Europe's effort to construct the techno-industrial base required for
long-term European independence.

Although the ratio of European-American arms sales remains un-
balanced, the gap has narrowed significantly in recent years, from seven
to one to less than three to one.[51] Between FY 1982 and FY 1985, U.S.
defense purchases from other NATO countries increased 65 percent to
reach $2.8 billion.[52] But the transatlantic rivalry continues, and Europe is
unlikely to compete successfully in the international arms market of the
twenty-first century without substantial progress in achieving European
security cooperation.

EUROPEAN SPACE AGENCY

Space technology is increasingly pertinent to defense policy for at least
two reasons: a) the synergism between space and weapons technologies;
and b) direct military applications in space. In Europe, civilian multilateral space cooperation is coordinated by the thirteen-member European
Space Agency (ESA).[53] France is the principal European proponent of
space research nationally, bilaterally, and within the ESA. France contributed 27 percent to ESA's 1986 budget, followed by Germany (24 percent), and Italy (15 percent); Britain paid 13 percent in 1986 but
subsequently withdrew from two of the ESA's largest programs.[54]

The Space Agency's attention is currently focused on three projects.
The least controversial is Ariane-5, which involves the new and heavier
version in the Ariane series of rockets for launching space vehicles. Ar-
iane-5 is planned for 1995 at a projected cost of nearly $4 billion. Hermès
is a second and much more controversial program to launch a two-man
space shuttle in 1998 at a cost approaching $5 billion. Some British

detractors dismiss Hermès as no more than a Dassault-Breguet testbed for new fighter-aircraft technologies.[55] The Federal Republic, after considerable hesitation, agreed to contribute 30 percent to the program's budget (compared to 45 percent from France). Other participants include Italy (12 to 15 percent), Spain, Belgium, the Netherlands, Sweden, Switzerland, Denmark, Ireland, and Austria.[56] The third program, Columbus, involves a European laboratory for the space station NASA (National Aeronautics and Space Administration) plans to launch in 1994. This space station will consist of four modules: three laboratories to be built by Europe (Columbus), Japan, and the United States, plus a fourth module for living quarters. Columbus, which is projected to cost more than $4 billion, was controversial because Washington demanded ultimate control over the entire project, and the Pentagon insisted that the space station could be expropriated for national security use, which would violate ESA regulations. Reportedly, these differences are now resolved.[57]

A stormy ESA meeting in November 1987 pitted France, which sought approval for all three projects, against Britain, which opposed them. *Le Monde* reported that Kenneth Clarke, Britain's Minister for Trade and Industry, "tried by every possible means to try to split Europe and vented his spite on the projects supported by the French. 'Ariane-5 is a despot's dream, and Hermès a cuckoo in a nest,' he proclaimed."[58] Clarke also declared that "The British refuse to associate themselves with programs dominated by the French."[59]

A German compromise, approved over vehement British objection, extended Hermès' research stage for three additional years at a cost of $585 million.[60] France is expected to finance 45 percent of both Ariane-5 (FRG 22 percent, Italy 15 percent) and Hermès (FRG 30 percent and Italy 12 to 15 percent) without British participation. For Columbus, the French and German roles are reversed, probably because its link to the American space program makes it more attractive to Bonn but less attractive to Paris. Germany will contribute 38 percent, followed by Italy (25 percent), France (15 percent maximum), and Britain (5.5 percent).[61]

Britain's policy toward the ESA is exceptionally negative. In recent years London has participated in most multilateral European initiatives, however reluctantly, if only to maintain minimal credentials as "good Europeans." The ESA is an exception. According to Kenneth Clarke, the organization

> simply piled up grandiose proposals, seeking to pursue every objective regardless of cost. . . . it has become largely divorced from the market place and

lacks the necessary commercial and industrial discipline in decision making.[62]

When the government decided to forego ESA projects, a storm was unleashed within British scientific and political circles. The tenor of the debate is illustrated by *The Times* editorial judgment that

> a failure to participate in these programmes would be the 20th-century equivalent of being bypassed by the coal, steam, and iron industries of the 19th century, and would secure for the Government the mantle of Ned Ludd.[63]

Sir Geoffrey Pattie, former Conservative minister for information technology, accused the government of "betraying" the country's scientific and industrial heritage.[64]

The British National Space Centre was created in November 1985 as "a focus for British space policy," and Roy Gibson (former head of the ESA) was named director-general. Britain's space budget of £116 million is surpassed by six other non-communist countries: United States £4500 million, France £600 million, Japan £500 million, Germany £450 million, Italy £300 million, and India £150 million.[65] Gibson resigned in 1987 when the government refused to make a substantial increase, although Gibson did agree that ESA's aspirations were "too ambitious and too costly."[66]

Admiral Sir James Eberle (director of the Royal Institute of International Affairs) and other critics of the government's policy argued that space was vital to Britain's economic and technological position and that the world had

> moved into a new generation of military systems in which space-based systems have become more important. . . . They are of special relevance to countries such as Britain with nuclear capabilities, where satellite-derived data are crucial for early warning about the intentions of others and for the credible deployment of nuclear weapons systems.[67]

Sir James also maintained that space research and development are so expensive that only international collaboration will permit Britain to keep abreast of these technologies. Michael Heseltine was the recent British defense minister who had the greatest personal commitment to development in space, and he made the argument that "The ESA is our only realistic journey into space. The industrial consequences of failing to follow it are incalculable and a decision to back out is not recoverable."[68]

Britain also withdrew support from the Hotol reusable spaceplane, the invention of Alan Bond, Britain's principal space scientist. Hotol's most innovative feature is an engine designed to burn atmospheric oxygen (with liquid hydrogen) at low altitudes and then enter orbit by switching to onboard tanks of liquid oxygen.[69] In early 1988, after Bond threatened to decamp from Britain to pursue his research elsewhere, the government appeared to drop its demand that space research be privately funded, and Hotol was expected to receive £15 million in government funds over three years. A private consortium including British Aerospace and Rolls-Royce was to match this sum.[70] In July, the government reversed course, concluding that, "The scale of funding required to develop Hotol or any similar concept to eventual production would be far too great for the U.K. to contemplate on a national basis."[71] The future of Britain's space program remains clouded but bleak, and it seems inevitable that Europe's multilateral space program will be increasingly a Franco-German effort, with Italy occupying the principal supporting role.

EUREKA

The European Research Coordination Agency (EUREKA) is another French initiative intended to defend European competitiveness from the American threat by promoting intra-European technical cooperation. One can debate whether EUREKA would exist without SDI, but SDI certainly reinforced concerns regarding Europe's competitive position in high technology fields. Unlike SDI, EUREKA is restricted to civilian projects; that was a condition for Bonn's participation. Nonetheless, many of the same technologies are involved in SDI and EUREKA: optical electronics, new materials, super-computers, lasers and particle beams, artificial intelligence, and high-speed microelectronics.[72]

EUREKA was established in April 1985. There are now nineteen members,[73] and following the sixth ministerial conference in June 1988, a total of 214 projects had been approved with an aggregate budget of Fr 26.5 billion. France is participating in 107 projects and Germany in 65.[74] France remains the most enthusiastic participant, but the Federal Republic overcame its initial hesitancy and also emerged as a strong proponent. Britain remains more skeptical, but after initial opposition London did fund research projects with public monies.

EUROPEAN COMMUNITY

The European Community is the focal point of European unification and is often considered the natural and inevitable focus for European security cooperation. Indeed, approximately two-thirds of the population in the twelve member countries favors the EC "developing towards becoming a 'United States of Europe',"[75] which would presume responsibility for European defense. And the French UDF described the EC's European Council as the ultimate organization "designated to conduct European defense developments at the multilateral level."[76] Nonetheless, fundamental changes would be required before the EC could fulfill this role.

Military goods are exempt from the EC's current free-trade regulations. So, the proposal discussed earlier, to expand the Common Market to include armaments, would be a substantial achievement. However, there is probably more support for Laurent Fabius's protectionist proposal that the EEC prohibit "purchases of military materiel outside the Community when one or more EEC countries manufactures a similar product. . . . "[77] Moreover, it was not until 1987 that the Single European Act explicitly empowered the EC to address "the political and economic aspects of security." Previously, leftist members of the European Parliament even argued that the Community was barred from addressing security issues.

As a focus for defense cooperation, the size and heterogeneity of the EC are major handicaps. From the security perspective, three members are particularly problematic. Ireland is formally neutral and has a conflictive relationship with Britain. Denmark is a relatively irresolute member of NATO (only Luxembourg and Iceland have lower levels of defense expenditures as a percentage of GDP), and gravitates toward the Nordic group on security questions. Greece is a NATO maverick whose defense policies conflict with those of other EC members. Considering these impediments, it is unsurprising that EC President Jacques Delors' efforts to extend the EC's role in the security sphere have failed conspicuously. In fact, even Delors seems to recognize that political and military unification are more probable in other venues, for he now predicts that the economic institutions will expand to include members of the Eastern Bloc.[78]

Since 1969, the European Political Cooperation (EPC) has achieved some modest success in coordinating foreign policy issues. The Political Committee, composed of political directors of the foreign ministries of the twelve member states, meets monthly to prepare for Council of Ministers meetings. There are also quarterly meetings of foreign ministers to address issues of political cooperation. Foreign ministers attend meetings of the European Council together with their heads of state or government, and daily contact among the Twelve is provided by the Coreu telex network.[79] This process facilitates foreign policy coordination within the Community, but deep cleavages remain, and defense policy issues are largely ignored.[80]

The anti-terrorism effort illustrates the fragile European consensus. At a Brussels meeting in January 1986, the EC agreed to embargo arms to "countries clearly implicated in supporting terrorism." The following October, after designating Syria as a sponsor of terrorist attacks including the April 1986 attempt to bomb an El Al flight from Heathrow Airport, Britain severed diplomatic relations with Syria and presented its evidence to the EC, which later sanctioned Damascus. Meanwhile, the Chirac government hoped that closer Franco-Syrian relations might facilitate the freeing of French hostages from Lebanon and forestall another bombing wave in Paris, where terrorist attacks killed ten persons and wounded more than 160 during the early fall of 1986. During a November 1986 interview by Arnaud de Borchgrave (editor of *The Washington Times*), Chirac also stated that Chancellor Kohl and Foreign Minister Genscher doubted London's accusation against Syria and believed that the affair was actually a plot by Israel's secret service (Mossad) and renegade elements within President Assad's entourage to destabilize the Syrian regime.[81] Bonn denied this report, as did Chirac (initially) until *The Washington Times* published a transcript of the interview which de Borchgrave had recorded without Chirac's knowledge. The overall effect was to sour Paris' relations with both London and Bonn.

Then, in the summer of 1987, France linked the wave of Parisian bombings to Walid Gordji, an Iranian diplomat based in Paris. An attempt to apprehend Gordji precipitated sieges at the Iranian and French embassies in Paris and Teheran, and caused France to dispatch the aircraft carrier *Clemenceau* to the Indian Ocean. During this test of wills, Foreign Minister Genscher angered the French by receiving the Iranian foreign minister in Bonn. A few months earlier, the French had hoped to extricate their citizens by dealing with Syria; now Germany hoped that Iran would help them obtain the release of their nationals from captivity in Lebanon.

The disarray continued in December 1987, when France resolved its conflict with Iran by permitting Walid Gordji to depart, and (temporarily) expelled opponents of the Iranian regime from France. In exchange, Iran permitted a French diplomat to leave Teheran and two French hostages were freed in Beirut. France's apparent capitulation to terrorist demands provoked an uproar in London: the Thatcher government was reportedly "seething,"[82] a *Times* editorial was entitled "French Betrayal," and an article in *The Manchester Guardian Weekly* was entitled "Another double cross by Chirac."[83] The French, in their turn, criticized Margaret Thatcher for applying a double standard by being more tolerant of Washington's "Iranscam" adventure than of France's more moderate conduct. André Fontaine wrote "that according to his British cousins Uncle Sam is entitled to an indulgence which is *a priori* refused to the 'natives'. . . . "[84]

In January 1988 a high-ranking German official (Wolfgang Schäuble) testified during a Dusseldorf terrorism trial. Schäuble said Bonn refused to grant Washington's request to extradite the alleged murderer of an American marine during a TWA hijacking in 1985 because Bonn feared for the safety of German hostages in Lebanon.

Terrorism illustrates the difficulty of convincing European governments to subordinate short-term national interests to pursue long-term European objectives. As *Le Monde* editorialized, "it is often when solidarity is most necessary that the task is most arduous."[85] This is especially true of the EC, because there is no dominant member to impose agreement as the United States sometimes does within NATO.

Moreover, the Community's difficulties extend well beyond foreign affairs. Even when confronted by an annual budget deficit nearing $6 billion, the EC proved chronically unable to resolve its budget crisis. The Common Agricultural Program (CAP) absorbs 70 percent of the EEC budget, with one-third (more than £10 billion) going just to *store* the agricultural surpluses.[86] CAP spending demanded control, but agreement was confounded by divisions between North and South, Britain and the others, and even between France and Germany.[87] As a result, the EC reached the brink of insolvency before a compromise was negotiated at an emergency European Council meeting in February 1988.

There is also controversy surrounding the possibility of a European central bank, as proposed by former French Finance Minister Edouard Balladur. Bonn's governing coalition was initially divided: Foreign Minister Genscher favored the concept, but Chancellor Kohl dismissed it as "neither realistic nor of current interest."[88] However, by April 1988 the German government had agreed to push the proposal at the June 1988 meeting of the European Council in Hanover. This left Britain as the principal opponent. The United Kingdom (like Greece, Spain, and Portugal) is not even a member of the existing European Monetary System, and just prior to the Hanover meeting Prime Minister Thatcher told the House of Commons that:

You will only have a European central bank when you have a United States of Europe under one sovereign government and not under 12. . . . That not being on the cards, I see no point in having anyone study a European central bank.[89]

In the end, the European Council voted to appoint a committee of experts, chaired by Commission President Delors, to study concrete steps for a European monetary union and a central bank. But Prime Minister Thatcher assented with the understanding that the bank was only a long-term possibility and no commitment was being made. As *The Times* wrote, "She made it plain she did not want a united Europe with a single currency and did not believe it would happen in her lifetime, if ever."[90]

The Community's chronic inability to resolve economic conflicts bodes poorly for security cooperation. As Josef Joffe has argued, if EC member governments will not compromise national prerogatives to solve budget crises, concessions are unlikely "in defense and foreign policy, the most jealously guarded bastion of *raison d'état*."[91]

The WEU security platform asserts that European integration will remain incomplete until it incorporates a security dimension. This is true, but progress toward this goal will probably occur at different speeds and in several bilateral and multilateral contexts. The EC is unlikely to assume the leading role, in part because neither France nor the FRG expects the EC to fulfill this function. As Jean Klein noted, the FRG looks first to NATO, while France considers the WEU the appropriate organization for addressing European security issues.[92]

As the common security platform demonstrates, the WEU is likely to remain the preeminent multilateral setting for addressing broad issues of European defense cooperation. The more heterogeneous and specialized institutions such as the IEPG and ESA fulfill important functions, but their roles are likely to remain relatively narrow and technical. France remains the principal advocate of multilateral European initiatives; Britain participates more reluctantly, and sometimes not at all. *Plus ça change, plus c'est la même chose* (The more things change, the more they remain the same.)

NOTES

1. Raymond Aron, "Historical Sketch of the Great Debate," in Daniel Lerner and Raymond Aron, eds., *France Defeats EDC* (New York: Frederick A. Praeger, 1957), pp. 3–4. For discussion of the EDC, also see

Edward Fursdon, *The European Defence Community: A History* (London: The Macmillan Press Ltd., 1980), and F. Roy Willis, *France, Germany, and the New Europe 1945–1967*, revised and expanded edition (London: Oxford University Press, 1968), pp. 130–84.

2. Ruth C. Lawson, ed., *International Regional Organizations: Constitutional Foundations* (New York: Praeger, 1962), p. 155.

3. Ibid.

4. Philippe de Schoutheete, *La coopération politique européenne* (Bruxelles: Editions Labor, 1980), p. 24.

5. See Nicole Gnesotto, "Union de l'Europe occidentale: La France, l'Europe, L'Alliance," *Défense nationale* 41 (June 1985): 42. This dispute foreshadowed the preamble that the Bundestag appended to the Elysée Treaty (1963) which was mentioned in Chapter 3.

6. William Wallace, "European Defence Co-operation: The Reopening Debate," *Survival* 26 (November/December 1984): 251–61 and Christopher Coker, "The Western European Union and European Security," in Robert J. Jackson, ed., *Continuity of Discord: Crises and Responses in the Atlantic Community* (New York: Praeger, 1985), pp. 158–59.

7. See Alfred Cahen, "Relaunching Western European Union. Implications for the Atlantic Alliance," *NATO Review* 34 (August 1986): 7.

8. As Ambassador François Puaux wrote of the German attitude toward the WEU, "it remains in their eyes a mark of the past." François Puaux, "La France, l'Allemagne et l'atome: Discorde improbable, accord impossible," *Défense nationale* 41 (December 1985): 17.

9. Prohibitions on warships and submarines were lifted in 1980.

10. Christopher Coker, *British Defence Policy in the 1990s: A Guide to the Defence Debate* (London: Brassey's Defence Publishers, 1987), p. 78.

11. Pascal Boniface, et al., *L'année stratégique*, (Paris: Editions J.-C. Lattes, 1985), p. 18.

12. See Peter Schmidt, "The WEU—A Union Without Perspective?" *Aussen Politik* 37 (1986): 399; Hernu's comment is cited in Kurt Becker, "La force de dissuasion nucléaire française et la sécurité de la République fédérale d'Allemagne," in Karl Kaiser and Pierre Lellouche, eds., *Le couple franco-allemand et la défense de l'Europe* (Paris: Economica, 1986), p. 218.

13. See Thierry Bréhier, "M. Giscard d'Estaing souligne la faiblesse de l'organisation politique de l'Europe," *Le Monde*, 18 April 1987; Jacques Isnard, "M. Hernu Dénonce l'absence d'une Europe de la défense," *Le Monde*, 17 March 1987; "Mme Veil pour une politique européenne de défense," *Le Monde*, 8 October 1987; and André Fontaine and Jacques Amalric, "M. Chirac expose au <<Monde>> sa politique étrangère," *Le Monde*, 8 July 1987.

14. Sir Geoffrey Howe, "The Atlantic Alliance and the security of Europe," *NATO Review* 35 (April 1987): 8.
15. Ibid., p. 9.
16. David Harvey and Dexter Jerome Smith, "In Defence of Europe," *A Bow Paper* (London: Bow Publications, 1987), p. 3.
17. See Harvey and Smith, "In Defence," pp. 7–8.
18. There is ongoing controversy within the FRG on this subject; Horst Telt-schik (national security adviser to Chancellor Kohl) and the *Frankfurter Allgemeine Zeitung* are among the prominent voices calling for a broader interpretation of the constitution. See Serge Schmemann, "Old Debate is Stoked in Bonn By Remarks on Military Role," *The New York Times*, 2 November 1987 and *The Week in Germany*, 16 October 1987, p. 3.
19. Quoted in Serge Schmemann, "Bonn, Citing Gulf Effort, Will Aid a NATO Fleet," *The New York Times*, 9 October 1987.
20. See Michael Evans, "UK Gulf ships set for Euro link," *The Times* (London), 21 January 1988, and "Les flottes française et italienne coordonner-ont leur action dans le Golfe," *Le Monde*, 24 September 1987.
21. *Platform on European Security Interests* (The Hague: Western European Union, October 27, 1987).
22. Ibid.
23. See Claire Tréan, "Les sept pays membres de l'Union de l'Europe oc-cidentale adoptent une plate-forme commune sur la sécurité," *Le Monde*, 28 October 1987.
24. See Jean d'Aubach (pseud.), "Pour une communauté stratégique," *Le Monde*, 30 October 1987.
25. "The Prime Minister's Visit to NATO," (New York: British Information Services, February 18, 1988), p. 4.
26. "M. Jean-Bernard Raimond plaide pour le regroupement à Paris de tous les organes de l'UEO," *Le Monde*, 3 December 1987.
27. Quoted in Camille Olsen, "Vers une candidature du Danemark à l'UEO?" *Le Monde*, 28 October 1987. However, the Danish parliament is considered unlikely to support an application for membership.
    According to *The Financial Times* (6 April 1987), Prime Minister Pa-pandreou said Greece made diplomatic inquiries about WEU member-ship; cited in *Keesing's Record of World Events*, Vol. 33 (May 1987), p. 31529.
28. See Elizabeth Pond, "Will the Rest of Europe Join In?", *The Christian Science Monitor*, 30 July 1987. This is Part 3 of a four part series on European defense issues.
29. See *News from France*, 4 November 1987.
30. Jacques F. Poos, "Prospects for the WEU," *NATO Review* 35 (August 1987): 18.

31. See Thierry Maliniak, "L'Espagne souhaite s'associer à la réflexion de Paris et de Bonn," *Le Monde*, 19 September 1987.

32. See James M. Markham, "The Alliance Enters the Age of Edgy Reassurance," *The New York Times*, 27 September 1987.

33. Quoted in Ingo Kolboom and Robert Picht, "Paris, Bonn, l'Europe," *Documents: Revue des questions allemandes*, (February 1985): 12.

34. The IEPG members are Belgium, Denmark, France, Greece, Italy, Luxembourg, the Netherlands, Norway, Portugal, Spain, Turkey, the United Kingdom, and West Germany.

35. See Jacques Isnard, "La France pourrait proposer un Eurêka militaire," *Le Monde*, 22 September 1987; also see, "Open Market In Defence: IEPG report on arms collaboration by Nato countries," *The Financial Times*, 10 February 1987.

36. "Make us bold, O lord, but not yet," *The Economist*, 26 September 1987.

37. *Statement on the Defence Estimates 1987*, Vol. 1 (London: Her Majesty's Stationery Office, 1987), p. 46.

38. See Eduardo Serra Rexach, "The Independent European Programme Group—on the right path," *NATO Review*, 34 (October 1986): 25.

39. See Shaun St. John, "Defence Equipment Collaboration: Some Legal and Financial Issues," *RUSI: Journal of the Royal United Services Institute for Defence Studies*, 132 (March 1987): 34–35.

40. European Defence Industry Study Team, *Towards a Stronger Europe*, Vol. 2 (Brussels: Independent European Programme Group, 1987), p. 119.

41. See "Ten steps to togetherness," *The Times* (London), 16 November 1987.

42. St. John, "Defence Equipment Collaboration: Some Legal and Financial Issues," *RUSI: Journal of the Royal United Services Institute for Defence Studies*, 132 (March 1987): 35. As Philip Towle wrote:

    Even if agreement can be reached to produce a standard aircraft or tank, the industrial work has to be shared between the partners. Experience suggests that jointly produced aircraft and tanks cost substantially more than those produced by individual countries, even though the costs are spread over a greater number of weapons. A militarily more effective method of procedure would be to give one country responsibility for combat aircraft, another for frigates or tanks and so on. But this would involve great industrial disruption and the disappearance of whole industries in the states involved.

    Europe Without America: Could We Defend Ourselves?, Occasional Paper No. 5 (London: Institute for European Defence and Strategic Studies, 1983), pp. 19–20. As was mentioned in Chapter 3, André Giraud shares this view.

43. Study Team, *Stronger Europe*, p. 4.

44. Ibid. In an October 3, 1984 speech before the Royal United Service Institute, Michael Heseltine advocated, "a common market in military pro-

curement within Western Europe comparable to that which exists in the United States." Quoted in William Wallace, "Shifts in British Defence Policy," in John Roper, ed., *The Future of British Defence Policy* (Aldershot: Gower, 1985), p. 110.

45. See Trevor Taylor, *Defence, Technology and International Integration* (London: Frances Pinter, 1982), p. 30.

46. Rexach, "The Independent European Programme Group," p. 31.

47. See Sam Nunn, "NATO challenges and opportunities: a three-track approach," *NATO Review* 35 (June 1987): 4–5 and Robin Beard, "NATO armaments co-operation: picking up the gauntlet," *NATO Review*. 35 (February 1987): 12–13.

48. See Eduardo Lachica, "Pentagon Turns More to European Arms," *The Wall Street Journal*, 10 February 1987; Bruce George, "Alliance Political Developments: Maintaining Consensus," in John Cartwright et al., *The State of the Alliance 1986-1987: North Atlantic Assembly Reports* (Boulder: Westview, 1987), pp. 170–72; and Jacques Isnard, "La défense divisée," *Le Monde*, 31 March 1987.

49. According to Study Team, p. 1, "The internal European market for armaments," is "40% of the size of that of the US...." Renaud Bachy of the Secrétariat général de la défense nationale estimated that annual U.S. spending equals $39 billion compared to eight billion for Europe. See Isnard, "La France pourrait proposer."

50. See Pearce Wright, "Britain's industries fail to match rivals' investment" *The Times* (London), 26 November 1987.

51. See International Institute for Strategic Studies, *Strategic Survey: 1985–86* (London: IISS, 1986), p. 87.

52. See Lachica, "Pentagon."

53. The ESA members are Austria, Belgium, Britain, Denmark, France, Ireland, Italy, the Netherlands, Norway, Spain, Sweden, Switzerland, and West Germany. Finland is an associate member, and Canada takes parts on a cooperative basis.

54. See James Eberle and Helen Wallace, *British Space Policy and International Collaboration*, Chatham House Papers 42 (London: Routledge & Kegan Paul, 1987), p. 68.

55. See "Per ardua ad ESA," *The Economist*, 7 November 1987.

56. See Jean-François Augereau, "Ariane-5, Columbus et Hermès," *Le Monde*, 10 November 1987.

57. See "Europe and US agree on co-operation," *The Times* (London), 26 January 1988.

58. Jean-François Augereau, "Britain odd-man-out in Europe's space race," *The Manchester Guardian Weekly*, November 29, 1987, p. 16 (translation of "L'Europe a affirmé sa détermination de ne pas <<jouer les seconds rôles>> dans la conquête de l'espace," *Le Monde*, 12 November 1987).

59. Quoted in Pierre Langereux, "Europe: à l'unanimité moins un," *Le Point*, 16 November 1987.

60. See Pearce Wright, "UK refuses to sign new European space plan," *The Times* (London), 11 November 1987; "Un <<oui mai>> allemand à l'Europe spatiale," *Le Monde*, 8–9 November 1987; and "Out of space," *The Times* (London), 9 November 1987.

61. Augereau, "L'Europe a affirmé,"; and *Survey of Current Affairs*, 18 (May 1988): 180.

62. Kenneth Clarke, "Putting space to work," *The Times* (London), 4 November 1987. Britain also contemplated withdrawal from the fourteen-member European Organization for Nuclear Research (CERN) but eventually agreed to remain if cost cutting procedures were implemented. See Walter Sullivan, "Britain to Remain a Part of Research Group," *The New York Times*, 21 December 1987.

63. "No space for Britain," *The Times* (London), 13 October 1987.

64. Robin Oakley, "Pattie attack over science," *The Times* (London), 30 January 1988.

65. See Pearce Wright, "Britain slips in world space race," *The Times* (London), 28 September 1987. In January 1988, the Select Committee on Science and Technology of the House of Lords recommended that the budget be increased to more than £200 million and that Britain participate in both Ariane-5 and Columbus. See Pearce Wright, "Peers urge £88m boost for space programme," *The Times* (London), 26 January 1988.

66. Pearce Wright, "Former space chief outlines European strategy," *The Times* (London), 16 October 1987.

67. Eberle and Wallace, *British Space Policy*, p. 13.

68. Michael Heseltine, "Little Britain ignores its space destiny," *The Times* (London), 19 October 1987.

69. See "Hotol: why this would have put us ahead," *The Times* (London), 2 August 1988. There is also a somewhat less revolutionary West German project for a spaceplane called Sänger; see "Piggy-backs in space," *The Economist*, 7 November 1987 and "Have we missed the plane?" *The Times* (London), 15 December 1987.

70. See Pearce Wright, "Top scientist in threat to quit space project," *The Times* (London), 13 October 1987 and "Hotol set for £5m boost," *The Times* (London), 19 January 1988.

71. Pearce Wright and Sheila Gunn, "Government refuses money to support Hotol space project," *The Times* (London), 26 July 1988.

72. See John Fenske, "France and the Strategic Defence Initiative: speeding up or putting on the brakes?" *International Affairs* 62 (Spring 1986): 235.

73. The EUREKA members are: Austria, Belgium, Britain, Denmark, Finland, France, Greece, Iceland, Ireland, Italy, Luxembourg, the Nether-

lands, Norway, Portugal, Spain, Sweden, Switzerland, Turkey, and West Germany.

74. See Camille Olsen, "Deux cent quatorze projets ont reçu le label Eurêka," *Le Monde*, 18 June 1988, and *The Week in Germany*, 17 June 1988, p. 8.

75. Source: *Eurobarometer* (Brussels: Commission of the European Communities, March 1987), p. 16. Surveys were conducted between January 9 and February 9, 1987 under the general coordination of Faits & Opinion, Paris. Sample sizes equaled FRG (1,057), France (1,000) and the United Kingdom (1,048).

76. Union pour la Démocratie Française, *Redresser la défense de la France* (Paris: UDF November 1985), p. 165. According to the UDF, progress must begin with the triangle of Paris-Bonn-London, but should eventually encompass a European Security Council in the EC context with a permanent secretariat and a military committee, pp. 162–65. Also see Michel Dobry, "Le jeu du consensus," *Pouvoirs* (September 1986): 58–59; Ricardo Petralla, "Pas d'Europe de la technologie sans politique militaire commune," *Le Monde Affaires*, 16 May 1987; and Joseph C. Rallo, *Defending Europe in the 1990s* (New York: St. Martin's, 1986), passim.

77. Laurent Fabius, "La défense de la France à l'aube du XXIe siècle," *Défense nationale* 43 (November 1987): 22.

78. See "M. Delors estime que <<l'Europe économique se fera à plus de douze y compris certains pays de l'Est>>," *Le Monde*, 21 November 1987.

79. See "European political cooperation," *European File*, No. 13/83 (Luxembourg: Office for Official Publications of the European Communities, August-September, 1983); and de Schoutheete, *La coopération politique*.

80. Alfred Cahen wrote that the Twelve, "have never succeeded in agreeing to put discussion of questions affecting security on a systematic basis within Political Cooperation." Cahen, "Relaunching Western European Union," pp. 8–9. But according to Bulmer and Paterson, "Although it would be misleading to argue that West German foreign policy and its relations with the East are conducted primarily through EPC, a higher priority is attributed to the multilateral level than in the British or French case." Simon Bulmer and William Patterson, *The Federal Republic of Germany and the European Community* (London: Allen & Unwin, 1987), p. 11.

81. "<<Qui était derrière le complot Hindawi?>>," *Le Monde*, 11 November 1986. (*Le Monde* published a French translation of *The Washington Times* English translation from the original French tape.)

82. Andrew McEwen, "British anger at Paris deal with Iranians," *The Times* (London), 1 December 1987.

83. See "French Betrayal," *The Times* (London), 1 December 1987 and

"Another double cross by Chirac," *The Manchester Guardian Weekly*, 6 December 1987.

84. André Fontaine, "La vertu outragée," *Le Monde*, 4 December 1987.

85. "Fausses notes européennes," *Le Monde*, 31 July 1987.

86. See James M. Markham, "Common Market is Divided on Finances," *The New York Times*, 6 December 1987, and Robin Oakley, "Europe's last chance to move mountains," *The Times* (London), 10 September 1987.

87. See Klaus Bohnhof, "Europeans fail to agree on farms and money," *The German Tribune*, 13 December 1987 (translated from *Kölner Stadt-Anzeiger*, 7 December 1987) and Dieter Schröder, "Weapons and wheat: tale of two summits," *The German Tribune*, 13 December 1987 (translated from *Süddeutsche Zeitung*, 7 December 1987).

88. Quoted in Steven Greenhouse, "Central Bank is Urged for Europe," *The New York Times*, 18 January 1988.

89. "Thatcher Rejects the Notion of a Central Bank for Europe," *International Herald Tribune*, 24 June 1988. According to Mrs. Thatcher, the bank "would only come about with the dissolution of this House." Michael Dynes, "European anger at bank rejection," *The Times* (London), 25 June 1988.

90. Richard Owen, "Summit reveals deep split," *The Times* (London), 29 June 1988.

91. Josef Joffe, *The Limited Partnership: Europe, the United States, and the Burdens of Alliance* (Cambridge: Ballinger, 1987), p. 187.

92. See Jean Klein, "Le débat en France sur la défense de l'Europe," *Stratégique* (quatrième trimestre 1984): 19.

6 EUROPEAN PUBLIC OPINION

Even in democracies, the public does not make defense policy, but public opinion does demarcate the policy alternatives available to political leaders. For example, even if they wished to, German politicians could not build a national nuclear deterrent—the German public would never accept it. The public's influence is applied in various ways: both indirectly, through interest groups and the media, and directly, through electoral punishment when politicians violate strongly held public attitudes. For example, CSU leader Franz Josef Strauss expressed his anxiety that NATO's short-range nuclear weapons might be traded away by stating that "Anyone who rejected [the triple-zero option] would meet a storm of opposition; he could never be reelected."[1]

Public opinion is important, but foreign policy is rarely a decisive electoral issue. In all Western democracies, issue voting more often involves domestic economic performance—especially unemployment and inflation. In France, the broadly-based defense policy consensus magnifies the difficulty of using security issues as a basis for the electoral decision. Subtle differences do divide the PS, RPR, and UDF, for example, concerning the proper role of French prestrategic nuclear weapons, but these distinctions are much too arcane to capture the attention of typical voters. Even in Britain and the Federal Republic, where previous defense consensuses have dissolved, the situation is not markedly different.

According to some analysts, German history and geography make in-

141

ternational affairs a relatively more salient political issue than elsewhere.[2] But foreign policy issues rarely decide German elections. The only possible exceptions were 1961, when it is sometimes argued that "the CDU/CSU profited greatly from the security issue. . . . "[3] and 1972. Although only 20 percent of the population considered foreign policy a very important issue in 1972, *Ostpolitik* was highly salient to those voters that switched their support from the CDU/CSU in 1969 to the SPD in 1972.[4]

Likewise, British elections are fought and decided principally on the basis of domestic issues. Defense policy may have contributed to the October 1951 Conservative victory, when the Tories promised to reduce Atlee's proposed level of defense spending. Again, in 1983, distaste for Labour's defense policy was magnified by the Falklands effect.[5] But these were exceptions. The 1987 general election was more typical. Labour's position on national defense diminished its electoral support and prevented Labour's unusually effective campaign from having more positive results. It probably did not cost Labour the election, although it did prompt Labour's retreat from unilateral nuclear disarmament after a third successive defeat by Margaret Thatcher.

Public opinion's principal effect, both in Western Europe and the United States, is to *exclude* certain alternatives. Especially in the Federal Republic, the INF treaty is an obvious recent example. Conservative German politicians were overwhelmed by the irresistible popular momentum created by Gorbachev's agreement to exchange the SS-20s and SS-4s for the Pershing 2s and the GLCMs without reductions of British and French nuclear forces or SDI limits. As discussed in Chapter 2, the German conundrum was partially self-inflicted: they were boxed in by their earlier justification for deploying INF. But the earlier argument was itself the product of politicians' perceptions of public attitudes. INF proponents knew that the German people would reject the contention that Pershing 2s and GLCMs were necessary to ensure that a European war would quickly escalate out of control if deterrence failed. Apart from a handful of defense intellectuals, there was no constituency for a European "doomsday machine." It was more persuasive to argue that the INFs were required to offset the Soviets' SS-20s; this was even reflected by applying the term *Nachrüstung* ("counterarmament") to the INFs. But the politicians were hoisted by their own petard when the Soviets accepted the double option. In both 1983 and 1987, the government's choices were severely constrained by public opinion. For this reason, public attitudes are a necessary ingredient of a comprehensive examination of future prospects for European defense cooperation.

Table 6–1. Nuclear Weapons in Western Europe: Develop or Dismantle? (percent).

Question: The UK and France have their own nuclear weapons. Would you prefer to see the countries of Western Europe

	Britain	France	Germany	Italy
Develop them further	9	17	8	5
Leave things as they are	52	40	35	13
Dismantle their own	34	32	57	79
Don't know	5	11	1	4

Source: David Fairhall, "Europe wary of American nuclear stance," *The Manchester Guardian Weekly*, 22 February 1987. The sample sizes were France (993), Germany (1,869), Italy (510), and Britain (1,463); the surveys were conducted between November 1986 and January 1987.

MILITARY POLICY

NATO doctrine asserts that European security requires both conventional and nuclear capabilities. This principle is endorsed by the German, French, and British governments, but nuclear deterrence receives only ambivalent public support. Public backing is strongest in France and weakest in the Federal Republic. As Table 6–1 indicates, a 1987 four-country survey revealed approximately one-third support for abandoning nuclear weapons in both France and Britain. However, further development of nuclear weapons received substantially greater support in France.

The French government conducts annual public opinion polls which indicate even higher levels of French support for nuclear deterrence. The questionnaire asks "Could a country like France assure its defense without the nuclear deterrent force?" The percentage of respondents who believed that nuclear weapons were essential to French security, that is, negative responses, increased from 56 percent in 1978 to 69 percent in 1986, while the positive responses declined from 25 percent to 18 percent.[6]

British attitudes toward nuclear deterrence have been stable in recent years. (See Table 6–2.) But like most public opinion, attitudes toward nuclear weapons are quite sensitive to precise question wording. This is illustrated by an October 1985 Gallup poll which asked, "Do you think that

Table 6–2.   British Nuclear Deterrent (percent).

Question: Britain is safer having its own nuclear weapons.

	1986	*1985*	*1984*
Agree	50	52	53
Disagree	36	35	31
Neither	9	9	6
Don't know	4	4	10

Source: Marplan Survey, Martin Linton, *The Guardian*, 26 September 1986.

Table 6–3.   German Support for Nuclear Deterrence by Party (percent).

Question: Are atomic weapons necessary to deter an attack on the Federal Republic or are conventional, that is nonatomic, weapons sufficient for deterrence?

	Total	*CDU/CSU*	*FDP*	*SPD*	*Green*
Atomic weapons necessary	26	40	31	15	11
Conventional sufficient	71	58	66	83	79

Source: "Affären wie in Kiel auch anderswo nöglich?" *Der Spiegel*, 2 November 1987. Survey conducted by EMNID-Institut between October 1 and October 18, 1987; N = 2,000 represents the 46 million adult West German citizens.

Britain should or should not continue to possess nuclear weapons *as long as the Soviet Union has them?*" When asked this way, with an explicit reference to Soviet nuclear capabilities, apparent support for the British deterrent increased to 68 percent of respondents, and apparent opposition dropped to only 26 percent.[7]

The Federal Republic has no national nuclear weapons, and Germans are, understandably, less supportive of nuclear deterrence. Table 6–3 presents findings from an October 1987 poll. It shows that even supporters of the CDU/CSU and FDP parties overwhelming rejected nuclear weapons. This is striking considering that these parties formed the governing coalition that authored the 1985 *White Paper* which explicitly based German security on America's nuclear guarantee.

Table 6–4. Nuclear Weapons Policy (percent).

	France	UK	FRG	USA
The use of nuclear weapons is not accept–able under any circumstances, not even if we are attacked with nuclear weapons.	27	24	31	14
Nuclear weapons should be used if we are attacked with nuclear weapons.	52	61	42	66
If we are attacked with non-nuclear weapons, we would be justified in using nuclear weapons to end the war quickly.	8	8	4	14
No answer/no opinion	13	7	23	6

Source: Connie de Boer, "The Polls: The European Peace Movement and Deployment of Nuclear Missiles," *Public Opinion Quarterly* 49 (Spring 1985): 125. Survey conducted by the Louis Harris Poll, September 10–November 4, 1983; the sample sizes were France (1,023), Britain (1,036), Germany (943), and the United States (1,246).

There is a widespread but erroneous impression that anti-nuclearism is stronger in Protestant Northern Europe than in the Catholic South. This misconception is based upon the massive anti-INF demonstrations in Northern Europe and the platforms of the Labour Party, the SPD, and other socialist parties. Actually, the lowest levels of support for nuclear deterrence are not found in the North, but in Spain and Italy. In 1983, 55 percent of Spanish respondents and 35 percent of Italian respondents agreed that the correct policy was to "Give up all nuclear weapons regardless of whether the Soviet Union does." This compared to 23 percent in Germany and 17 percent in Great Britain.[8]

The prevailing European attitude toward nuclear weapons is that of "non-war." Thus, there is substantially more public support for possessing nuclear weapons as a deterrent than for using nuclear weapons if deterrence fails—especially if the attack is non-nuclear. Table 6–4 demonstrates this point with findings from a multi-country survey from late 1983; it is confirmed by more recent polls from individual countries. For example, a 1987 French survey found that a majority of respondents supported the use of French nuclear weapons only if Western Europe were attacked by nuclear weapons; see Table 6–5. As mentioned in Chapter 3, a German defense ministry study found that 35 percent of commissioned officers and 65 percent of non-commissioned officers thought there were

Table 6–5.   French Willingness to Use Nuclear Weapons (percent).

Question: According to you, should France use its nuclear force?

	Yes	No	No Opinion
If the USSR uses its nuclear weapons to launch an attack against Western Europe.	<u>52</u>	33	15
If the USSR invades French territory.	41	<u>48</u>	11
If the USSR invades Germany.	20	<u>66</u>	14

Source: Michel Colomès, "Sommet Reagan-Gorbatchev: l'esprit de défense des Français," *Le Point,* 7 December 1987. SOFRES survey conducted November 21–25, 1987; N = 1,000.

Table 6–6.   European Public Opinion and Nuclear First Use (percent).

Question: Should NATO fall back upon the use of nuclear weapons if it is being threatened by a defeat in a conventional war?

	Yes	No
France	29	<u>62</u>
Great Britain	27	<u>66</u>
West Germany	11	<u>80</u>

Source: *Newsweek* (international edition), 7 October 1985. The poll was conducted by Gallup between September 18–23, 1985. The sample size exceeded 500 in each country.

no circumstances which could justify using nuclear weapons. There is virtually no public support for actually implementing NATO's policy of nuclear first use, as Table 6–6 demonstrates with findings from 1985.

EUROPE AND AMERICA

According to the British, French, and German governments, America's conventional and nuclear guarantees are essential to NATO-European security. The publics' attitudes are more complex. German opinion is affected by that country's geographical exposure and dovish orientation. The French are influenced by their commitment to both European and

Table 6–7. Support for INF, 1985 (percent).

Question: Are you for or against the continued stationing of U.S. Pershing II missiles and cruise missiles in Western Europe as long as there is no arms control agreement?

	UK	France	FRG
For	41	36	28
Against	46	49	66

Source: *Newsweek* (international edition), 7 October 1985. The poll was conducted by Gallup between September 18–23, 1985. The sample size exceeded 500 in each country.

Table 6–8. U.S. Nuclear Weapons Based in Europe (percent).

Question: Do you approve or disapprove of the decision by certain European governments to allow the Americans to base nuclear weapons in Europe?

	UK	France	FRG	Italy
Approve	35	23	33	17
Disapprove	56	60	66	78
Don't know	9	17	1	5

Source: David Fairhall, "Europe wary of American nuclear stance," *The Manchester Guardian Weekly*, 22 February 1987. The sample sizes were France (993), Germany (1,869), Italy (510), and Britain (1,463); the surveys were conducted between November 1986 and January

French autonomy, while British opinion is affected by strong minority support for nuclear unilateralism and ambivalence toward the United States.

These concerns are illustrated by opinion toward the INF deployments. Although the governments supported the Euro-missile deployments, Table 6–7 indicates that in 1985, INF was opposed by the publics in all three countries: narrowly in Britain, more strongly in France (where no American INFs were deployed), and by a margin exceeding two-to-one in the Federal Republic. More recently, a four-country survey revealed even stronger opposition to basing American nuclear weapons in Europe. (See Table 6–8.)

Nuclear deterrence is central to NATO's strategy, and the United States provides virtually all of NATO's nuclear capability. Therefore, opposition to American nuclear weapons in Europe appears inconsistent

Table 6–9.   German Attitudes Toward NATO (percent).

	Oct/Nov 1984	Oct/Nov 1985	April/May 1986
Peace is only secured by NATO	<u>57</u>	<u>60</u>	<u>62</u>
Peace is only secured by a neutralized Western Europe without NATO	20	15	19
Undecided	21	21	19

Source: Helmut Fogt, *Friedenssicherung und westliches Bündnis in der Einschätzung der Bevölkerung 1984 bis Mitte 1986*, Internal Study No. 4/1986 (Sankt Augustin bei Bonn: Konrad Adenauer Stiftung, July 1986), p. 7. The sample sizes were 1984 (3,060), 1985 (3,816), and 1986 (5,017).

Table 6–10.   French Opinion and the U.S. Nuclear Guarantee (percent).

Question: Faced by the nuclear and conventional forces of the USSR and the Warsaw Pact, can France currently assure her defense alone without American nuclear protection?

Yes	20
No	<u>69</u>
No opinion	11

Source: "Défense: les Français croient en l'Europe," *L'Express*, 24 April 1987. The survey was conducted by Louis Harris, April 2–6, 1987; N = 1,001 adults aged eighteen and above.

with the rather broad public support for NATO membership. For example, in the Federal Republic a three-to-one majority believes the Atlantic Alliance strengthens German security. (See Table 6–9.)[9]

French opposition to American nuclear deployments is even more contradictory, for it conflicts with the opinion expressed by greater than a three-to-one majority in 1987 that French security depended upon the American nuclear umbrella. (See Table 6–10.) Similarly, in September 1986 45 percent of a British sample said that removing American nuclear bases from the United Kingdom would make them feel less safe com-

Table 6–11.   Confidence in the U.S. Nuclear Guarantee (percent).

Question: How much do you trust the USA to defend Western Europe, even with the risk of an atomic attack upon its own territory?

	UK	France	FRG
Very confident	16	9	9
Quite confident	26	37	33
Not very confident	33	34	34
Completely nonconfident	24	15	18
No opinion	1	5	6

Source: *Newsweek* (international edition), 7 October 1985. The poll was conducted by Gallup between September 18–23, 1985 with samples exceeding 500 in each country.

pared to 31 percent who would feel more safe (24 percent were indifferent or had no opinion).[10]

To repeat, nuclear deterrence is central to NATO's strategy and overwhelmingly provided by the United States. So the likelihood of successful deterrence must depend, at least partially, upon the credibility of the American nuclear guarantee. In 1985, a Gallup poll (Table 6–11) indicated considerable homogeneity among the three publics in their expectation " . . . that the USA would defend Western Europe—even with the risk of an atomic attack on their own territory." In each country, between 42 and 46 percent of the population expressed confidence in the American nuclear pledge.

More recent French findings are quite confusing. Although a survey near the end of 1987 (Table 6–12) found a similar level of confidence (38 percent), an earlier 1987 survey (Table 6–13) revealed a much higher level of confidence in the American commitment—78 percent. And in 1986, with the explicit reference to nuclear weapons omitted, 86 percent (compared to only 10 percent) thought that "in case of conflict we could count on United States aid."[11] These disparities may arise from differently worded questions or from situational factors. For example, the INF treaty was about to be signed when the second 1987 survey was conducted, which may have diminished French confidence. Nonetheless, these poll results do not demonstrate significant differences among the three countries concerning confidence in the U.S. guarantee.

THE POLITICS OF EUROPEAN DEFENSE COOPERATION

Table 6–12. French Confidence in the U.S. Nuclear Guarantee (percent).

Question: In case of a military attack against Western Europe, do you believe that the United States would use its nuclear force to come to the aid of the European countries?

Yes, they would use it	<u>38</u>
No, they would not use it	37
No opinion	25

Source: Michel Colomès, "Sommet Reagan-Gorbatchev: l'esprit de défense des Français," *Le Point,* 7 December 1987. SOFRES survey conducted November 21–25, 1987; N = 1,000.

Table 6–13. French Confidence in the U.S. Nuclear Guarantee (percent).

Question: Today, the United States possesses nuclear weapons based in Europe. If Europe were threatened by the Soviet Union and Warsaw Pact forces, could she count on America's nuclear engagement?

Yes, definitely	41
Yes, perhaps	37
No, probably not	8
No, certainly not	3
No opinion	11

Source: "Défense: les Français croient en l'Europe," *L'Express,* 24 April 1987. The survey was conducted by Louis Harris, April 2–6, 1987; N = 1,001 adults aged eighteen and above.

EUROPEAN COOPERATION

Since 1945, the United States has been the ultimate guarantor of Western European security, but other security options are conceivable. These include national autonomy, neutralism, European cooperation, and various hybrids. For example, France has pursued a mixed strategy of autonomy and alliance, and a united Europe could be neutral rather than the second pillar of the Atlantic Alliance. There is at least some minority support for these policy alternatives in all three countries, but also rather distinct national preferences, as Table 6–14 indicates. The French are most likely

Table 6–14.   Defense Alternatives (percent).

Question: Most Western European countries are linked to the USA for their defence in NATO. Do you think the Western European countries should maintain their military links with the US through NATO, create a common European defence independent of the US and NATO, or should each European country be fully responsible for its own defence?

	UK	France	FRG[12]	Italy
Links with US and NATO	<u>41</u>	26	<u>54</u>	19
Common European defence	23	<u>35</u>	19	<u>38</u>
Own defence	26	20	25	31
Don't know	10	20	2	12

Source: David Fairhall, "Europe wary of American nuclear stance," *The Manchester Guardian Weekly*, 22 February 1987. The sample sizes were France (993), Germany (1,869), Italy (510), and Britain (1,463); the surveys were conducted between November 1986 and January 1987.

Table 6–15.   European Defense Alternatives (percent).

Question: If there were to be a common Western European defence independent of the US and NATO, which of these three possibilities is in your opinion the most desirable?

	UK	France	FRG	Italy
Nuclear, Franco–Britain based	13	8	12	3
Nuclear, all countries involved	<u>35</u>	<u>35</u>	14	14
Conventional	<u>35</u>	25	29	<u>70</u>
None of these	4	13	<u>44</u>	6
Don't know	13	18	2	7

Source: David Fairhall, "Europe wary of American nuclear stance," *The Manchester Guardian Weekly*, 22 February 1987. The sample sizes were France (993), Germany (1,869), Italy (510), and Britain (1,463); the surveys were conducted between November 1986 and January 1987.

to value European unity as an end in itself. Germany and Britain have comparatively small constituencies for a European approach to security issues; their publics tend to see the European option primarily as a makeshift replacement if NATO founders. In fact, 44 percent of Germans reject *all* forms of European defense (Table 6–15). Most Germans favor either the status quo (54 percent prefer continued links with the United States through NATO) or an autonomous non-nuclear defense. British

Table 6–16.   British Opinion Regarding a European Army (percent).

Question: A number of ideas are being considered which it is said will bring the member states of the European Community closer together. Do you support or oppose the idea of a fully integrated armed services to defend Europe?

	Support	Oppose	Don't know
Total	<u>58</u>	29	14
Conservative	<u>60</u>	30	10
Labour	<u>55</u>	30	16
Other party	<u>60</u>	28	12
Stay in Common Market	<u>65</u>	24	11
Get out of Common Market	<u>51</u>	36	13

Source: Survey conducted in Great Britain for the European Democratic Group of the European Parliament by Market and Opinion Research International (MORI). The sample size was 2,003; the survey was conducted between September 7–14, 1987.

opinion is similar. According to *Libération*, "like the Germans, if the Atlantic Alliance were abandoned [the British] would lean toward a strictly national defense rather than toward a common European defense."[13] Nonetheless, as Table 6–16 indicates, a British survey in September 1987 revealed a remarkably high level of support (58 percent) for a European army. There was even majority support for a European army among British respondents who favored withdrawal from the EEC!

British and German reserve toward defense cooperation parallels their general apathy toward European institutions. In the 1950s, Britain was the principal skeptic, and Germany was an ardent partisan of European integration. During this period, Britain still hoped to retain its status as one of the wartime "Big Three" and would not limit her horizons to Europe nor pay the economic cost of EEC entry. Germans, in contrast, were strong advocates of European unity. "Europe" was an honorable surrogate for discredited German nationalism, and European institutions provided a context for establishing the FRG's legitimacy.

As time passed, opinion altered in both countries. Britain's international position deteriorated. The Empire was lost, and it became clear that neither the special Anglo-American relationship nor the Commonwealth was sufficient to maintain Britain's global position. Consequently, public support for European unity increased, although it still lags behind that of the six original EEC members. Concurrently, the Federal Republic became increasingly well-integrated into the postwar international

Table 6–17. United States of Europe? (percent).

Question: Are you personally for or against the European Community developing towards becoming a 'United States of Europe'?			
	FRG	*France*	*UK*
For—very much	20	24	14
For—rather	<u>36</u>	<u>50</u>	<u>38</u>
Against—rather	10	12	21
Against—very much	7	3	16
No opinion	27	11	11

Source: *Eurobarometer* (Brussels: Commission of the European Communities, March 1987), p. A8. Surveys were conducted between January 9 and February 9, 1987 under the general coordination of Faits et Opinion, Paris. Sample sizes equaled FRG (1,057), France (1,000), and the United Kingdom (1,048).

Table 6–18. Reinforce EC? (percent).

Question: Do you favor reinforcing the European Community?				
	France	*UK*	*FRG*	*Spain*
Yes	<u>88</u>	<u>65</u>	<u>77</u>	<u>69</u>
Moderately	10	24	12	25
No	2	11	11	6

Source: "Cadres: à la recherche d'une entreprise européenne," *Le Monde Affaires,* 10 October 1987. The surveys were conducted during September 1987 by l'Institut Motivaction International. The sample equaled 1,200 managers in four countries.

system, and West Germans became somewhat more nationalistic and preoccupied with *Deutschlandpolitik.* The *immobilisme* of European institutions, and their role as principal paymasters, also disillusioned some Germans.

Between 1962 and 1984, the proportion of Germans expressing strong support for European unification declined among all age groups. During these years, French support was relatively uniform and remained slightly below the German level into the mid-1980s.[14] But as tables 6–17 and 6–18 indicate, the French are now substantially more supportive of European goals than the Germans and much more so than the British. In recent years, French support for European defense initiatives has been especially strong. This orientation is probably reinforced by France's lesser dependence upon the United States (see Table 6–19). When asked

Table 6–19.   French Autonomy or European Defense (percent).

Question: In the years to come, would you prefer a common European defense, including the French nuclear force, or that France preserve a totally independent national defense?

	November 1983	April 1987
A common European defense	<u>47</u>	<u>54</u>
An independent French defense	39	35
No opinion	14	11

Source: "Un sondage Figaro-Sofres: l'opinion des Français sur les rapports Est-Ouest," *Le Figaro,* 21 April 1987. The survey was conducted by SOFRES, April 7–11, 1987; N = 1,000 adults aged eighteen and above.

in April 1987, "Are you rather favorable or rather unfavorable to establishing a common European defense," 88 percent of the French were favorable and only 7 percent were unfavorable (5 percent with no opinion).[15]

EUROPEAN NEUTRALISM

Germans resent the fact that their closest allies, the Americans and the French, chronically suspect that the FRG is on the brink of succumbing to neutralist tendencies. They point out that the Federal Republic has repeatedly demonstrated loyalty to the West during more than three decades. It remains true, nonetheless, that Germans continue to be fascinated by the possibility of unification which is enshrined in their Basic Law. Moreover, substantial evidence supports Theo Sommer's assertion that "Two thirds of all West Germans would like a united Germany. . . . "[16] In fact, a secret government survey described by *Bild* in 1987 found that 71 percent of the West German population favored the reunification of a nonaligned Germany.[17] But as Theo Sommer wrote, "What we [Germans] may regard as a pleasant dream is regarded as a nightmare by our neighbors in East and West."[18] Italian Foreign Minister Giulio Andreotti unleashed a furor in 1984 by remarking that "There are two German states, and two it should be."[19] But Andreotti only said aloud what nearly all Europeans believe. Throughout Europe a divided Germany is seen as one positive result of World War II, and not only because

Table 6–20. German and French Attitudes Toward Reunification (percent).

Question: In your opinion, which is more important, the reunification of Germany or the Federal Republic's membership in the Western world?

	FRG	France
The FRG's membership in the Western world	57	40
The reunification of Germany	41	31
No opinion	2	29

Source: "La réunification allemande? Sondage Gallup international: Français et allemands répondents," *Géopolitique* (Winter 1984/85):8. The samples were of adults aged eighteen and older. The German poll was conducted between December 4–6, 1984 (N = 535) and the French poll during December 13–14, 1984 (N = 809).

of nineteenth and twentieth century German bellicosity and the Third Reich's barbarism. The more fundamental problem is the difficulty of incorporating a powerful united Germany into a stable European balance of power.

Considering international opinion, it is fortunate that Germans appear to value European unification more than German reunification. For example, in December 1984, West Germans agreed (Table 6–20) by a margin of 57 percent to 41 percent that West German membership in the Western world was more important than reunification.[20] And in August 1983, West Germans preferred European unity over German unification by a margin of 60 percent to 36 percent.[21]

Furthermore, West Germans have few illusions concerning the likelihood of reunification. GDR leader Erich Honecker made an unprecedented and historic visit to the Federal Republic in September 1987. One poll conducted during his visit found that only 19 percent of West Germans considered the trip a step toward reunification.[22] A second poll during the visit found that only 8 percent considered reunification likely, 58 percent said it was unlikely, and 33 percent thought it was impossible.[23] This is similar to the finding of an August 1983 survey. The German polling organization EMNID asked, "Do you expect the division between the GDR and the FRG to dissolve in the foreseeable future resulting in a single Germany?" Seven percent of respondents answered yes, 33 percent were uncertain, and 60 percent said no.[24]

Germany belongs to *Mitteleuropa*, and the tie connecting East and West Germans is natural and deep. Indeed, 50 percent of the East Ger-

Table 6–21.   German Equidistance (percent).

Question: Should we work together equally closely with the United States and the Soviet Union in the future, or more closely with the Soviet Union or more closely with the United States?

	5/73	1/80	1/82	5/84	5/85	1/86	1987
More closely with the United States	36	<u>49</u>	42	41	43	33	31
Equally closely	<u>54</u>	41	<u>44</u>	<u>48</u>	<u>45</u>	<u>54</u>	<u>58</u>
More closely with the USSR	3	2	2	2	1	2	
Undecided, no reply	7	8	12	9	11	11	

Source: Elisabeth Noelle-Neumann, "A Lesson in the Defense of Western Europe," in Elisabeth Noelle-Neumann, *Die deutsch-amerikanischen Beziehungen und die öffentliche Meinhung: Dokumentation des Artikels in der Frankfurter Allgemeinen Zeitung Nr. 146 vom 28. Juni 1985* (Allensbach: Institut für Demoskopie Allensbach, n.d.), Table 1; Elisabeth Noelle-Neumann, "Attitudes on Western Defense: German Youth and the Greens" (mimeo, Institut für Demoskopie Allensbach, 1986), p. 24; and James M. Markham, "Gorbachev Gains in West Germany," *The New York Times*, 17 May 1987. Surveys were conducted in the FRG and West Berlin among the population aged sixteen and over.

mans and one-third of the West Germans have relatives across the border, and many prominent West and East Germans (including Hans-Dietrich Genscher, Hannelore Kohl, and Erich Honecker) were born in the other German state. Many West Germans also regard the less industrialized and environmentally blighted East as a more authentic embodiment of traditional German culture which is now lost to the FRG. By the end of 1986, nearly 90 percent of the West German public favored improved relations with the GDR (German Democratic Republic), up from approximately two-thirds in 1979,[25] and Bonn was committed to strengthening inter-German cooperation even in times of East-West friction.[26] Moreover, despite harboring few illusions regarding prospects for reunification, Germans have not abandoned the dream. As Chancellor Kohl told a *Frankfurter Allgemeine Zeitung* interviewer in late 1987, "The German Question is open. We do not reconcile ourselves to the division of Germany and Berlin."[27] However, West Germans continue to rank their ties with NATO and the European Community above inter-German relations.

German neutralism is a particular concern, but many Americans and

Table 6–22. German Neutralism (percent).

Question: There are different opinions about what relations between the Federal Republic and other nations should be like. Could you read what these two people are saying? Which of them would you agree with?

	6/82	6/83	5/84
The alliance with America and the other friendly nations of the Western world has secured peace and freedom for more than 30 years. As a neutral nation, we would be too weak to defend ourselves in case of an attack.	67	60	60
The freedom of the Federal Republic would not be threatened either if it were neutral. And we can do more for world peace and for countries getting along with each other if we do not belong to either of the two power blocs.	21	21	26
Undecided	12	19	14

Elisabeth Noelle-Neumann, "A Lesson in the Defense of Western Europe," in Elisabeth Noelle-Neumann, *Die deutsch-amerikanischen Beziehungen und die öffentliche Meinung: Dokumentation des Artikels in der Frankfurter Allgemeinen Zeitung Nr. 146 vom 28. Juni 1985* (Allensbach: Institut für Demoskopie Allensbach, n.d.), Table 2

conservative Europeans express a more generalized fear of what Timothy Garten Ash labels "equilateralism." This is the view "that the United States and Soviet Union are equal, and that our side—that is, Europe—should distance itself equally (and as far as possible) from both."[28] Equilateralism is related to both disillusionment with the United States and an improving Soviet image. As Table 6–21 indicates, between 1982 and 1986 there was increased support in the Federal Republic for a more equidistant position between the superpowers; however, support for explicit neutralism rose only slightly (from 21 percent to 26 percent) between 1982 and 1984 (Table 6–22).[29]

A related trend is seen in the United Kingdom, where confidence in U.S. policies has substantially eroded during the 1980s, as Table 6–23 indicates. But the reverse is true of France; French confidence in the United States grew between 1976 and 1986, (Table 6–24), and there is a clear preference for the United States over the Soviet Union (Table 6–25).

Table 6–23.   British Confidence in U.S. Policy (percent).

Question: How much confidence do you have in the ability of the United States to deal wisely with present world problems?

Year/(Number of Surveys)	A Great Deal/ Considerable Amount	Little	Very Little/ None at All
1985 (4)	24	28	41
1984 (5)	23	25	47
1983 (6)	23	26	45
1982 (5)	27	27	40
1981 (3)	30	25	36
1980 (4)	33	25	32
1979 (4)	28	25	36
1978 (2)	36	23	28
1977 (2)	48	22	22
1976 (1)	33	27	26
1975 (6)	30	26	31
1974 (7)	33	24	31
1973 (7)	28	26	32
1972 (6)	30	25	31
1970 (2)	29	28	27

Source: Gordon Heald and Robert J. Wybrow, *The Gallup Survey of Britain* (London: Croom Helm, 1986), p. 187.

Table 6–24.   French Confidence in U.S. Policy (percent).

Question: Would you say you have confidence, or no confidence in the United States' foreign policy?

	1986	1982	1976
Confidence	51	42	33
No confidence	42	41	58
Don't know	7	17	9

Source: *News From France,* 27 May 1986. Survey conducted by Gallup International for the French-American Foundation and *L'Express,* April 1986.

Table 6–25.   French Opinion of Soviet and U.S. Policies (percent).

Question: Overall, do you have a very good, rather good, rather bad, or very bad opinion of the Soviet/US international policy?

| | Soviet | | American | |
	4/87	11/85	4/87	11/85
Very good	1	0	2	4
Rather good	17	9	<u>41</u>	<u>39</u>
Rather bad	<u>43</u>	<u>36</u>	31	22
Very bad	19	23	8	5
No opinion	20	32	18	30

Source: "Un sondage Figaro-Sofres: l'opinion des Français sur les rapports Est-Ouest," *Le Figaro*, 21 April 1987. The survey was conducted by SOFRES, April 7–11, 1987; N = 1,000 adults aged eighteen and above.

Table 6–26.   Opinions of Reagan and Gorbachev (percent).

Question: Whom do you trust more to reduce tensions between the Soviet Union and the United States, President Ronald Reagan or Soviet leader Mikhail Gorbachev?

	UK	FRG	France	USA
Reagan	19	16	<u>23</u>	<u>62</u>
Gorbachev	<u>39</u>	<u>24</u>	16	17
Neither/Don't know	42	60	61	21

Source: Nicholas Beeston, "Britons regard Reagan as the 'bad' guy," *The Times* (London), 8 December 1987. Surveys: UK, Mori, 2,004 adults November 6–10, 1987; France, BVA, 919 adults November 14–19, 1987; FRG, Sample Institute, 1,850 adults November 7–16, 1987.

These assessments of U.S. and Soviet policies are strongly influenced by perceptions of the American and Soviet leaders, and much of the trend toward equilateralism and equidistance was related to dislike of President Reagan (especially in the FRG and the UK) and the popularity of General Secretary Gorbachev. This was manifested in a striking manner by a survey near the end of 1987 (Table 6–26) which found a much higher British assessment of Gorbachev's commitment to peace compared to Reagan's. This survey also found (Table 6–27) that a majority of the British public had an unfavorable opinion of President Reagan (by a margin of 54 to 31

Table 6–27.   Reagan and Gorbachev: Favorable and Unfavorable Opinions (percent).

	UK	FRG	France
Reagan			
Favorable	31	<u>38</u>	<u>37</u>
Unfavorable	<u>54</u>	36	35
Gorbachev			
Favorable	<u>68</u>	<u>59</u>	<u>39</u>
Unfavorable	14	14	28

Source: Nicholas Beeston, "Britons regard Reagan as the 'bad' guy," *The Times* (London), 8 December 1987. Surveys: UK, Mori, 2,004 adults November 6–10, 1987; France, BVA, 919 adults November 14–19, 1987; FRG, Sample Institute, 1,850 adults November 7–16, 1987.

Table 6–28.   German Opinion of Soviet and American Disarmament Policies (percent).

Question: My trust in the peace and disarmament policies of the US and the Soviet Union is

	US	USSR
Very great or relatively great	<u>52</u>	<u>59</u>
Relatively small or very small	47	40

Source: "Affären wie in Kiel auch anderswo nöglich?" *Der Spiegel,* 2 November 1987. Survey conducted by EMNID-Institut between October 1 and October 18, 1987; N = 2,000 represents the 46 million adult West German citizens.

percent) and a very favorable opinion of Gorbachev (by a margin of 68 percent favorable to 14 percent unfavorable). The Germans shared both sentiments, but to a somewhat lesser extent, as Tables 6–27 and 6–28 indicate.

EUROPEAN PACIFISM

Despite fears on both sides of the Atlantic that European pacifism is growing, there continued to be substantial evidence of resolve to defend European security. Admittedly, most Europeans assessed the Soviet threat more modestly than Americans tended to do, and Gorbachev's relative

Table 6–29.   French Willingness to Risk One's Life (percent).

Question: In each of the following cases, do you think it would justify risking your life by fighting?

	November 1987			December 1983		
	Yes	No	DK	Yes	No	DK
The invasion of countries allied to France such as West Germany	32	<u>59</u>	9	35	<u>49</u>	16
The invasion of French territory	<u>75</u>	19	6	<u>79</u>	14	7

Source: Michel Colomès, "Sommet Reagan-Gorbatchev: l'esprit de défense des Français," *Le Point,* 7 December 1987. SOFRES survey conducted November 21–25, 1987; N = 1,000. The 1983 survey question referred to "The invasion of France by a foreign army."

popularity compared to Ronald Reagan's reinforced this tendency. Nonetheless, in 1987, a clear majority of the German public (56 percent) believed that the Bundeswehr should respond to aggression against the Federal Republic; this percentage had remained constant for a decade, although German support for nuclear retaliation declined from 19 to 11 percent.[30]

Being less dovish than the Germans, the French public was even more willing to oppose aggression. As Table 6–29 indicates, 75 percent of French respondents were prepared to risk their lives if French territory were attacked, and 52 percent were prepared to retaliate with nuclear weapons if France were attacked with nuclear weapons (Table 6–5).

A European defense community must be built on the foundation of Franco-German cooperation, so it is significant that Frenchmen were substantially less willing to defend the FRG by either conventional or nuclear means (see Table 6–29 and Table 6–5). Despite the growing interdependence between the two countries' defense policies, and the competition between President Mitterrand and Prime Minister Chirac to claim credit for Franco-German solidarity prior to the 1988 presidential election, opinion surveys revealed no change in the French public's reluctance to contribute to German defense.

NOTES

1. Quoted in David C. Morrison, "NATO Has Pre-Treaty Tremors," *National Journal*, 28 November 1987.
2. See for example Kendall L. Baker, Russell J. Dalton, and Kai Hildebrandt, *Germany Transformed: Political Culture and the New Politics* (Cambridge: Harvard University Press, 1981), p. 105.
3. Hans D. Klingemann and Charles Lewis Taylor, "Partisanship, Candidates and Issues: Attitudinal Components of the Vote in West German Elections," in Max Kaase and Klaus von Beyme, eds., *Elections & Parties* (London and Beverly Hills: Sage Publications, 1978), pp. 123–24.
4. See David B. Conradt, *The German Polity*, 2nd ed. (New York: Longman, 1982), p. 136.
5. See David Capitanchik and Richard C. Eichenberg, *Defence and Public Opinion*, Chatham House Papers 20 (London: Routledge & Kegan Paul, 1983), p. 15.
6. For the 1986 results, see Jean-Paul Le Bourg, "Opinion et défense en 1986," *Armées d'aujourd'hui* (February 1987). The 1986 survey was conducted by Sofres between September 27–October 1, 1986; N = 1,000 adults aged eighteen and older. For earlier results, see Jean-Paul Le Bourg, "Opinion et défense en 1985," *Armées d'aujourd'hui* (October 1985): 15.
7. See Gordon Heald and Robert J. Wybrow, *The Gallup Survey of Britain* (London: Croom Helm, 1986), p. 197 (emphasis added).
8. Cited in Josef Joffe, *The Limited Partnership: Europe, the United States, and the Burdens of Alliance* (Cambridge: Ballinger, 1987), p. 128. Joffe explains this phenomenon in terms of the differing political structures of Northern and Southern Europe, especially the positions of the democratic socialist parties; see pp. 110–19.
9. Similar findings for a longer but less current timespan are contained in Hans Rattinger, "The Federal Republic of Germany: Much Ado About (Almost) Nothing," in Gregory Flynn and Hans Rattinger, eds., *The Public and Atlantic Defense* (Totowa, NJ: Rowman & Allenheld, 1985), p. 143, and William K. Domke, Richard C. Eichenberg, and Catherine M. Kelleher, "Consensus Lost? Domestic Politics and the 'Crisis' in NATO," *World Politics* 39 (April 1987): 382–407.
10. See, "79% fear Labour would upset US," *Sunday Telegraph*, 28 September 1986. The survey was conducted September 19–22, 1986; N = 967.
11. Source: "La confiance quand même: Sondage l'Express-Gallup International," *L'Express*, 30 May 1986. The poll was conducted April 16–19, 1986; N = 1,033.
12. Although West Germans are more supportive of NATO than the French,

the level of support has declined during the 1980s as is indicated by the following survey responses:

The Federal Republic has several possibilities as to how to align its foreign policy. Various possibilities are described in this list. Which of them do you consider the best; which of these should the Federal Republic especially emphasize?

	9/80	7/83	3/84	5/85
Pursue a policy of neutrality between the superpowers in the East and in the West	31%	38%	38%	34%
Continue to stand by the United States	56%	47%	36%	37%
Pursue an independent policy with the countries of the European Community	40%	38%	35%	38%
Take a neutral position with friendly cooperation with the Soviet Union	16%	15%	8%	5%
Work closely together with the Soviet Union	4%	5%	2%	1%
Undecided	9%	8%	9%	11%

Source: Elisabeth Noelle-Neumann, "A Lesson in the Defense of Western Europe," in Elisabeth Noelle-Neumann, *Die deutsch-amerikanischen Beziehungen und die öffentliche Beziehungen: Dokumentation des Artikels in der Frankfurter Allgemeinen Zeitung Nr. 146 vom 28. Juni 1985* (Allensbach: Institut für Demoskopie Allensbach, n.d.), Table 4.

13. Carlos de Sa Rego, "Le parapluie de l'Oncle Sam a perdu de ses charmes," *Libération*, 16 February 1987. *Libération* was the French sponsor of the four-country survey.

14. Groupe d'Etudes sur les Conflits et les Stratégies en Europe, Fondation pour les Etudes de Défense Nationale, *Sécurité et Défense de l'Europe: Le Dossier Allemand*, Collection les sept épées (troisième trimestre 1985): 185–86.

15. Source: "Défense: les Français croient en l'Europe," *L'Express*, 24 April 1987. The survey was conducted by Louis Harris, April 2–6, 1987; N = 1,001 adults, aged eighteen and above.

16. Theo Sommer, "German identity faces a double dilemma over the wish for reunification," *The German Tribune*, 5 July 1987 (translated from *Die Zeit*, 26 June 1987).

17. Cited in "Rumeurs à Bonn à propos de la réunification," *Le Monde*, 14 May 1987.

A survey of 535 West German adults conducted between December 4–6, 1984 found that 67 percent (compared to 31 percent) agreed that "If the reunification of Germany resulted in the neutralization of Germany and of Western Europe, I would be ready to accept it." Source: "La réunification allemande? Sondage Gallup international: Français et allemands répondents," *Géopolitique* (Winter 1984/85): 8.

An EMNID survey of March 1980 indicated that 67 percent of the West German public (compared to 28 percent) believed that the FRG should "strive for reunification with the German Democratic Republic as is called for in the constitution. . . ." Michael Wolffs, *Einstellungen der Bevölkerung zu Heimat, Vaterland und Nation* (Sankt Augustin bei Bonn: Konrad Adenauer Stiftung, June 1984), p. 11.

18. Sommer, "German identity."
19. Quoted in Joffe, *The Limited Partnership*, p. 40.
20. However, German opinion is not necessarily consistent, for 67 percent of respondents (compared to 31 percent) agreed that "If the reunification of Germany resulted in the neutralization of Germany and of Western Europe, I would be ready to accept it."
21. Wolffs, *Einstellungen*, p. 17. The EMNID survey had a sample of 1,003.
22. See Serge Schmemann, "Leaders of 2 Germanys Agree to Disagree," *The New York Times*, 9 September 1987.
23. See Serge Schmemann, "A Saar Town Welcomes Home 'Der Erich'," *The New York Times*, 11 September 1987. The survey was conducted for the television program "Report;" N = 10,000.
24. Wolffs, *Einstellungen*, p. 15.
25. See *Aktueller Politischer Dienst* (Bielefeld: EMNID-Institut, November 1986), p. 19.
26. See Manfred Wörner, "Security and Defence: Perceptions and Policies of the Federal Republic of Germany," *RUSI: Journal of the Royal United Services Institute for Defence Studies* 131 (March 1986): 17.
27. Johann Georg Reismüller, "A re-united Germany cannot be ruled out forever, says Chancellor Kohl," *The German Tribune*, 13 December 1987 (translated from *Frankfurter Allgemeine Zeitung*, 30 November 1987).
28. Timothy Garton Ash, "Equilateralism," *The New Republic*, September 1986.
29. Noelle-Neumann, "A Lesson in the Defense," Table 2.
30. See André Ancian, "RFA: la <<fin>> du danger soviétique," *Le Point*, 7 December 1987 which describes results of an EMNID Institute survey, and Richard C. Eichenberg, "Public Opinion and National Security in Western Europe and the United States," in Linda P. Brady and Joyce P. Kaufman, eds., *NATO in the 1980s: Challenges and Responses* (New York: Praeger, 1985), p. 240.

7 THE FUTURE

Germany, France, Britain, and America will largely determine the future of European defense cooperation. Other countries including the Soviet Union, will affect the process at the margins, but they will not be key players. Germany and the United States are the decisive actors: Germany primarily for geopolitical reasons and the United States because she has led the Western Alliance for over forty years. Britain is more marginal both geographically and politically. Notwithstanding Margaret Thatcher's status as the dean of European leaders, London is simply less influential today than in the early fifties when the United Kingdom opted out of the EDC. France is more crucial than Britain, but France cannot construct Europe alone. Germany is the fundamental European actor because French options are dependent upon German behavior. The dominant chain of influence runs from Washington to Bonn to Paris to London.

THE GIVENS

The central issue is how to defend the Federal Republic, and tinkering with the status quo cannot provide a long-term solution. Nor is the obvious alternative to replace America's noncredible nuclear guarantee with a suspect French or "European" nuclear umbrella. The *obvious* alternative is to equip the Federal Republic with a German nuclear deterrent which

165

could credibly threaten nuclear reprisals if the FRG were attacked. An invulnerable retaliatory force would give the Federal Republic the same margin of security now enjoyed by Britain and France, for as François Mitterrand argued, "One does not doubt the resolution of a country whose independence is at stake. . . . "[1] A German force would obviate the problem of "extending" nuclear deterrence, whether by the United States, France, or some hypothetical "European" entity. Nuclear deterrence cannot easily be shared; *conventional* deterrence can. A German nuclear deterrent, combined with a conventional allied force, could safeguard German security with high confidence.

The option of German nuclear weapons has received some serious consideration in recent years, most notably in France by André Glucksmann. But as André Fontaine wrote, "André Glucksmann is not alone in wishing that the West Germans possess them."[2] And Anne-Marie Le Gloannec wrote that during 1983–84 not only Glucksmann but also Michel Tatu, Simone Veil, and Jacques Chirac suggested the possibility of "giving" nuclear weapons to the Germans.[3] Foreign ministry official François Gorand (pseud.) presented a somewhat different rationale. He argued that affirming Germany's right to possess nuclear weapons would address the lack of trust among Europeans, "even if they do not wish to exercise it and perhaps not even to see it bestowed."[4]

Nonetheless, this option appalls most Germans. As Chapter 3 established, it is the Germans themselves, more than other Europeans, who refuse to contemplate this alternative.[5] According to Glucksmann, German aversion to nuclear weapons is an anticipatory reaction which assumes that her neighbors would never accept a nuclear Germany. This may partially explain German attitudes, but the roots of German dovishness are actually much deeper, as Hans-Peter Schwarz argued. Furthermore, although the INF Treaty and possible 50 percent reductions in the superpowers' strategic arsenals strengthen the argument for independent European nuclear forces, their effect upon German public opinion is quite different. Progress toward nuclear disarmament created a political atmosphere which further precluded the nuclear option even without the legal constraints of the NPT (Non-Proliferation Treaty) and WEU. According to Chancellor Kohl, "We do not possess nuclear weapons, and we do not wish to possess them at any price. It is the hard core of our policy."[6]

In France, the principal political given is refusal to rejoin NATO's integrated military structure. As French leaders reshaped Gaullist principles to fit new strategic conditions, this refusal remained one of three surviving precepts. The others were nonsharing of the nuclear decision and faith in proportional deterrence, that is, deterrence by threats of nuclear reprisals whose damage would be disproportionate to an enemy's possible gain from attacking France. Nonintegration remains a deeply held principle of French defense policy, but it is less rigid than Bonn's renunciation of nuclear weapons. Indeed, the French government reportedly examined the integration option during 1987 before it was eventually rejected by Prime Minister Chirac, who feared a negative political backlash.[7] If one recalls the initial denunciation of Giscard d'Estaing's call for an "enlarged sanctuary" in 1976, and the subsequent metamorphosis during the next decade, eventual acceptance of reintegration cannot be rejected categorically.

French integration would be facilitated if, as Henry Kissinger and others propose, SACEUR were a European rather than an American. It would certainly be consistent with recent French support for European defense cooperation, as illustrated by the Franco-German Defense Council, the Franco-German brigade, and the WEU security platform. In fact, former National Assembly president Jacques Chaban-Delmas specifically recommended that France join a separate European command that would have equal status to the United States within NATO.[8] Similarly, the Socialist Party's executive bureau advocated multilateral units with the "understanding that such units could only be under another European commander."[9] Likewise, François Heisbourg argued that if U.S. troops were withdrawn, France should reconsider its refusal to defend a portion of Germany's eastern border. According to Heisbourg:

> If the 'hole' to fill were of limited size—equal or smaller than the 2nd Army Corps, for example, being about 50,000 men—and if some vacant infrastructures were available, it would be difficult for France to evade a West German request.[10]

Of course, reintegration would require substantial changes in French defense policy; for example, clarification of the First Army's ambiguous mission, which currently includes conducting the "deterrent maneuver" to evaluate an adversary's intentions prior to using prestrategic nuclear weapons as described in Chapter 3. Reintegration remains unlikely, but it may become possible in the foreseeable future and could erase a principal barrier to closer Franco-German cooperation.

In Britain, there are no givens. The United Kingdom lacks both France's broadly-based defense consensus and Germany's searing historical experience, which forged a distinctive German repudiation of power politics. There is a weak parallel between British and American adjustment to lost hegemony, but Britain has progressed further down this road, which the United States is just entering. There are neither domestic nor systemic influences which impel Britain toward or away from particular strategic alternatives. Britain is likely to continue along its present path: contracting defense commitments, maintenance of the independent deterrent, and increased but reluctant participation in European arrangements.

America's eventual action is not in doubt. Ultimately, hegemonic decline will compel a diminished American commitment to Europe. Two hegemonic states have dominated the modern international system: Great Britain, from the Napoleonic epoch until World War I, and the United States, from 1945 until the late 1970s.[11] Hegemony is maintained by a combination of economic and military capabilities. Of the two, economic power is the more essential, in part because military power is derived from it.[12] Notably, the one unifying theme that links the heterogenous American advocates of devolution is an appreciation of declining American *relative* power since 1945.

Chapter 4 discussed how, a full generation after Britain lost hegemonic status, postwar British leaders still clung to delusions of imperial grandeur. This failure to adjust obligations to diminished resources accelerated Britain's eventual decline and may have deepened the decline as well.[13] The United States stands in considerable danger of repeating Britain's error. Certainly the Reagan administration seemed oblivious that the price of creating a fleeting impression of renewal was to undermine permanently the indispensable foundation for sustained American power.

The United States has lived beyond its means for at least two decades. Initially, American profligacy was financed by an inflationary monetary policy (Johnson to Carter). When that approach failed, the United States shifted to massive foreign borrowing, which more than doubled the cumulative American budget deficit during the Reagan presidency and transformed the United States from the world's principal creditor to its largest debtor nation. The crash of world financial markets in October 1987 signaled the failure of that approach. As Robert Gilpin predicted prior to the collapse, unless the United States can

> borrow abroad to finance hegemony or domestic welfare, it will be required to lower domestic consumption, to decrease capital consumption further, and/or to reduce significantly its overseas military commitments in Western Europe, East Asia, or elsewhere.[14]

That time has come. The United States will retreat from increasingly onerous global responsibilities: the only question that remains is how quickly American adaptation to relative decline will occur.

There is no viable candidate to replace America's global leadership: Japan is too small and lacks military power, and the EC countries are too small individually and too fragmented collectively. Therefore, American leaders will serve both U.S. and allied interests by acting prudently to preserve a diminished but substantial version of global leadership. An attempt to postpone the inevitable will end by quickening the pace of America's decline.

In contrast, President Reagan continued to reassure Europeans that the status quo would endure. For example, his November 1987 broadcast to Europe asserted that

> the commitment of the United States to the Alliance and to the security of Europe . . . remains unshakable. Over 300,000 American servicemen with you on the continent and our steadfast nuclear guarantee, underscore this pledge. Those who worry that we will somehow drift apart or that deterrence has been weakened are mistaken on both counts.[15]

But the next president will not be obligated by these assurances: troop withdrawals could commence immediately, as pessimistic Europeans expect. Even Reagan administration officials, including Defense Secretary Frank Carlucci and former Navy Secretary James Webb, raised the possibility of troop withdrawals. Unlike Caspar Weinberger, Carlucci acknowledged from the outset that overwhelming budget deficits compelled reduced military spending. When faced with fiscal constraints, Carlucci's priority was to maintain readiness and sustainability. He acknowledged that this would require force reductions and might include small cuts in NATO forces.[16] Meanwhile, in January 1988 (shortly before his abrupt resignation) Navy Secretary Webb presented a National Press Club speech which echoed many of the themes discussed in Chapter 1: America's declining share of the global product, the full economic recovery of Western Europe and Japan, and the shift of American interests toward Asia and Latin America. Webb pointed out that during the preceding decade these regions accounted for 86 percent of "legal" immigration into the United States, and in 1986 Asian trade exceeded Atlantic trade by 75 percent. Arguing that America was "a maritime power" with global interests and that no other region was better equipped than Europe to provide for its own defense, Webb concluded that force reductions should emphasize Army and Air Force deployments in Western European, rather than naval personnel.[17]

Despite this pressure for change, there is deep-seated resistance to altering well-established US policy. There was advance speculation that *Discriminate Deterrence*, the January 1988 report of the Defense Department's Commission on Integrated Long-Term Strategy, would recommend European troop withdrawals. This was plausible, considering that Zbigniew Brzezinski and Henry Kissinger were among the thirteen commissioners, all former civilian and military national security officials. The report was controversial—especially its recommendation that "The Alliance should threaten to use nuclear weapons not as a link to a wider and more devastating war . . . but mainly as an instrument for denying success to the invading Soviet forces."[18] This view aroused a storm of protest from Europeans fearful of a limited nuclear war.[19] But despite the market crash, and Secretary Carlucci's support of force reductions, the report hewed to the orthodox line and did not explicitly recommend troop withdrawals. At approximately the same time, Senate Minority Leader Robert Dole was "unequivocal and emphatic" in assuring *Times* columnist Geoffrey Smith that "there would be no rundown of American troops in Europe."[20]

The likelihood of troop withdrawals was also reduced by prospects for new conventional arms control talks. During the 1970s, the beginning of the MBFR undercut support for Senator Mansfield's campaign to withdraw troops from Europe. In the 1980s, the Congress may be similarly reluctant to press for unilateral reductions as new conventional arms talks begin. Moreover, withdrawal of the INFs seems to demand strengthened rather than weakened conventional forces.

We are present at the collision of an immovable object with an irresistible force. According to Samuel Huntington, "no administration has seriously considered a reduction in American commitments in Western Europe, East Asia or the western hemisphere. These have been assumed to be fixed and unalterable."[21] Yet hegemonic decline is inevitable. Pierre Dommergues wrote that

> Great Britain, France, Spain, Rome, all knew an epoch when the cost of external wars and/or the maintenance of imperial order, even if it remained constant in absolute terms, became insupportable because the relative wealth of the empire contracted. Such is certainly the case of the United States today.[22]

This reality is increasingly apparent as the exceptional attention paid to historian Paul Kennedy's *The Rise and Fall of the Great Powers* illustrates. This volume documents how "Great Powers in relative decline instinctively respond by spending more on 'security,' and thereby divert potential resources from 'investment' and compound their long-term dilemma."[23] Devolution must eventually occur, but there is intense American inertia to surmount, so change may prove less imminent than many Europeans fear. Indeed, devolution may be postponed until the corrosive effect of excessive commitments upon the underpinnings of American power becomes even more overt and destructive.

"BALANCING" OR "BANDWAGONING"?

Europeans are increasingly aware that the status quo is changing. In the summer of 1987, *The Economist* wrote that "An America which is no longer much richer than Europe is unlikely to go on forever spending 7% of its GNP on defence, of which it uses a third or more for Europe's benefit, when most European countries spend only 3–4% of theirs."[24] In Germany, former SPD party manager Peter Glotz even advocated an arms control agreement to remove U.S. and Soviet forces from Western and Eastern Europe because, "It does not make much sense to wait until the U.S. Congress forces a president at some time to unilaterally reduce the presence of U.S. troops."[25]

This raises a fundamental question: as America reduces its contribution to European security, will Europeans assume a larger role? According to Richard Perle, the "key question" raised by the INF Treaty was whether Europeans would "abandon themselves once more to the illusions of detente or, on the contrary, have done with a dangerously comfortable dependence regarding the United States?"[26] The saliency of this choice will increase as America's European commitment diminishes, and the Federal Republic will largely decide the European answer.

German behavior is pivotal to prospects for a unified European defense, but Germany's response is complicated by her divided status, popular rejection of power politics, the absence of a national security consensus, and Germany's relatively precarious geopolitical position. There is little doubt that as Germany's confidence in the U.S. guarantee erodes, Bonn will be tempted to resolve its security concerns by *"bandwagoning"* with the East, that is through a policy of neutralism and accommodation with the Soviet Union. But in the end, German policy (supported by public opinion) is more likely to *balance* against the Soviet threat by reinforcing links to France and other Western European allies.

This may appear counterintuitive, especially to Americans who are deeply conditioned by views such as those John F. Kennedy expressed in Great Falls, Montana in September 1963 that the United States is "the keystone in the arch of freedom." So, "If the United States were to falter, the whole world . . . would inevitably begin to move toward the Communist bloc."[27] This bandwagoning assumption, that without the American shield Western allies would submit to Soviet domination, is a commonly held belief; it assumes that appeasement is the natural reaction when states are confronted with an external threat.[28]

In contrast, the balancing hypothesis builds upon a central assumption of balance-of-power theory—that whenever possible, nation-states act to prevent domination by other states. When a country bandwagons, it makes itself dependent upon the continued goodwill of the dominant state. This is a hazardous strategy. States are much more secure when they are self-reliant, so policymakers will opt for bandwagoning only if their state is too weak to balance or when allies are unavailable.[29]

But the Federal Republic is neither too weak nor too isolated: it is the fourth largest global economy, the most populous state in Western Europe, and already enjoys close security relations with all of the principal West European powers. Furthermore, German leaders are well aware of the dangers. Chancellor Kohl's "great objective" is to make the general direction of Germany's future policy "irreversible." "That means, among other things, that Rapallo is excluded."[30]

Former German defense minister (and now NATO secretary-general) Manfred Wörner argued that

> neither neutralism nor pacifism are options of German policy . . . [because] the road into the no–man's-land between East and West would end under Soviet hegemony. For us there is neither security nor freedom, nor a representation of our national interests, outside the Alliance, let alone against NATO.[31]

Or, as Chancellor Kohl expressed it, "The western integration of the Federal Republic of Germany is part of our *raison d'état.*"[32] According to Kohl, Bonn's integration with the West is a necessary condition for successful negotiations with the East, because it provides an essential base of power. Therefore, the FRG would probably balance with its Western European allies against the Warsaw Pact, even if the Soviets offered the package Bonn's allies most fear: reunification with neutrality.[33]

Furthermore, despite recurrent rumors, not even Gorbachev is likely to extend the unification/neutralism offer. The Soviet Union has as much reason as any Western European country to fear the destabilizing consequences that German unification could have upon the Central European balance of power. Although the population of a unified Germany would equal less than 25 percent of the Soviet Union's, its GNP would equal approximately 40 to 45 percent of the Soviet GNP, and doubtless more in the future unless Gorbachev's "restructuring" succeeds. Considering both the historical record and perceived threats to Soviet security from the United States, China, Japan, France, Britain, and others, Moscow is likely to fear not only a neutral Germany but even a unified Communist Germany.[34] As in the past, the Kremlin is more likely to embrace Marshal Zhukov's 1955 assertion that "You have your Germans and we have ours. It is much better this way."[35]

Of course, it is not *certain* that Europe will balance when the United States withdraws. Josef Joffe makes the bandwagoning argument and claims that

> the Soviet Union would not necessarily be the great federator but would loom as the paramount power—with the chance to use its overweening strength to play one West European state against another and to dictate the terms of its relationship to them all. *History, at any rate, does not assure us that the weak will always band together against the strong.*[36]

And more specifically, Joffe argues that Willy Brandt's *Ostpolitik* was "inspired" by Senator Mansfield's campaign to withdraw U.S. troops from Europe.[37] However, the process of normalizing East and West European relations that *Ostpolitik* initiated is now extolled by all German political parties, indeed throughout Western Europe. Even in the United States, where the Nixon administration initially distrusted *Ostpolitik* as a form of bandwagoning, Henry Kissinger eventually concluded that "the new link between Bonn and Moscow was not the result of a weak-kneed Chancellor Brandt but that it was a historical inevitability."[38] *Ostpolitik* can hardly be used to demonstrate that American disengagement would lead to "Finlandization."

In fact, despite American politicians' beliefs, history confirms an overwhelming tendency for states to balance. As Stephen Walt wrote, "every attempt to achieve hegemony in Europe since the Thirty Years War has been thwarted by a defensive coalition formed precisely for the purpose of defeating the potential hegemon."[39] And Zbigniew Brzezinski argued that "there is little reason to expect that a self-reliant France and a generally prosperous Western Europe would acquiesce in overt Soviet domination."[40]

There are excellent reasons rooted in *Realpolitik* why West Germany should opt for its Western anchor rather than entrusting its freedom to the Kremlin's good graces. But it must be recognized that Germany's choice to balance is less inevitable than France's or Britain's, because defending Germany against the Soviets is comparatively difficult and the perceived price of independence is higher.

Balancing and bandwagoning are ideals: real world nation-state behavior is more complex and involves combinations which are predominately one or the other. The geography, history, political culture, and power of Germany differs from that of France, Britain, or the United States. Germany's approach to balancing will reflect these differences. For example, the British Labour Party's defense program isolated it from the political mainstream (despite some resonance from the Liberals), while the SPD and Green agendas influenced not only the FDP but even the CDU. The political culture of the Federal Republic is strikingly different from that of France or the United States, and this difference will translate into a more nuanced and less blatant form of balancing.

FRANCE AND GERMANY

According to Jacques Chirac, France and Germany now confront "the same [question] General de Gaulle tried unsuccessfully to put to his principal allies: how to act so Europeans can, in the context of their alliance with the United States, take charge of their destiny."[41] There has been concrete progress toward this goal in recent years. Even in 1982, when the Elysée Treaty's defense component was belatedly implemented, virtually no one foresaw the subsequent achievements: French soldiers serving under a German commander during exercises deep within the FRG; a Defense Council established to harmonize military policy and operational plans; a permanent bilateral brigade serving under rotating French and German commanders; arms cooperation revitalized by the multibillion dollar helicopter program; and a revolution in French military doctrine, as François Mitterrand and Jacques Chirac competed to reshape French policy concerning tactical nuclear weapons and the automaticity of French participation in Germany's forward defense.

Especially in Britain and Germany, some observers disparage the alleged superficiality of Franco-German _rapprochement_. They dismiss Franco-German cooperation as a series of dramatic but ultimately empty gestures, what one German defense industry executive characterized as "purely symbolic bullshit."[42] This criticism has some substance, for the basic structure of European defense is unaltered. As _The Economist_ editorialized concerning the brigade and the Defense Council, "so far they will not add a man or a franc to Europe's defense."[43] The United States remains the ultimate guarantor, and it is Britain, not France, that continues to make the larger ongoing contribution to Central European defense. But, although nothing fundamental has yet changed, Bonn and Paris are establishing the essential foundation for change. De Gaulle's error was to pursue grand initiatives such as the Elysée Treaty and the Fouchet Plan without preparing the political terrain. The result was worse than failure: a residue of recriminations and the ossification of the European system for a generation. But now Paris is pursuing a policy of "small steps" which, above all, avoids forcing Bonn to choose between Europe and America.[44]

Criticism of Franco-German cooperation also overlooks the political import of symbolic acts. Prime Minister Thatcher (like Jacques Chirac) disdains symbolic gestures such as Chancellor Kohl and President Mitterrand joining hands on the Verdun battlefield in 1984, and such gestures are absent from Anglo-French and Anglo-German relations. But that gesture graphically dramatized reconciliation between the nations after generations of hostility and warfare. Verdun was an ideal choice. World War II sites, for example, Oradour-sur-Glane, resound with Nazi barbarism, and even more than President Reagan's visit to the Bitburg cemetery, a visit there would inevitably divide rather than unite. Verdun was the perfect choice to symbolize reconciliation, for it was both a Franco-Prussian and First World War battlefield which has special significance because of the 1916 battle. In December 1915, Chief of the General Staff Erich von Falkenhayn prepared a memorandum to the Kaiser describing the forthcoming battle as attacking

> objectives for the retention of which the French General Staff would be compelled to throw in every man they have. If they do so _the forces of France will bleed to death_—as there can be no question of a voluntary withdrawal—whether we reach our goal or not.[45]

Falkenhayn's prediction was only half right. In the end, both nations nearly bled to death, suffering combined losses of 420,000 killed and

800,000 gassed or wounded in that single battle.[46] There could not be a better site than Verdun to memorialize a commitment to a wholly new era in Franco-German history.

These accomplishments were barely conceivable in the recent past, which is evidence of their significance. Considering this impressive headway, prospects for future progress should not be underrated, even though the new Defense Council confronts major obstacles to Franco-German defense cooperation. A principal impediment is Bonn's continued preference for its American guarantor and Paris' detachment from the Western Alliance. Bonn and Paris also have divergent perceptions of East-West relations and arms control, which many Germans consider the essence of security policy but which the French tend to view with considerable skepticism. Finally, with the nonbelligerency issue resolved, nuclear policy remains the true Gordian knot of Franco-German relations—especially the implications of French prestrategic forces and the possibility of French extended deterrence.

Alfred Grosser describes "a French ambition to exercise global responsibilities," and considering its size, France is unusually preoccupied with national greatness.[47] In 1984 L'Express reported survey results from several countries (including the United States, Japan, Brazil, the FRG, Britain, and Spain) reporting the degree to which France was perceived as "a great, a medium, or a small power," and respondents were asked where France ranked in importance compared to other European states.[48] More recently, the French became obsessed with national "decline," and a 1987 poll revealed that 73 percent (compared to 23 percent) of the French public would make personal sacrifices "so France remains a great world economic power." However, only 40 percent (compared to 52 percent) would sacrifice to make France a global military power.[49]

French aspirations for greatness reinforce Franco-German cooperation. Germany lacks comparable aspirations, but with only 4 percent of the global product, France cannot fulfill her dreams alone.[50] She needs the Federal Republic. As Stanley Hoffmann recognized many years ago, "It is through Europe that France can still pretend to a certain grandeur."[51] Or, as Paul-Jean Franceschini asserted, less tactfully, "Without Germany solidly fastened to her, France is nothing more than an ambition without means."[52]

When combined, France and Germany constitute 9.5 percent of the global product (close to the Soviet Union with 13 percent and Japan with 11 percent), while the whole EC produces 20 percent.[53] Therefore, by influencing Europe, or at least the Franco-German tandem, France obtains access to the resources required to fulfill aspirations such as EUREKA and the European space program, which were discussed in Chapter 5.

But many Germans, who already resent being cast as paymasters for the European Community, have no enthusiasm for a division of labor which permits Paris to define the goals and requirements (for example, the Helios surveillance satellite) while Bonn pays the bills. This relationship is inherently unequal, and according to Francophobes such as *Der Spiegel* publisher Rudolf Augstein, the Federal Republic is expected to make concrete economic concessions while France reciprocates with hollow pledges of security.[54]

There are, in fact, two perceptions of French attitudes toward German power. One argues that "The French no longer fear that the Bundeswehr will become too strong, but to the contrary that it will not be strong enough. France not only has an interest that a solid 'glacis' exist east of the Rhine but equally that it be in the hands of a militarily powerful ally."[55] The second maintains that "As Giscard d'Estaing reminded the French National Assembly in 1976, the French have always considered it important for the military balance in Europe that their own forces should never be inferior to those of the Federal Republic."[56] Along these lines, Josef Joffe wrote that

> treaties of friendship and cultural summits, joint military manoeuvres, and the growing ramifications between ministerial bureaucracies, however, cannot disguise the fact that the official and semi-official France views its new friends with the keen eye of skepticism and recurrent apprehensiveness.[57]

The author's assessment of current thinking is that the French are much less worried that Germany will prove too strong than that she will prove too weak. Moreover, the mutual fears that the other partner might attempt some unilateral advantage, which are an undeniable characteristic of the Franco-German relationship, are actually less intense between France and Germany than between other pairs of European allies.

"TRIUMVIRATE"

At the rhetorical level, all European governments support increased European power and unity, but there is also a high level of mutual distrust. France fears Germany's economic power, the Benelux countries fear domination by their larger neighbors, the Germans fear French political hegemony, and Britain and Italy fear Franco-German condominium.

France and Germany are the dominant members of the European Community and the essential core of a strengthened European pillar. This predominant status derives from their geographical positions, their economic and military power, and their increasingly intimate bilateral relationship. Not surprisingly, their European partners fear and resent Franco-German preeminence. Both Britain and Italy are fearful that NATO could be undermined by Franco-German bilateralism. For example, Margaret Thatcher cautioned against "sub-structures which could sap the Atlantic Alliance."[58] And while she acknowledged that bilateral military cooperation "has a useful role to play, whether between France and Germany or between France and Great Britain," this was true, she argued, only if, "it has the clear and demonstrable effect of reinforcing NATO and not to erode or sap its unity."[59] According to Mrs. Thatcher, "military cooperation should be within the framework of NATO and enhance its efficiency—otherwise it could undermine it."[60] She also questioned whether the Franco-German brigade served any purpose, and compared it negatively to Britain's contribution to "the front line defense elbow to elbow with our stalwart allies."[61]

Italy shares London's fear that the Alliance might be weakened, and Foreign Minister Giulio Andreotti warned that unilateral European efforts "risk encouraging some Americans who want to drastically reduce their role in Europe."[62] According to Andreotti, in the defense sphere, "an autonomous European policy would be an error."[63]

This concern with NATO's well-being is sincere and legitimate, but other factors also impinge. As the third and fourth-ranking European powers, British and Italian self-esteem is particularly sensitive to perceived slights or evidence of marginalization. In addition, much of Britain's influence derives from the close Anglo-American relationship, and it would undoubtedly suffer if NATO's importance declined.

France and Germany deny any intention to exclude or to dominate. Chancellor Kohl argued that Franco-German cooperation "is directed against no one and excludes no one."[64] He also expressed some irritation that "If Franco-German relations are good our partners suspect us of wishing to create a *directoire*. If our relations are not good, we are accused of fleeing our historic obligations." Kohl also observed that the history of recent decades demonstrates "that if Paris and Bonn don't budge nothing moves in Europe."[65]

President Mitterrand expressed similar assurances. During the celebration of the Elysée Treaty's twenty-fifth anniversary, he explicitly asserted that "There is no Franco-German axis. There is, on the other hand, a strong will in Paris and in Bonn to join our ambitions and our means to advance European unity."[66] And earlier, at Naples, Mitterrand asserted that France and Germany "will not create European defense; we will do it with those that want it, but who wants it? If one wishes it, one must say so."[67] Mitterrand also reiterated his hope that Italy and Spain would eventually join the Franco-German initiatives, although he also rued the complexity even of bilateral Franco-German relations.[68]

These efforts to mollify their European partners were somewhat ritualistic, and at a deeper level both countries considered Britain's criticisms misguided. The French faulted London's failure to appreciate how Franco-German cooperation helped to anchor the Federal Republic more firmly to the West, and the Germans believed their bilateral links to France served the common goal of reinforcing France's ties to NATO.[69] Bonn also reproached London, and especially Prime Minister Thatcher, for failing to match France's empathy with Germany's security concerns.[70]

These tensions illustrate the lack of cohesion and leadership that bedevil efforts to strengthen the European Pillar. While American leadership has not immunized NATO from recurrent crises, Philip Towle is clearly correct to argue that "An alliance or federation without the USA would be even more difficult to hold together. The Federal Republic of Germany (FRG), Italy, France and Britain would be rivals for the dominant position while the other states would resent their predominance."[71] And, as The Economist argued, there is no obvious leader:

> France has the best nuclear technology, West Germany has the strongest economy. Neither seems ready to accept the other's leadership, or to create a Europe in which 'French' and 'German' are no longer words that mean much. The same applies, perhaps even more strongly, to Britain.[72]

Nearly everyone talks of "Europe," but "Europe" does not exist and may never exist. Europe is merely shorthand for some conglomeration of sovereign states: twelve in the EC and seven in the WEU.

Although France and Germany are the essential nucleus of the European Pillar, and likely to be the most active and influential participants, a Franco-German-British triumvirate could eventually evolve. In fact, a triumvirate could be a necessary condition for British participation. There is already some evidence of an embryonic "European triangle," as William Wallace labeled it, which has emerged "on a number of occasions in the last five years."[73] There was, for example, a Paris meeting of the three defense ministers in September 1983; another was scheduled for London in May 1984 until Italy forestalled it. In December 1986 George Shultz met his British, French, and German counterparts in London, and after Reykjavik an informal defense committee emerged composed of key advisers to Thatcher, Kohl, Mitterrand, and Chirac.

Historically, the stimulus for European defense cooperation has been negative: anti-German in the case of the WEU and anti-Soviet in NATO's case. This pattern persists; all of the principal participants are reacting to various negative stimuli including American withdrawal (Germany), German neutralism (France), or regional isolation (United Kingdom). But all three countries are strongly cross-pressured. For example, Germany tries to cultivate the Franco-German relationship as a hedge against U.S. abandonment without accelerating the process of American disengagement. Germany is unlikely to jump into French arms until pushed from the American nest, so fears of abandonment by the United States are a useful catalyst for European integration. The dilemma is how to create a genuine European Pillar *within* the Alliance without destroying the Alliance in the process. As André Giraud said, "we're facing a house of cards that we have to rearrange without collapsing the original structure."[74]

NEXT STEPS

In 1985, NATO-wide military expenditures equaled 5.5 percent of combined GDP: 6.9 percent for the United States and 3.5 percent with the United Staters excluded.[75] Considering the relative affluence of Japan, Western Europe, and the United States, there is no obvious reason why America's defense spending should be more than six times larger than Japan's nor approximately twice that of the Federal Republic. This is especially so considering that America is *more* physically secure than her allies. Many Europeans assert that the United States enjoys the advantages of superpower status, but these advantages are rarely specified and remain invisible to most Americans. For example, a study of 120 members of Washington's "foreign policy elite," found that only 2 percent agreed that the United States derived most of the benefits from the Atlantic alliance: 70 percent thought benefits were shared equally between

Europe and America, and 29 percent believed that Europe reaped most of the benefits.[76]

From the American perspective, the differential level of burden looks like a residual "free rider" problem inherited from the era of American hegemony, not an equitable division of the collective burden. Fortunately, it is no longer Americans alone who believe that this situation must change. In early 1988, *The Times* editorialized that "This is a serious disparity. Americans cannot be expected to bear this burden indefinitely, however much their presence in Western Europe assures them of their status as a superpower."[77] And following the October 1987 stock market crash, Josef Joffe wrote in the *Süddeutsche Zeitung* that it is difficult to justify an international economy in which the two most successful economies pay 1 percent and 3 percent of GNP for defense, while the United States pays over 6.5 percent and Britain 5 percent.[78]

NATO (and Japan) should strive to achieve an equivalent level of defense spending, for example, 5.5 percent of GNP, throughout the alliance. Calculations should include such pertinent but typically invisible costs as conscription and military exercises which would erase much of the apparent differential between British, French, and German spending. The failure to achieve NATO's goal of 3 percent increases in inflation-adjusted defense expenditures demonstrated the extreme difficulty of increasing European military spending. But the contention that Europe cannot or will not spend more, so the United States must, is no longer defensible. The United States is no more capable of allocating 6.5 percent of GNP to defense than Germany, France or Britain. The United States has the largest budget deficit, the least generous social welfare system, and the greatest public aversion to high taxation.[79] Considering Europe's very large stake in avoiding the self-destruction of the American economy, it must confront the bitter reality that the United States is no longer Europe's rich uncle.

Germany, in particular, has a lengthy list of reasons why the status quo must remain intact: (1) a German nuclear deterrent force is out of the question; (2) French and British guarantees are rejected as inherently less credible than American commitments; (3) conventional defense is prohibitively expensive (both financially and demographically) and risks a limited European war; (4) forward defense is inviolable; (5) counterattacks against second-echelon WTO forces are "too offensive"; (6) tank barriers along the inter-German border are politically unacceptable because they would institutionalize Germany's divided status. But international affairs are dynamic, not static. America's international position has changed fundamentally during the four decades of the Atlantic Alliance, and these changes must be acknowledged, even by the Europeans.

The traditional division of military responsibilities is one example. American defense policy has consistently assumed that the United States should provide the nuclear deterrent while Europe contributed the bulk of the forces.[80] This approach was never totally successful because each party provided the component it valued less. As Morton Halperin has written:

> Telling American allies that they should increase their conventional capability so that the United States can reduce its reliance on nuclear weapons is like telling young children that if they eat their vegetables they will not be given any dessert. Allies in Europe do not want to reduce reliance on nuclear devices.[81]

European governments always feared that too large a conventional capability would either make possible a reprise of World War II or tempt American withdrawal because Europe appeared adequately defended. This created a bizarre situation. Europeans, who most valued a policy of "non-war" through nuclear deterrence, were principally responsible for conventional deterrence, and Americans, who wanted a strengthened conventional "firebreak" between European and central war, were responsible for the nuclear deterrent.

The incongruities of this strategy were magnified as mutual vulnerability eroded the credibility of extended deterrence. Now that the United States can no longer extend nuclear deterrence either safely or credibly, Europeans must assume this responsibility and choose their preferred blend of nuclear and conventional capabilities.

Although America's global responsibilities and fiscal constraints will compel some reduction of European troop deployments, and Europeans should assume overall command of NATO forces as Henry Kissinger has recommended, the United States should continue to make a significant contribution to Europe's conventional defense. If Alliance responsibilities are realigned, and NATO becomes more European-centered, French reintegration may become possible.

Some experts fear that the United States would withdraw troops from Europe if the nuclear umbrella were removed. In fact, at the 1988 Wehrkunde conference in Munich, Secretary Carlucci said that if Europe were denuclearized he would "wonder if we should maintain our troops here."[82] Richard Perle went further, saying that unless the short-range tactical nuclear weapons which will remain following the INF withdrawals were modernized, he did not "know how we could in good conscience leave 325,000 American troops in Europe hopelessly unprotected."[83] François Heisbourg said of the triple option that the German public wanted both "the denuclearization of Europe and the 300,000 American GIs. They should know that 'no nukes is no troops'—without atomic weapons the Americans will not remain."[84]

Elimination of all land-based nuclear weapons from Europe would revolutionize Western European security, but neither Bonn nor any other NATO government advocates this option, which is vehemently opposed by the United States, France, and Britain. Domestic German politics may preclude replacing the obsolescent eighty-eight Lance missiles as well as other TNF modernizations approved at Montebello in 1983, but the actual denuclearization of NATO-Europe is unlikely, and there is no reason why U.S. troops deployed in Europe should not retain nuclear arms.

There is also concern that the French or British might use their nuclear weapons and involve American forces in a limited nuclear war, against Washington's wishes. Of course, that threat already exists, for example, if France chose to employ its prestrategic weapons. Moreover, this entails a slight risk that 100,000 or 200,000 American combatants might become involved in a limited nuclear war. However abhorrent, this danger is insignificant when compared to the risks of Flexible Response, which Europeans interpret as America's promise to unleash global nuclear warfare if Europe is attacked. How can the option of placing American troops in Europe with fewer tactical nuclear weapons be too risky when it is manifestly less dangerous to American interests than current declaratory policy?

The United States must also address its acceptance of an altered Atlantic relationship. As the United States disengages, American influence will diminish, and Europe will inevitably pursue a more independent course. Euro-American differences are endemic, and include divergent attitudes toward the Soviet threat, economic and political-military policies in the Third World, arms control, and international economic policy. These perennial issues of conflict will probably endure between Europe and America but also within Europe, as illustrated by the disputes over terrorism, the proper degree of stimulation of the FRG economy, and the "triple zero option." American leaders claim to support European unification, but they also prefer to deal with docile allies. Unfortunately, less tidy decision making is an inevitable consequence of diminished hegemony and the shift to a more decentralized security system.[85]

CONCLUSION

In the future, as in the past, European defense cooperation will be strongly influenced by American behavior. This was true of the EDC and the Paris Accords, which were necessitated by Washington's demand for German rearmament to confront the Soviet threat. It continued through the WEU's reactivation, EUREKA, and the European security platform which responded to SDI, Reykjavik, double zero, and the prospect of American disengagement. In fact, shifts in American behavior are correlated with what Alfred Cahen called the "intermittence of the European reflex."[86]

This pattern is likely to continue. While the United States maintains a large conventional troop presence in Europe and the nuclear guarantee (however incredible), Germany and Britain will adhere tightly to their Atlantic partner, and France will cling to the remaining shreds of national autonomy. But European behavior will alter as the United States disengages. As a first step, geopolitical imperatives and existing patterns of political and military cooperation could produce a variant of the Franco-German defense community envisioned by former Chancellor Schmidt. This is contingent upon German balancing, but if Bonn is prepared to deepen the Franco-German partnership, Paris will certainly respond. The Franco-German core could then broaden to encompass a Franco-German-British triangle, probably within the WEU, which may expand to include Iberia and perhaps a portion of Scandinavia.

It is impossible to predict the precise pattern of future events, but the broad outlines are quite distinct. The European security system is evolving in two directions: toward American disengagement and toward European unification. Both processes remain inchoate, but both are likely to persist. Most Europeans fear American disengagement, but many consider it a prerequisite for European unity. With both bilateral and multilateral institutions in place, and public and official support for European defense cooperation, the political environment has never been brighter for new European initiatives.

NOTES

1. François Mitterrand, *Réflexions sur la politique extérieure de la France: Introduction à vingt-cinq discours (1981–1985)* (Paris: Fayard, 1986), p. 96.

2. See André Glucksmann, *La force du vertige* (Paris: Bernard Grasset, 1983), pp. 137–38 and André Fontaine, "Un coup de jeune pour l'Europe? II. Où l'on reparle de défense," *Le Monde*, 31 May 1984.

3. Anne-Marie Le Gloannec, "Les Allemands et la dissuasion française ou les ambiguïtés franco-allemandes," in Karl Kaiser and Pierre Lellouche, eds., *Le couple franco-allemand et la défense de l'Europe* (Paris: Economica, 1986), pp. 91–92.

4. François Gorand (pseud.), "Les Européens et la politique Européenne de défense," *Politique étrangère* (Winter 1984): 947.

5. However, one rare exception argues that "The guarantee of American nuclear protection, or some other equivalent one, is the condition for the future renunciation of the national nuclear option by the FRG." Kurt J. Lauk, *Die nuklearen Optionen der Bundesrepublik Deutschland* (Berlin: Duncker & Humblot, 1979), p. 14.

6. Quoted in Luc Rosenzweig and Daniel Vernet, "Le chancelier Kohl expose au <<Monde>> sa conception de la sécurité européenne," *Le Monde*, 20 January 1988.

7. See Jean-Paul Pigasse, "Libres propos," *L'Express*, 13 November 1987.

8. See Harry Anderson et al., "The New French Connection," *Newsweek*, 1 February 1988.

9. See Parti Socialiste, *Réflexions sur la sécurité européenne* (Paris: Parti Socialiste, October 1987), p. 3.

10. François Heisbourg, "Défense Française: L'impossible statu quo," *Politique internationale* (Summer 1987): 148.

11. Robert Gilpin dates the end of American economic hegemony from October 1979, when Bonn refused to support the dollar and forced the Carter administration to pursue a restrictive monetary policy. "This was the first time in the postwar era that the United States made a major change in its domestic economic policy in response to foreign pressure." Robert Gilpin, *The Political Economy of International Relations* (Princeton: Princeton University Press, 1987), p. 332.

12. See Gilpin, *The Political Economy*, p. 76, and Robert O. Keohane, *After Hegemony: Cooperation and Discord in the World Political Economy* (Princeton: Princeton University Press, 1984), p. 32.

13. As Stephen Blank wrote:

    Eventually, although not until the second half of the 1960s, British political leaders came to see that the international role Britain had sought to play since

1945 was beyond its capacity. By then, however, enormous damage had been inflicted on the domestic economy. Moreover, largely because of the retardation of economic growth that had been the result of these earlier policies, Britain was in a poor position to cope effectively with the new challenges of the 1970s, domestic and international.

Stephen Blank, "Britain: The Politics of Foreign Economic Policy, the Domestic Economy, and the Problem of Pluralistic Stagnation," in Peter J. Katzenstein, ed., *Between Power and Plenty: Foreign Economic Policies of Advanced Industrial States* (Madison: The University of Wisconsin Press, 1978), p. 91.

14. Gilpin, *The Political Economy*, p. 351.
15. President Ronald Reagan, "Remarks by the President to Worldnet," (Washington, DC: Office of the White House Press Secretary, November 3, 1987), pp. 4–5.
16. According to *Defense Daily*, Defense Secretary Carlucci noted that "America's NATO contribution might have to be sacrificed slightly." "Technology R&D Supported," *Defense Daily*, 26 January 1988. Carlucci also described European force levels as not "immutable." See "US troops pullout hint," *The Times* (London), 1 December 1987.
17. Webb said that "An improved situation in Europe, absent a stand-down of conventional forces taken out of that theater, may well increase rather than decrease Soviet pressure in other areas." James H. Webb, Jr., remarks at the National Press Club, January 13, 1988; broadcast by National Public Radio. Also see Richard Halloran, "Navy Secretary Suggests Forces in Europe Be Cut," *The New York Times*, 14 January 1988.
18. The Commission on Integrated Long-Term Strategy, *Discriminate Deterrence* (Washington, D.C.: U.S. Government Printing Office, January 1988), p. 30.
19. Michael Howard, François de Rose, and Karl Kaiser warned of Europe becoming "a zone of guaranteed limited nuclear war." Michael Howard, François de Rose, and Karl Kaiser, "Battleground Europe," *The Times* (London), 10 February 1988, p. 10. German Defense Ministry official Lothar Rühl cautioned against a "limited nuclear war in Europe"; see "Christian Democrats Fear U.S. Betrayal," *Insight*, 15 February 1988 (reprinted from *Süddeutsche Zeitung*). Also see Michael Evans, "Europe cool on Pentagon high-tech arms report," *The Times* (London), 13 January 1988.
20. Geoffrey Smith, *The Times* (London), 17 November 1987. It is noteworthy, however, that Senator Dole opened his campaign for the 1988 Republican presidential nomination by arguing that "It's high time for those who owe their own security to America's military might to assume their rightful role, and bear their rightful burden in the defense of our common

interests." Quoted in Bernard Weintraub, "Dole Will Seek Presidential Nomination," *The New York Times*, 10 November 1987.

21. Samuel P. Huntington, "Coping With the Lippmann Gap," *Foreign Affairs* (1988): 457.

22. Pierre Dommergues, "L'Amérique s'interroge sur la meilleure façon de gérer son déclin," *Le Monde Diplomatique* 34 (October 1987): 20.

23. Paul Kennedy, *The Rise and Fall of the Great Powers: Economic Change and Military Conflict from 1500 to 2000* (New York: Random House, 1987), p. xxiii. Also see Robert Gilpin, *War & Change in World Politics* (New York: Cambridge University Press, 1981), pp. 156–85.

24. "Europe's braver colours," *The Economist*, 11 July 1987.

25. *Insight*, 5 October 1987.

26. Richard Perle, "N'abusez pas du parapluie américain," *L'Express*, 2 October 1987.

27. Quoted in Seyom Brown, *The Faces of Change: Constancy and Change in United States Foreign Policy From Truman to Johnson* (New York: Columbia University Press, 1968), p. 217.

28. The most comprehensive analysis of balancing and bandwagoning is contained in Stephen M. Walt, *The Origins of Alliances* (Ithaca: Cornell University Press, 1987); also see Stephen M. Walt, "Alliance Formation and the Balance of World Power," *International Security* 9 (Spring 1985): 3–43 and Kenneth N. Waltz, *Theory of International Politics* (Reading, MA: Addison-Wesley, 1979), pp. 125–28.

29. See Walt, *The Origins of Alliances*, pp. 29–31.

30. Quoted in Rosenzweig and Vernet, "Le chancelier Kohl expose." The Rapallo Treaty (1922) between Germany and the Soviet Union is a symbol for Germany siding with the East rather than the West.

31. Manfred Wörner, "Security in the 1990s," Speech to the Chicago Council on Foreign Relations, October 30, 1987.

32. Quoted in Johann Georg Reismüller, "A re-united Germany cannot be ruled out forever, says Chancellor Kohl," *The German Tribune*, 13 December 1987 (translated from *Frankfurter Allgemeine Zeitung*, 30 November 1987). Kohl also described European integration as "the second priority field for Bonn's foreign policy" after German-American relations, and he told *Le Monde* that "Liberty is more important than unity. . . . The Federal Republic of Germany is not for sale." Quoted in Rosenzweig and Vernet, "Le chancelier Kohl."

33. Jean-Pierre Chevènement acknowledged that substantial West German support exists for a united but neutral country. But in his opinion

   such an evolution would maintain Germany without defense and would create a zone of fragility and destabilization in Central Europe. Furthermore, any attempt to create a European Europe, that is to say independent from both the

United States as well as the USSR, would be indefinitely postponed. No, this is not a good step: Germany cannot reasonably found its security on the perpetual benevolence of the USSR, be it that of Mr. Gorbachev, any more than on American protection.

Quoted in Jacques Amalric and Jean-Louis Andréani, "M. Chevènement: il faut une volonté politique franco-allemande," *Le Monde*, 24 September 1987.

34. On the potential threat to the Soviet Union of a Communist Germany, see Richard Rosecrance, *The Rise of the Trading State: Commerce and Conquest in the Modern World* (New York: Basic Books, 1986), p. 36.

35. Quoted in Ronald Steel, *Pax Americana*, revised edition (New York: Viking Press, 1970), p. 103.

36. Josef Joffe, *The Limited Partnership: Europe, the United States, and the Burdens of Alliance* (Cambridge: Ballinger, 1987), p. 188 (emphasis added). Joffe also argues that "After WWII, Europe coalesced *because* it was secure not to safeguard security," p. 187.

37. See Joffe, *The Limited Partnership*, p. 189.

38. Henry Brandon, *The Retreat of American Power* (New York: Dell, 1974), p. 77.

39. Walt, *The Origins of Alliances*, p. 29.

40. Zbigniew Brzezinski, *Game Plan: A Geostrategic Framework for the Conduct of the U.S.-Soviet Contest* (Boston: The Atlantic Monthly Press, 1986), p. 204. According to Melvyn Krauss, "the removal of U.S. subsidies can be expected to increase, not decrease, European defense efforts on its own behalf." Melvyn Krauss, *How NATO Weakens the West* (New York: Simon & Schuster, 1986), p. 37.

41. Michel Colomès (interviewer), "Défense: la ligne Chirac," *Le Point*, 5 October 1987.

42. Quoted in David G. Morrison, "NATO Has Pre-Treaty Tremors," *National Journal*, 28 November 1987. Yves Boyer has stated that "when you leave the world of declarations and enter the world of action, I see very little progress and little prospect of real cooperation." Quoted in *Insight*, 31 August 1987. According to West Germany's commissioner for Franco-German cultural affairs, Lothar Späth, cooperation between the two countries consists primarily of friendly meetings between the countries' leaders rather than of substantive relationships. See *The Week in Germany*, 8 May 1987.

43. "It takes two to decouple," *The Economist*, 28 November 1987.

44. See Pascal Boniface and François Heisbourg, *La puce, les hommes et la bombe: l'Europe face aux nouveaux défis technologiques et militaires* (Paris: Hachette, 1986), pp. 253–55.

45. Quoted in Alistair Horne, *The Price of Glory: Verdun 1916* (New York: Penguin Books, 1964), p. 44 (emphasis added).

46. See Horne, *The Price of Glory*, p. 328.

47. Alfred Grosser, "Un optimisme mesuré mais légitime," *Le Monde*, 23 January 1988.

48. See *L'Express*, 3 February 1984.

49. See Georges Valance, "Enquête sur le déclin de la France," *Le Point*, 22 June 1987. The survey was conducted by Ipsos between June 11–12, 1987; the sample equaled 800 respondents aged fifteen and older.

50. See *Le Point*, 11 January 1988.

51. Quoted in Anthony Hartley, "The British Bomb," *Survival* 6 (July/August 1964): 174.

52. Quoted in Ingo Kolboom, "La politique de sécurité de la France: un point de vue allemand," in Karl Kaiser and Pierre Lellouche, eds., *Le couple franco-allemand et la défense de l'Europe* (Paris: Economica, 1986), p. 71.

53. See *Le Point*, 11 January 1988.

54. See Rudolf Augstein, "'Warnschläge, präzise, wirksam und begrenzt,'" *Der Spiegel*, 21 December 1987.

55. Ingo Kolboom and Robert Picht, "Paris, Bonn, l'Europe," *Documents: Revue des questions allemandes* 40 (February 1985): 10.

56. Christopher Coker, *A Nation in Retreat: Britain's Defence Commitment* (London: Brassey's Defence Publishers, 1986), p. 62. And, of course, Giscard d'Estaing is a Germanophile.

57. Josef Joffe, "The ambivalent relationship: France and the 'mysterious Germans,'" *The German Tribune*, 9 November 1986 (translated from *Süddeutsche Zeitung*, 29 October 1986).

58. "Paris-Bonn and Co?" *Le Monde*, 28 November 1987.

59. "Un <<tandem>> qui souvent irrite ou inquiète . . ." *Le Monde*, 21 January 1988. Similarly, Defense Secretary Carlucci said Franco-German cooperation was "highly desirable to the extent that it aimed to reinforce the Atlantic Alliance rather than weakening it." "Le secrétaire américain à la défense a interrogé M. Mitterrand sur ses idées en matière de dissuasion nucléaire," *Le Monde*, 13 January 1988.

60. Quoted in Howell Raines, "Britain and France Stay at Odds On Economic and Defense Policy," *The New York Times*, 30 January 1988.

61. Quoted in "Thatcher: la défense de l'Europe, c'est d'abord l'OTAN," *L'Express*, 5 February 1988. She asked the interviewers, "What exactly is this Franco-German brigade for?"

62. Quoted in Harry Anderson, et al., "The New French Connection," *Newsweek*, 1 February 1988.

63. "Un <<tandem>> qui souvent irrite ou inquiète. . ." *Le Monde*, 21 January 1988.

64. "Paris-Bonn and Co?"

65. "Un entretien avec le chancelier Kohl," *Le Monde*, 20 January 1988.

66. "<<Il n'y a pas d'axe franco-allemand>>, déclare le président de la République," *Le Monde*, 24–25 January 1988.

67. "Paris-Bonn and Co?"

68. See Claire Tréan, "MM. Mitterrand et Goria n'ont pu surmonter toutes
les divergences sur les finances de la défense européennes," *Le Monde*,
28 November 1987.

69. In fact, during a *L'Express* interview, Prime Minister Thatcher said explicitly that the reintegration of France into NATO was "the path to follow."
Quoted in "Thatcher: la défense de l'Europe."

70. See Richard Owen, "West German plea to Thatcher for defence sympathy," *The Times* (London), 12 December 1987.

71. Philip Towle, *Europe Without America: Could We Defend Ourselves?*
Occasional Paper No. 5 (London: Institute for European Defence and
Strategic Studies, 1983), p. 13.

72. "If NATO became WETO," *The Economist*, 21 March 1987.

73. William Wallace, "Shifts in British Defence Policy," in John Roper, ed.,
The Future of British Defence Policy (Aldershot: Gower, 1985), p. 112.

74. Quoted in Tim Carrington, "Kohl Stance on Nuclear Arms Intensifies
Allied Concern About European Defense," *The Wall Street Journal*, 8
February 1988.

75. See Caspar W. Weinberger, Secretary of Defense, *Report on Allied Contributions to the Common Defense: A Report to the United States Congress* (Washington, D.C.: U.S. Department of Defense, April 1987), p.
72.

76. See Bärd Bredrup Knudsen, "From Ideology to Foreign Policy 'Schools
of Thought' to Policy Preferences: American Foreign Policy Elites and
Europe." Paper presented at the International Studies Association Annual
Convention, Washington, D.C., March 1985, p. 9. Knudsen interviewed
between November 1981 and April 1983. The interviewees came from
the State Department, the Defense Department, the U.S. Senate, "think
tanks," and academe.
    The advantages of economic dominance are more apparent. One privi-
lege is the option of borrowing one's own currency, whose value can be
manipulated, from foreigners. Japanese lenders who loaned the U.S. dollars in the mid-1980s will experience very large exchange rate losses if
they reconvert to yen.

77. "Security at a price," *The Times* (London), 13 January 1988.

78. See Josef Joffe, "Germany: a time for action and an end to the myth
about the political dwarf," *The German Tribune*, 20 December 1987
(translated from *Süddeutsche Zeitung*, 5 December 1987).

79. For a comparison of American and European social welfare programs,
see David P. Calleo, *Beyond American Hegemony: The Future of the
Western Alliance* (New York: Basic Books, 1987), pp. 109–13. Also see

Eric Willenz, "Why Europe Needs the Welfare State," *Foreign Policy* (Summer 1986): 88–107.

80. For example, a recent report of the Democratic Leadership Council asserts that

the United States should do what it does best, providing, for example, the nuclear components, rapid reinforcements, air and naval superiority, highly mobile light army units (that could be used in other parts of the world or on short notice) and technological leadership.

For its part, our European allies should emphasize the heavily-armored ground forces needed to blunt an initial Soviet attack, and large manpower reserves.

Democratic Leadership Council, *Defending America: Building a New Foundation for National Strength* (Washington, D.C.: Democratic Leadership Council, September 1986), p. 21.

81. Morton H. Halperin, *Nuclear Fallacy: Dispelling the Myth of Nuclear Strategy* (Cambridge, MA: Ballinger, 1987), p. 112.

82. Quoted in "Washington met en garde l'Europe contre une dénucléarisation totale," *Le Monde*, 9 February 1988.

83. Carrington, "Kohl Stance on Nuclear Arms."

84. Quoted in Elie Marcuse, "L'Alliance monte au filet," *L'Express*, 5 February 1988.

85. Based upon 120 interviews with members of the "foreign policy elite" in Washington conducted from late 1981 through early 1983, Knudsen found that 57 percent favored European defense cooperation, 33 percent were ambiguous, and 10 percent were opposed. See Knudsen, "From Ideology to Foreign Policy," p. 11.

86. Quoted in Bridget Bloom, "Europe applies the brake on veteran defence vehicle," *The Financial Times*, 7 May 1986.

INDEX

United States (*cont.*)
  hegemonic decline of, 168–169,
    170, 183
  and IEPG, 126
  and intelligence cooperation, 98–99
  and "Iranscam," 132
  and nuclear proliferation, 98
  space budget of, 128
  and WEU, 122
United States, public opinion in. *See*
  Public opinion, U.S.
United States commitment, 1
  attitudes toward, 21
  and British policy, 88
  burden of, 180–181
  and changes in Atlantic relation-
    ship, 183–184
  European rivalry prevented by, 179
  European role after reduction of,
    171
  European worries over, 16
  and Franco-German relations, 70
  and German policy, 52
  importance of, 14, 15–16
  nuclear deployment, 11
  "Platform" on, 119
  questioning of, 1
  rationale for, 12–14
  and U.S. decline, 168–169, 170
  and U.S. defense budget, 12
United States commitment,
  conventional, 11–12
  attempts to reduce, 16–18, 19–20,
    22
  and budget/trade deficit, 18, 22,
    43n.69
  European doubts over, 22, 32–33
  future decline of, 169–171
  and modernization vs. readiness, 19
  and nuclear, 16
  support for, 20–22
United States commitment, nuclear,
  22–24. *See also* Nuclear
  deterrence
  and conventional, 16
  and denuclearization fears, 30–32
  as dubious, 23–24
  and European conventional forces,
    182–183
  European doubts over, 32–33
  public opinion on, 149–150
  and SDI, 24–30

"United States of Europe," 91,
  130

Vegetius, 3
Veil, Simone, 166
Verdun, symbolic reconciliation at,
  175–176

Wallace, William, 92, 94, 102, 180
Walt, Stephen, 173
Warner, John, 125
Warsaw Treaty Organization (WTO),
  6. *See also* NATO-Warsaw Pact
  relation
Watt, David, 87
Webb, James, 169
Weinberger, Caspar, 12–13, 13–14,
  19, 20, 26–27, 169
Western European Union (WEU), 2,
  34, 115, 116–122, 133
  and Britain, 88, 117, 118, 121
  "Platform" of, 119–120, 133, 167
  possible expansion of, 184
  and Rome Declaration, 70
West Germany (FRG), 1, 2–3. *See
  also* Franco-German relations
  and Anglo-French relations, 94
  antiwar sentiment in, 3, 7–8n.3, 69
  "bandwagoning" vs. "balancing"
    by, 171–174
  and Britain, 100–103
  defense contribution of, 12
  defense policy of, 52, 53, 58
  defense spending of, 6, 126
  and denuclearization, 31–32
  and ESA, 126, 127
  and EUREKA, 129
  and European central bank, 132
  in Franco-German-British trium-
    virate, 179–180
  and future of European defense
    cooperation, 165
  and INF treaty, 31, 142
  invisible defense costs for, 12
  military R & D spending by, 126
  and NATO vs. EC, 133
  and non-nuclear deterrence, 6
  and nuclear deterrence, 58–59
  nuclear weapons for, 59–60, 98,
    102, 165–166

ABOUT THE AUTHOR

David Garnham is an associate professor of political science at The University of Wisconsin-Milwaukee. He received a B.A. from Cornell University and an M.A. and a Ph.D. from the University of Minnesota. His research interests include defense policy and quantitative studies of international conflict. He has written several chapters in edited volumes as well as articles for many scholarly journals.